**TEACHER'S PET PUBLICATIONS**

LITPLAN TEACHER PACK
for
The Canterbury Tales
based on the tales by
Geoffrey Chaucer

Written by
Mary B. Collins

© 1994 Teacher's Pet Publications
All Rights Reserved

This **LitPlan** for Chaucer's
The Canterbury Tales
has been brought to you by Teacher's Pet Publications, Inc.

Copyright Teacher's Pet Publications 1994

Only the student materials in this unit plan (such as worksheets,
study questions, and tests) may be reproduced multiple times
for use in the purchaser's classroom. No other portion of
this document may be reproduced in any way without
the written consent of Teacher's Pet Publications, Inc.

For any additional copyright questions,
contact Teacher's Pet Publications.

www.tpet.com

TABLE OF CONTENTS - *The Canterbury Tales*

Introduction	5
Unit Objectives	8
Reading Assignment Sheet	9
Unit Outline	10
Study Questions (Short Answer)	13
Quiz/Study Questions (Multiple Choice)	33
Pre-reading Vocabulary Worksheets	71
Lesson One (Introductory Lesson)	123
Nonfiction Assignment Sheet	129
Oral Reading Evaluation Form	134
Writing Assignment 1	132
Writing Assignment 2	136
Writing Assignment 3	143
Writing Evaluation Form	137
Vocabulary Review Activities	138
Extra Writing Assignments/Discussion ?s	141
Unit Review Activities	144
Unit Tests	147
Unit Resource Materials	189
Vocabulary Resource Materials	251

ABOUT THE AUTHOR
Geoffrey Chaucer

CHAUCER, Geoffrey (1340?-1400). Called the Father of the English Language as well as the Morning Star of Song, Geoffrey Chaucer, after six centuries, has retained his status as one of the three or four greatest English poets. He was the first to commit to lines of universal and enduring appeal a vivid interest in nature, books, and people. As many-sided as Shakespeare, he did for English narrative what Shakespeare did for drama. If he lacks the profundity of Shakespeare, he excels in playfulness of mood and simplicity of expression. Though his language often seems quaint, he was essentially modern. Familiarity with the language and with the literature of his contemporaries persuades the most skeptical that he is nearer to the present than many writers born long after he died.

--- Courtesy of Compton's Learning Company

INTRODUCTION

This unit has been designed to develop students' reading, writing, thinking, and language skills through exercises and activities related to *The Canterbury Tales* by Geoffrey Chaucer. It includes twenty-seven lessons, supported by extra resource materials.

It is based on the Coghill modern translation of Chaucer's tales which stays very close to the old text, mostly substituting modern spellings for the Old English words, but also occasionally substituting modern words for archaic ones. The poetry remains intact, though not always exactly word-for-word the same as Chaucer's. This author thinks the Coghill translation is a good one for most high school students who want to enjoy the stories, learn about Chaucer and his times, and consider the main ideas presented by Chaucer rather than studying Old English and the exact text created by Chaucer's poetic genius.

This unit can be used for either the Old English version or the modern translation. If you use the Old English version, the vocabulary words chosen won't match, making the vocabulary sections of the unit non-applicable. However, you will still be able to use the study guides, tests, writing assignments and other portions of the unit.

The materials in this literature unit plan are based on the Prologue and thirteen of the tales--tales by the Knight, the Miller, the Reeve, the Shipman, the Prioress, the Nun's Priest, the Pardoner, the Wife of Bath, the Friar, the Summoner, the Clerk, the Merchant, and the Franklin. For each of these tales there are short answer study questions, multiple choice study/quiz questions, vocabulary worksheets, vocabulary and text word search puzzles, vocabulary and text crossword puzzles, and extra worksheets.

The **introductory lesson** introduces students to *The Canterbury Tales*. Students are given the materials they will be using during the unit including the **group project** through which most of the background and reading of the tales will take place. Students are grouped into pairs. Each pair of students is assigned a tale. One student of the pair is responsible for getting background information about the character type. For example, he/she would find out what Reeves were in the 1300s--where they fit in the social classes, what their jobs were, what function they served in society, what their daily lives were like, etc. The other student will be responsible for reading the story (or a summary of the story if you choose) to the class. In the text there are often references to various gods or historical figures. Both students in the group will create a little reference sheet to go along with their tale on which these names will be listed with a short explanation of who they were. During the reading of the tales, the reader will pause when he/she comes upon one of these key names, and the background person will give a brief explanation of the person named.

This takes care of 26 of your students. What about the others? If you have more students, divide them into two groups. One group will be responsible for creating a presentation lasting 1/2 class period giving background information about life in England in the 1300's. The other group will be responsible for creating a presentation lasting 1/2 class period giving background information about Chaucer's life. If you have too many students for just these two groups, consider adding a third person to a few of the tale pairs, especially for long tales like the Knight's. Have two Knights do the reading--split the tale in half.

The idea behind the pattern for this unit is to simulate the experience of the group traveling to Canterbury and yet still get meaning and an education from the stories told. After being given time to prepare their presentations, different pairs of students will tell their tales each day, dressed in appropriate costumes of the day. Most of the people who tell tales are described in the Prologue to the tales. Students should transform themselves into their characters as much as possible. The person giving background information should dress appropriately also. For example the person giving background information for the Knight might dress as a squire. The person giving background information for the Prioress might dress as a nun or a monk, friar or priest, and so on. Ideally, students in your class should just listen to the presentation being made as the other travelers listened to the tale-tellers. However, if you have a class of students who will not pay attention, you might have them follow along in the text in their books.

During the time scheduled for students to make and listen to the presentations of the tales, students will do the vocabulary worksheet, preview the study questions and read the prologue of the tale to be done in the next class period on the night before. That way, they will have some familiarity with the tale and the more difficult words that will be used, and you won't have to take class time reading the prologue to each tale. After each tale is read or presented, discuss the study questions so you are sure students understand what they just heard. After all the tales have been presented, there is time for a short review of all the tales.

The **study guide questions** are fact-based questions; students can find the answers to these questions right in the text. These questions come in two formats: short answer or multiple choice. The best use of these materials is probably to use the short answer version of the questions as study guides for students (since answers will be more complete), and to use the multiple choice version for occasional quizzes. It might be a good idea to make transparencies of your answer keys for the overhead projector.

The **vocabulary work** is intended to enrich students' vocabularies as well as to aid in the students' understanding of the text. Prior to each tale, students will complete a two-part worksheet for approximately 10 vocabulary words in the upcoming tale. Part I focuses on students' use of general knowledge and contextual clues by giving the sentence in which the word appears in the text. Students are then to write down what they think the words mean based on the words' usage. Part II nails down the definitions of the words by giving students dictionary definitions of the words and having students match the words to the correct definitions based on the words' contextual usage. Students should then have an understanding of the words when they meet them in the text.

After each tale, students will go back and formulate answers for the study guide questions. Discussion of these questions serves as a **review** of the most important events and ideas presented in the reading assignments.

After students complete reading the work, there is a **vocabulary review** lesson which pulls together all of the fragmented vocabulary lists for the reading assignments and gives students a review of all of the words they have studied.

Following the vocabulary review, a lesson is devoted to the **extra discussion questions/writing assignments**. These questions focus on interpretation, critical analysis and personal response, employing a variety of thinking skills and adding to the students' understanding of the text.

There are three **writing assignments** in this unit, each with the purpose of informing, persuading, or having students express personal opinions. The first assignment is to inform: students take the information gathered through research and organize it into a composition. The second assignment is to express personal opinions: students choose one tale as the "winner" of the free meal offered by the Host. The third assignment is to persuade: students choose one composition from a list related to the tales.

In addition, there is a **nonfiction reading assignment**. Students are required to read a piece of nonfiction related in some way to *The Canterbury Tales*. This assignment may be fulfilled through the background research students will do relating to their characters. After reading their nonfiction pieces, students will fill out a worksheet on which they answer questions regarding facts, interpretation, criticism, and personal opinions. Before and during the tale presentations, students make **oral presentations** about the nonfiction pieces they have read, giving background information and additional information to the text. This not only exposes all students to a wealth of information, it also gives students the opportunity to practice **public speaking**.

The **review lesson** pulls together all of the aspects of the unit. The teacher is given four or five choices of activities or games to use which all serve the same basic function of reviewing all of the information presented in the unit.

The **unit test** comes in two formats: all multiple choice-matching-true/false or with a mixture of matching, short answer, multiple choice, and composition. As a convenience, two different tests for each format have been included. There is also an advanced short answer version of the unit test.

There are additional **support materials** included with this unit. The **resource sections** include suggestions for an in-class library, crossword and word search puzzles related to the play, and extra vocabulary worksheets. There is a list of **bulletin board ideas** which gives the teacher suggestions for bulletin boards to go along with this unit. In addition, there is a list of **extra class activities** the teacher could choose from to enhance the unit or as a substitution for an exercise the teacher might feel is inappropriate for his/her class. **Answer keys** are located directly after the **reproducible student materials** throughout the unit. The student materials may be reproduced for use in the teacher's classroom without infringement of copyrights. No other portion of this unit may be reproduced without the written consent of Teacher's Pet Publications, Inc.

The **level** of this unit can be varied depending upon the criteria on which the individual assignments are graded, the teacher's expectations of his/her students in class discussions, and the formats chosen for the study guides, quizzes and test. If teachers have other ideas/activities they wish to use, they can usually easily be inserted prior to the review lesson.

UNIT OBJECTIVES - *The Canterbury Tales*

1. Through reading Chaucer's *The Canterbury Tales* students will gain a better understanding of fourteenth-century English society.

2. Students will demonstrate their understanding of the text on four levels: factual, interpretive, critical and personal.

3. Students will be exposed to several different forms of literature.

4. Students will see how Chaucer uses the framing device as a structure for his tales.

5. Students will get background information about Chaucer, his times and *The Canterbury Tales*.

6. Students will compare and contrast medieval and modern ideas.

7. Students will be given the opportunity to practice reading aloud and silently to improve their skills in each area.

8. Students will answer questions to demonstrate their knowledge and understanding of the main events and characters in *The Canterbury Tales* as they relate to the author's theme development.

9. Students will enrich their vocabularies and improve their understanding of the play through the vocabulary lessons prepared for use in conjunction with the play.

10. The writing assignments in this unit are geared to several purposes:
    a. To have students demonstrate their abilities to inform, to persuade, or to express their own personal ideas
       Note: Students will demonstrate ability to write effectively to <u>inform</u> by developing and organizing facts to convey information. Students will demonstrate the ability to write effectively to <u>persuade</u> by selecting and organizing relevant information, establishing an argumentative purpose, and by designing an appropriate strategy for an identified audience. Students will demonstrate the ability to write effectively to <u>express personal ideas</u> by selecting a form and its appropriate elements.
    b. To check the students' reading comprehension
    c. To make students think about the ideas presented by the play
    d. To encourage logical thinking
    e. To provide an opportunity to practice good grammar and improve students' use of the English language.

11. Students will read aloud, report, and participate in large and small group discussions to improve their public speaking and personal interaction skills.

READING ASSIGNMENT SHEET - *The Canterbury Tales*

Date Assigned	Reading Assignment	Completion Date
	Prologue	
	Knight's Tale	
	Miller's Tale	
	Reeve's Tale	
	Shipman's Tale	
	Prioress's Tale	
	Nun's Priest's Tale	
	Pardoner's Tale	
	Wife of Bath's Tale	
	Friar's Tale	
	Summoner's Tale	
	Clerk's Tale	
	Merchant's Tale	
	Franklin's Tale	

UNIT OUTLINE - *The Canterbury Tales*

1 Introduction	2 Prologue	3 Library	4 Library	5 Writing Assignment 1
6 Background	7 Knight	8 Knight	9 Miller	10 Reeve
11 Shipman	12 Prioress	13 Nun's Priest	14 Pardoner	15 Wife of Bath
16 Friar	17 Summoner	18 Clerk	19 Merchant	20 Franklin
21 Writing Assignment 2	22 Vocabulary	23 Extra ?s	24 Discussion	25 Writing Assignment 3
26 Review	27 Test			

STUDY GUIDE QUESTIONS

SHORT ANSWER STUDY GUIDE QUESTIONS - *The Canterbury Tales*

The Prologue

1. Who did the narrator meet at the Tabbard Inn?
2. Why was everyone at the Tabbard?
3. What were they going to Canterbury to see?
4. Describe the Knight.
5. Describe the Squire.
6. Describe the Yeoman.
7. Describe the Prioress
8. What other people were in the Nun's group?
9. Describe the Monk.
10. Describe the Friar.
11. Describe the Merchant.
12. Describe the Clerk.
13. Describe the Sergeant At Law.
14. Describe the Franklin.
15. What tradesmen were there?
16. Describe the Cook.
17. Describe the Shipman.
18. Describe the Doctor.
19. Describe the Wife of Bath.
20. Describe the Parson.
21. Describe the Miller.
22. Describe the Manciple.
23. Describe the Plowman.
24. Describe the Reeve.
25. Describe the Pardoner.
26. Describe the Summoner.
27. Describe the Host.
28. What game does the host propose to the pilgrims?

The Canterbury Tales Short Answer Study Guides Page 2

The Knight's Tale
1. How did Arcita and Palamon become Theseus's prisoners?
2. About what did Arcita and Palamon argue in the tower when they were prisoners?
3. Why was Arcita released from prison?
4. What was the one condition of Arcita's release?
5. How and why did Arcita return to Athens?
6. How did Palamon get out of prison?
7. Why did Theseus spare the lives of Palamon and Arcita when they were fighting in the woods?
8. What solution to the knights' problem did Theseus have?
9. Who won the battle for Emily's hand?
10. What happened to Arcita?
11. How did Palamon come to be married to Emily?

The Miller's Tale
1. What is the Miller's condition as he begins to tell his tale?
2. Who is Nicholas?
3. Describe the carpenter's wife, Alison.
4. How did Nicholas get the carpenter out of the way so he and Alison could sleep together?
5. Identify Absalom.
6. What joke did Alison and Nicholas play on Absalom?
7. How did Absalom get even with Alison and Nicholas?
8. Why did the village people think the carpenter was crazy?

The Canterbury Tales Short Answer Study Guides Page 3

The Reeve's Tale
1. What does the Reeve vow to do through his story?
2. Who is Simpkin?
3. Identify Molly.
4. Why did Alan and John go to the miller's?
5. What did the miller do to get the best of Alan and John?
6. Why did John and Alan stay overnight at the miller's?
7. How did the miller and his guests pass the evening?
8. How did John and Alan get even with the miller?
9. How did Alan and John get away from the miller's house?

The Shipman's Tale
1. Who are the three main characters of the Shipman's tale?
2. Where did the merchant have to go first?
3. What was the merchant's wife's complaint to Sir John?
4. What does the merchant's wife ask of Sir John, and what does she offer in return?
5. Why does Sir John want to borrow 100 francs from the merchant?
6. What 'repayment' does Sir John get from the merchant's wife?
7. Why did Sir John tell the merchant he paid back the loan to the merchant's wife?
8. What is the merchant's wife's reaction to the merchant's complaint that she didn't tell him Sir John had paid back his debt?
9. What does the merchant decide about his wife's little escapade?

The Canterbury Tales Short Answer Study Guides Page 4

The Prioress's Tale
1. What is the prologue to the Prioress's tale?
2. What is the setting for this tale?
3. Who is the main character?
4. What did the little boy decide to do?
5. What happened to the little boy?
6. What was unusual about the little boy's death?
7. Where did the Christian people take the boy?
8. What was the boy's answer when asked how he could sing with a slit throat?
9. What happened when the monk took the grain of seed away?

The Nun's Priest's Tale
1. Identify Chanticleer and Pertelote.
2. What was Chanticleer's dream?
3. To what did Pertelote attribute dreams?
4. What was Pertelote's suggested remedy?
5. Explain the significance of the Latin phrase that Chanticleer tells Pertelote means "Woman is man's delight and all his bliss."
6. Summarize the story of the shipmates.
7. State the reason for Chanticleer's stories to Pertelote.
8. Why did the fox flatter Chanticleer?
9. What happened to Chanticleer?
10. How did Chanticleer escape?

The Canterbury Tales Short Answer Study Guides Page 5

The Pardoner's Tale
1. Of what use is the bone?
2. For what use is the mitten and under what condition will it work?
3. Describe the "trick" which has been worth a hundred marks a year to the Pardoner.
4. What is the Pardoner's purpose? What is he supposed to do?
5. What is ironic about how the Pardoner gets people to repent from the sin of avarice?
6. What bargain or agreement did the rioters make at the tavern?
7. They met an old man as they began their journey. What was the old man's problem?
8. Where does the old man send the rioters?
9. What did they find where the old man sent them?
10. Why did they have to bring the treasure home at night?
11. Why was one youth sent to town?
12. What plan did the two other youths make to kill the one when he returned from town?
13. What plan did the one who went to town make to kill the two others when he got back?
14. Who died, and how did it happen?

The Friar's Tale
1. Why did the Friar tell a story about a Summoner?
2. What did the archdeacon punish most?
3. For whom did the summoner work?
4. Why did the summoner have informers?
5. Who was the yeoman?
6. Why didn't the fiend take the horses, cart and hay?
7. What had the old woman done to be summoned to court?
8. What happened to the summoner?
9. What is the moral of the Friar's story?

The Canterbury Tales Short Answer Study Guides Page 6

The Wife of Bath's Tale

1. What does the Wife of Bath think of marriage?
2. How many husbands has the Wife of Bath had?
3. The Wife of Bath talks about Solomon, Abraham, Jacob, and others from the Bible. What is her point?
4. On what commandment does the Wife of Bath like to dwell?
5. What is the Wife of Bath's complaint about husbands?
6. "No empty-handed man can lure a bird," said the Wife of Bath. Explain what she meant.
7. The Wife of Bath says she was her fourth husband's purgatory. Explain.
8. The Wife's fifth husband beat her. Why did she stay with him?
9. What lies did the Wife of Bath tell Johnny?
10. What book did Johnny like to read?
11. What was the result of the fight between the Wife of Bath and her fifth husband?
12. Why did the Friar promise to tell a tale poking fun at a Summoner?
13. What did the knight do to warrant the punishment of beheading?
14. Who saved the knight, and under what condition was he let go?
15. What deal did he make on his way home after the year was almost ended?
16. What was the answer to the Queen's question?
17. What did the woman ask of the knight in return for saving his life?
18. The knight kept his word and married her, but he was miserable. What options did the old woman give him?
19. What did the knight choose?
20. Why did the old woman promise him both beauty and fidelity?

The Canterbury Tales Short Answer Study Guides Page 7

The Summoner's Tale
1. Where did the Summoner say all the friars were in hell?
2. What was the main objective of the friar's preaching at church at Holderness?
3. What characteristic of the friars does the Summoner's story accentuate?
4. Identify Thomas.
5. Did the friar know about the woman's baby's death prior to her telling him about it?
6. Who did the friar use as examples showing the necessity of fasting?
7. Thomas says he's given all his money to various friars and now he has no more to give. What is the friar's response?
8. Why is the friar's lecture to Thomas about ire ironic?
9. What is the point of the two stories the friar uses as examples about anger?
10. What was Thomas's "gift" to the friar?
11. What was the squire's solution to the problem of dividing the gift?

The Clerk's Tale
1. What did the Host ask of the Clerk?
2. What did the marquis' vassals want him to do?
3. Why did the marquis choose Griselda?
4. What promise did Griselda make to the marquis?
5. How did the marquis test Griselda's faithfulness to him?
6. What was Griselda's reaction to each of the tests?
7. What was Griselda's reward for keeping her promise?

The Canterbury Tales Short Answer Study Guides Page 8

The Merchant's Tale
1. Describe the Merchant's marriage.
2. Why did January want to have a young wife?
3. What did Placebo think of January's idea?
4. What was Justinus's advice?
5. Identify May.
6. Identify Damian.
7. What misfortune befell January?
8. How was January's handicap cured?
9. How did May overcome January's accusations?

The Franklin's Tale
1. Why was Dorigen so sad?
2. Why didn't Dorigen like the rocks?
3. What unusual incident happened to Dorigen at the garden party?
4. What promise did Dorigen make to Aurelius?
5. How did Aurelius get rid of the rocks?
6. What noble gesture did Arveragus make on behalf of Dorigen?
7. What was Aurelius's response when Dorigen told him she and been set free to keep her word?
8. The magician also did a noble deed. What was it?

ANSWER KEY: SHORT ANSWER STUDY QUESTIONS
The Canterbury Tales

The Prologue

1. Who did the narrator meet at the Tabbard Inn?
    He met 29 pilgrims.
2. Why was everyone at the Tabbard?
    They were on their way making a pilgrimage to Canterbury.
3. What were they going to Canterbury to see?
    They were going to see the shrine of Thomas a Becket.
4. Describe the Knight.
    He had been in many battles. He was a true, a perfect gentle knight.
5. Describe the Squire.
    He was the son of the knight, twenty-ish, agile and strong, fashionable and happy-go-lucky.
6. Describe the Yeoman.
    The Yeoman was the Squire's servant. He was a woodsman, a Robin Hood type character.
7. Describe the Prioress
    Her name was Madam Eglantyne. She spoke French, was dainty, pleasant, sensitive, and the picture of medieval beauty (although her wide forehead was a sign that she wasn't very bright).
8. What other people were in the Nun's group?
    There was another nun, and there were three priests.
9. Describe the Monk.
    He was bald and fat. He had a preference for fine clothes and luxuries. He didn't care at all for the hard work at the monastery. He liked to ride.
10. Describe the Friar.
    He takes bribes for easy penance, and he knows the taverns and barmaids better than he does the lepers and beggars. He is rather aristocratic; too good for the lepers. He lisps, and his name is Hubert.
11. Describe the Merchant.
    He has a forked beard and motley coat. He is careful with money, a good negotiator, and always tells his opinions about business.
12. Describe the Clerk.
    He is an Oxford student. He didn't say much, didn't have a job, and just loved to learn for the sake of learning.
13. Describe the Sergeant At Law.
    He seemed wise. He made a lot of money as a lawyer. He knew the law by rote, and seemed busier than he really was.
14. Describe the Franklin.
    He looked a little like Santa Claus. He liked to eat, drink and be merry. He was a country gentleman with a dagger and a silk purse.

15. What tradesmen were there?

    A haberdasher, dyer, carpenter, weaver, and carpet-maker were there.
16. Describe the Cook.

    He was a master of his trade. He had a sore on his knee, and was physically a rather disgusting character.
17. Describe the Shipman.

    He was from Dartmouth, didn't ride well, had little conscience about killing the enemy, and was a good navigator. He seems, actually, like a pirate.
18. Describe the Doctor.

    The Doctor knew medicine well, and took kickbacks from the pharmacist. He was not particularly religious. He was dressed in red and blue/gray garments, and he loved gold.
19. Describe the Wife of Bath.

    She was a large woman, and somewhat deaf. She had a red complexion and wore a wide hat and spurs. She had been married five times, and she went on many pilgrimages (possibly man-hunting).
20. Describe the Parson.

    He was truly Christ-like; patient, giving, holy and virtuous, and didn't believe in pomp or glory. He practiced what he preached.
21. Describe the Miller.

    The Miller had a football-player build. He had a red beard, wart on his nose, and a filthy mouth. He cheated his customers and in his spare time played the bagpipes.
22. Describe the Manciple.

    He was a shrewd buyer. Lawyers with all their knowledge were no match for him. He purchased well and kept the extra money for himself. He stole the lawyers blind.
23. Describe the Plowman.

    He was the Parson's brother. He was an honest worker who paid his taxes on time.
24. Describe the Reeve.

    He was old, choleric, and thin. He was a good manager and good carpenter, feared by the farm workers. He usually brought up the rear of the party, lagging behind.
25. Describe the Pardoner.

    He sang in a strong voice. He had long, yellow hair, bulging eyes, and was baby-faced. He carried a bunch of false relics to sell.
26. Describe the Summoner.

    The Summoner had a red face full of sores. He ate onions and drank too much. He would take bribes. He had a garland of flowers on his head and held a cake like a shield.
27. Describe the Host.

    His name was Harry Bailly. He was manly, good natured, and happy.
28. What game does the host propose to the pilgrims?

    He proposed that they each tell two stories on the way to and from Canterbury. The winner with the best story would get a free meal at the expense of the other travelers. The host would ride along and be the judge. Anyone who wouldn't abide by his rule would have to pay everyone's way.

The Knight's Tale

1. How did Arcita and Palamon become Theseus's prisoners?
   Theseus went to slay Creon at Thebes. After he had won and conquered the city, pillagers found Arcita and Palamon, knights who had fought against Theseus. They were wounded, so the pillagers took them to Theseus's tent. He ordered that they would be kept perpetual prisoners.
2. About what did Arcita and Palamon argue in the tower when they were prisoners?
   Each one had seen and fallen in love with Emily, the Queen's sister. They argued about which of them first saw Emily and could claim her for his own.
3. Why was Arcita released from prison?
   Duke Perotheus, a great friend of Duke Theseus, also happened to have known and loved Arcita in former years. At Perotheus's request, Theseus set Arcita free without ransom.
4. What was the one condition of Arcita's release?
   He was never to return to any lands of Duke Theseus again, or he would be killed.
5. How and why did Arcita return to Athens?
   He went disguised as a lowly servant looking for work so that he might see Emily again.
6. How did Palamon get out of prison?
   He poisoned the guard and escaped.
7. Why did Theseus spare the lives of Palamon and Arcita when they were fighting in the woods?
   The Queen and Emily begged his mercy, and after consideration, he agreed to let the knights live.
8. What solution to the knights' problem did Theseus have?
   Each was to return to Athens in one year with 100 knights, and there would be a contest. The winner of the contest would marry Emily.
9. Who won the battle for Emily's hand?
   Arcita did.
10. What happened to Arcita?
    There was an earth tremor as he was taking his victory round. His horse stopped and stumbled, and Arcita was thrown out of the saddle upon his head with his breast shattered by the saddle bow. He later died.
11. How did Palamon come to be married to Emily?
    After a sufficient period of mourning, a certain number of years, Theseus sent for Palamon. Theseus and his parliament gave permission for Palamon to marry Emily, and they lived happily ever after.

The Miller's Tale

1. What is the Miller's condition as he begins to tell his tale?
   He is drunk.

2. Who is Nicholas?
> He is a student (mostly interested in astrology and telling the future) who has come to board with the carpenter and the carpenter's new wife.

3. Describe the carpenter's wife, Alison.
> She is young and beautiful.

4. How did Nicholas get the carpenter out of the way so he and Alison could sleep together?
> He pretended to have had a premonition of a second great flood that would destroy the world, and he convinced the carpenter to make preparations to save the three of them. The carpenter was to get three tubs and hang them under the roof. On the night the flood was to happen, the three would spend the night in the separate tubs. They did so, and when the carpenter fell asleep, Alison and Nicholas climbed out of their tubs and ran off to the bedroom.

5. Identify Absalom.
> He was the parish clerk who loved Alison, too. He also wanted Alison for himself.

6. What joke did Alison and Nicholas play on Absalom?
> When Absalom came to Alison's window pleading for a kiss, she agreed. She opened her window and stuck out her behind, which unsuspecting Absalom kissed.

7. How did Absalom get even with Alison and Nicholas?
> He went to the blacksmith's shop and borrowed a hot iron. When he came back for another kiss, he put the hot iron on the bare behind that was stuck out of the window.

8. Why did the village people think the carpenter was crazy?
> When Nicholas's behind got burned, he began yelling, "Help! Water!" The carpenter, thinking the flood had come, cut the ropes holding the tub which fell to the floor. People came to see what the commotion was all about, and they saw the carpenter (broken arm and all) in a tub ranting about a flood. Nicholas pretended not to know what the carpenter was talking about, and brushed him off as having gone crazy, an explanation the people easily accepted and joked about.

The Reeve's Tale

1. What does the Reeve vow to do through his story?
> He vows to pay back the Miller for making a carpenter look like a fool.

2. Who is Simpkin?
> He is the miller who steals and cheats his customers and bullies everyone.

3. Identify Molly.
> Molly is the miller's daughter.

4. Why did Alan and John go to the miller's?
> They were taking corn from the college to be milled. The Warden was tired of being cheated and these two students thought they could outwit the miller.

5. What did the miller do to get the best of Alan and John?
> He let their horse go, and when they went to find it, he took 1/2 bushel of their flour.

6. Why did John and Alan stay overnight at the miller's?
> They were tired and wet after chasing their horse, and it was too late to travel.

7. How did the miller and his guests pass the evening?
> They ate dinner and drank a lot of ale.

8. How did John and Alan get even with the miller?
> Alan slept with Molly; John tricked the miller's wife into sleeping with him. In the morning, they took their flour and the cake that had been made with part of it, and left. They had slept with both women, had a free meal, had a free night's lodging, and left with all of their goods.

9. How did Alan and John get away from the miller's house?
> While the miller was fighting with Alan and John, his wife hit him on the head with a stick (by mistake) and knocked him out.

The Shipman's Tale

1. Who are the three main characters of the Shipman's tale?
> The merchant, his wife, and their friend, a monk (Sir John) are the main characters.

2. Where did the merchant have to go first?
> He had to go to Bruges on business.

3. What was the merchant's wife's complaint to Sir John?
> Her husband won't give her enough money to buy what she needs, especially clothes, to maintain her social position.

4. What does the merchant's wife ask of Sir John, and what does she offer in return?
> She asks for 100 francs to buy clothes with and promises to repay him and do "some little task" he might want.

5. Why does Sir John want to borrow 100 francs from the merchant?
> He says he is going to buy cattle, but he actually intends to give it to the merchant's wife to buy clothes.

6. What 'repayment' does Sir John get from the merchant's wife?
> She sleeps with him while the merchant is away on business.

7. Why did Sir John tell the merchant he paid back the loan to the merchant's wife?
> This way he didn't have to have any money out of pocket. He used the merchant's 100 francs to loan to the merchant's wife and then claimed that he had paid back his loan to the merchant's wife. The merchant had been duped into, in effect, giving his wife 100 francs for clothes. The wife had slept with Sir John for nothing; he hadn't really lent her any money at all.

8. What is the merchant's wife's reaction to the merchant's complaint that she didn't tell him Sir John had paid back his debt?
> She stayed calm and collected. She admits Sir John gave her the money for clothes but wisely omits the part about her doing him a favor. She tells her husband she will pay him back for the 100 francs in bed.

9. What does the merchant decide about his wife's little escapade?

    There is no use in reprimanding her for her foolishness. He just tells her to be a bit more thrifty in the future.

The Prioress's Tale

1. What is the prologue to the Prioress's tale?

    It is a prayer. The Prioress is asking for guidance from Mary as she tells this tale to glorify the Lord.

2. What is the setting for this tale?

    It is in a Christian town in Asia.

3. Who is the main character?

    A little boy of seven, a widow's son, is the main character.

4. What did the little boy decide to do?

    He decided to learn to sing *O Alma Redemptoris* in Latin.

5. What happened to the little boy?

    The Jewish people hired a murderer who slit the boy's throat.

6. What was unusual about the little boy's death?

    He kept singing the song even though his throat had been cut.

7. Where did the Christian people take the boy?

    They took him to the nearest abbey.

8. What was the boy's answer when asked how he could sing with a slit throat?

    He said Christ willed it so that he could sing to the honor of Christ's mother.

9. What happened when the monk took the grain of seed away?

    The boy died peacefully.

The Nun's Priest's Tale

1. Identify Chanticleer and Pertelote.

    Chanticleer is a rooster and Pertelote is his favorite hen.

2. What was Chanticleer's dream?

    He dreamed that an animal unfamiliar to him (we know as a fox) murdered him.

3. To what did Pertelote attribute dreams?

    She said he must have indigestion.

4. What was Pertelote's suggested remedy?

    She suggested that he should take a laxative.

5. Explain the significance of the Latin phrase that Chanticleer tells Pertelote means "Woman is man's delight and all his bliss."

    Chanticleer has not translated this properly. It actually means, "woman is man's worst enemy." This mistranslation is ironic because Pertelote, in brushing off Chanticleer's concern, actually is helping to lead to Chanticleer's downfall. Also the mistranslation adds to the comic element of the mock-heroic tone.

6. Summarize the story of the shipmates.
> One shipmate had a dream that they would be killed at sea if they left port on a certain date. The other mate brushed off the concerns of the first. they put out to sea, and their ship did go down.

7. State the reason for Chanticleer's stories to Pertelote.
> The stories are Chanticleer's way of trying to convince Pertelote that dreams should be taken seriously. They also foreshadow Chanticleer's own future.

8. Why did the fox flatter Chanticleer?
> He wanted to put Chanticleer at ease. Also, as Chanticleer sang, he stretched his neck and closed his eyes, making an easy target for the fox.

9. What happened to Chanticleer?
> The fox hauled him away and prepared to make a meal of him.

10. How did Chanticleer escape?
> He appealed to the fox's sense of superiority and told him not to miss a chance to shout a few insults at the other animals. The fox opened his mouth to shout some insults, and Chanticleer escaped.

The Pardoner's Tale

1. Of what use is the bone?
> It would cure various animals' snake bites or other sores, and it could help make the cattle business good. It was also a cure for jealousy.

2. For what use is the mitten and under what condition will it work?
> It will increase the yield of grain provided the wearer has made a donation to the church.

3. Describe the "trick" which has been worth a ;hundred marks a year to the Pardoner.
> The Pardoner preaches that the very sinful members of his flock cannot make an offering, but that the virtuous members may, and he will absolve them.

4. What is the Pardoner's purpose? What is he supposed to do?
> He does everything he can to make money. He is supposed to be concerned with saving souls.

5. What is ironic about how the Pardoner gets people to repent from the sin of avarice?
> The Pardoner is very guilty of the sin of avarice himself. He sees ways of getting people to repent from avarice as a means for acquiring more money for the church.

6. What bargain or agreement did the rioters make at the tavern?
> They agreed to go hunt down Death.

7. They met an old man as they began their journey. What was the old man's problem?
> The old man had to roam the earth until he had found someone who would trade youth for age.

8. Where does the old man send the rioters?
> He sends them up the road to an oak tree.

9. What did they find where the old man sent them?
> They found eight bushels of gold.

10. Why did they have to bring the treasure home at night?
> They were afraid someone would see them and think they had stolen it.

11. Why was one youth sent to town?
    One went to town to buy food and drink so they would have something to eat while waiting for nightfall.
12. What plan did the two other youths make to kill the one when he returned from town?
    They decided one would talk to him and the other would come up from behind and stab him.
13. What plan did the one who went to town make to kill the two others when he got back?
    He was going to poison the two.
14. Who died, and how did it happen?
    All three died. The two stabbed the one, and then they unknowingly drank the poisoned wine.

The Friar's Tale
1. Why did the Friar tell a story about a Summoner?
    He was mad at the Summoner for reprimanding him during the Wife of Bath's turn.
2. What did the archdeacon punish most?
    He punished lechery most.
3. For whom did the summoner work?
    He technically worked for the archdeacon, but he pocketed extorted money for his living.
4. Why did the summoner have informers?
    He wasn't interested in bringing the guilty to justice and reformation; he wanted to extort money from them. Therefore, the more guilty people he could find, the more money he would make. Informers helped him find guilty people.
5. Who was the yeoman?
    He was a fiend from hell.
6. Why didn't the fiend take the horses, cart and hay?
    He knew that the farmer didn't mean his curse.
7. What had the old woman done to be summoned to court?
    Nothing.
8. What happened to the summoner?
    The old woman cursed him to hell, and the fiend took him there.
9. What is the moral of the Friar's story?
    Summoners should repent and quit their vices before the devil gets them.

The Wife of Bath's Tale
1. What does the Wife of Bath think of marriage?
    She thinks it is a misery and a woe.
2. How many husbands has the Wife of Bath had?
    She has had five husbands.
3. The Wife of Bath talks about Solomon, Abraham, Jacob, and others from the Bible. What is her point?
    Lots of Christians had several wives. She is defending her five marriages by proclaiming examples of how others in good stead with the church have had many marriages.

4. On what commandment does the Wife of Bath like to dwell?
>   She dwells on the one that husbands should love their wives.

5. What is the Wife of Bath's complaint about husbands?
>   She had many complaints which basically involve husbands' complaints about their wives and how their complaints are unfounded or the husbands' own fault. For instance, she says if husbands would "try out" their wives before marriage, they wouldn't think the wives had hidden their "vices." Husbands, she says, don't trust their wives; they have to spy on them all the time for fear of infidelity. Husbands "hide the keys of coffer doors" and seem to forget that their valuables are common property between man and wife. She says husbands think women contrive ways to make their husbands miserable.

6. "No empty-handed man can lure a bird," said the Wife of Bath. Explain what she meant.
>   Her husband had to do something nice for her or bring her something before she would be nice to him or let him sleep with her.

7. The Wife of Bath says she was her fourth husband's purgatory. Explain.
>   She knows she was hateful to him and that his life was miserable because of her.

8. The Wife's fifth husband beat her. Why did she stay with him?
>   She said of all her husbands, she loved him most of all.

9. What lies did the Wife of Bath tell Johnny?
>   She told him that she dreamed the night away thinking of him, and that as she lay there he tried to kill her. We get the impression that she probably told other lies to try to get Johnny's attentions.

10. What book did Johnny like to read?
>   It was a book with a collection of stories about hateful wives.

11. What was the result of the fight between the Wife of Bath and her fifth husband?
>   She was partially deaf, but they lived happily ever after.

12. Why did the Friar promise to tell a tale poking fun at a Summoner?
>   After the Wife of Bath's prologue, the Summoner insulted the Friar.

13. What did the knight do to warrant the punishment of beheading?
>   He raped a young maiden.

14. Who saved the knight, and under what condition was he let go?
>   The Queen saved him. He was let go under the condition that he would come back in one year to tell her what one thing women wanted above all else.

15. What deal did he make on his way home after the year was almost ended?
>   He met an old woman who told him the answer to the Queen's question under the condition that he would grant her next request if it would be in his power to do so.

16. What was the answer to the Queen's question?
>   The knight told the Queen that all women want to be masters of their husbands and lovers.

17. What did the woman ask of the knight in return for saving his life?
>   She asked him to marry her.

18. The knight kept his work and married her, but he was miserable. What options did the old woman give him?
    He could have her old and faithful or young and perhaps not so faithful.
19. What did the knight choose?
    He left the decision up to the old woman.
20. Why did the old woman promise him both beauty and fidelity?
    By giving her the choice, he allowed her mastery over him, her husband.

The Summoner's Tale

1. Where did the Summoner say all the friars were in hell?
    He said one would find them under Satan's tail, up his behind.
2. What was the main objective of the friar's preaching at church at Holderness?
    He wanted money to pay for trentals, masses for the deceased in Purgatory.
3. What characteristic of the friars does the Summoner's story accentuate?
    It accentuated their asking for money and charitable donations for their cause(s).
4. Identify Thomas.
    He was a sick man whose house the friar visited. Thomas had given generously to the friars and had little left for himself.
5. Did the friar know about the woman's baby's death prior to her telling him about it?
    No, probably not, or he most likely would have expressed his regrets or made some comment about it upon entering the home. His whole vision speech is a fabrication.
6. Who did the friar use as examples showing the necessity of fasting?
    Moses, Aaron, Jesus, Elijah
7. Thomas says he's given all his money to various friars and now he has no more to give. What is the friar's response?
    Thomas is ill because he has so little faith; he should give more. He should have given all his donations to him instead of spreading the money about.
8. Why is the friar's lecture to Thomas about ire ironic?
    After Thomas gives the friar his "gift" for the friar to share with others at the convent, the friar is furious and spends the rest of the story ranting and raving in anger.
9. What is the point of the two stories the friar uses as examples about anger?
    Anger makes people senseless.
10. What was Thomas's "gift" to the friar?
    He passed gas in the friar's hand.
11. What was the squire's solution to the problem of dividing the gift?
    He would have a wheel with 12 spokes placed on its side, have the friars kneel and place their nose at the end of each spoke, he upright at the axle-hole. Thomas seated over the axle-hole passes gas. He said the sound and smell would travel equally to each spoke's end.

The Clerk's Tale

1. What did the Host ask of the Clerk?

   He asked Clerk to tell a cheerful tale of adventure instead of preaching.

2. What did the marquis' vassals want him to do?

   They wanted him to find a wife and get married.

3. Why did the marquis choose Griselda?

   She was beautiful in both looks and deeds.

4. What promise did Griselda make to the marquis?

   "And here I promise never willingly
   To disobey in deed or thought or breath"

5. How did the marquis test Griselda's faithfulness to him?

   Over a period of years, he took both children away and then threw her out of the castle back home to her father empty-handed. He then asked her to come back and clean and decorate his home for his new wife.

6. What was Griselda's reaction to each of the tests?

   Perfect, mild-mannered submission to the marquis' will, and total loyalty in her love for him.

7. What was Griselda's reward for keeping her promise?

   Both children were brought back, she remained the wife of the marquis, and they lived happily ever after.

The Merchant's Tale

1. Describe the Merchant's marriage.

   He says he is married to a shrew and if freed would never marry again.

2. Why did January want to have a young wife?

   A young, beautiful wife, he thinks, would keep him from adultery. He also thinks a young wife will be easier to handle than an older one, and she won't have turned into a pest yet.

3. What did Placebo think of January's idea?

   He completely agreed. Of course, we get the idea that he would agree with anything January would say, just to ingratiate himself to January.

4. What was Justinus's advice?

   Choosing a wife needs careful consideration and long investigation. He does not think a young wife is a good idea.

5. Identify May.

   January's new wife.

6. Identify Damian.

   Damian was one of January's squires. He lusted after May, gave her a note, and they contrived a way to get together.

7. What misfortune befell January?

   He became blind.

8. How was January's handicap cured?

    When May stepped on his back to climb into the pear tree to meet Damian, January regained his sight just in time to catch May and Damian in the act.

9. How did May overcome January's accusations?

    She just kept telling him over and over that he really didn't see what he thought he saw. His vision was still a bit fuzzy.

The Franklin's Tale

1. Why was Dorigen so sad?

    Her husband, Arveragus, had gone off to do his knightly work for two years, and she missed him.

2. Why didn't Dorigen like the rocks?

    She thought they had no useful purpose; they were a menace and useless. They reminded her of accidents that could befall her husband.

3. What unusual incident happened to Dorigen at the garden party?

    Aurelius professed his love for her.

4. What promise did Dorigen make to Aurelius?

    If he would clear the coasts of all those dreadful rocks, she would love him most.

5. How did Aurelius get rid of the rocks?

    He hired a magician to perform an optical illusion.

6. What noble gesture did Arveragus make on behalf of Dorigen?

    He released her to keep her word to Aurelius.

7. What was Aurelius's response when Dorigen told him she and been set free to keep her word?

    He gave her back her freedom and allowed her to be with her husband.

8. The magician also did a noble deed. What was it?

    He released Aurelius from his debt.

MULTIPLE CHOICE STUDY GUIDE/QUIZ QUESTIONS - *The Canterbury Tales*

The Prologue

1. Who did the narrator meet at the Tabbard Inn?
    a. He met the King of England
    b. He met the Archbishop of Canterbury
    c. He met 29 pilgrims
    d. He met St. Thomas a Becket

2. Why was everyone at The Tabbard?
    a. There was a band of highwaymen on the road and the people were afraid to travel. They were waiting for the King's soldiers to come and escort them.
    b. They were on their way making a pilgrimage to Canterbury.
    c. They had come to celebrate the baptism of the King's youngest son.
    d. Over half the group had taken ill. They were recuperating at the inn.

3. What were they going to see?
    a. They were going to see the relics of the True Cross.
    b. They were going to see a special presentation of the Passion play.
    c. They were going to see a spring that was supposed to have miraculous healing powers.
    d. They were going to see the shrine of St. Thomas a Becket.

4. He has been in many battles. He was true and gentle.
    a. The Knight
    b. The Yeoman
    c. The Sergeant at Law
    d. The Merchant

5. He was the son of the Knight, in his twenties, agile, strong, and happy-go-lucky.
    a. The Plowman
    b. The Squire
    c. The Reeve
    d. The Pardoner

6. He was the Squire's servant. He was a woodsman, a Robin Hood type character.
    a. The Host
    b. The Shipman
    c. The Yeoman
    d. The Manciple

7. She spoke French, was dainty and pleasant, and the picture of medieval beauty.
    a. The Prioress/Nun
    b. The Wife of Bath
    c. The Cook
    d. The Weaver

Canterbury Tales Multiple Choice Questions Page 2
Prologue Page 2

8. These people were in the nun's group.
   a. One priest and three students
   b. Four nuns
   c. Two converts, one priest, and one nun
   d. One nun and three priests

9. He was bald and fat. He had a preference for fine clothes and luxuries. He didn't like hard work, but he did like to ride.
   a. The Knight
   b. The Monk
   c. The Squire
   d. The Franklin

10. He takes bribes for easy penance. He knows the taverns and barmaids better than he does the lepers and beggars. He is rather aristocratic, and he lisps.
    a. The Pardoner
    b. The Parson
    c. The Friar
    d. The Summoner

11. He has a forked beard and a motley coat. He is careful with money, a good negotiator, and always tells his opinions about business.
    a. The Haberdasher
    b. The Shipman
    c. The Merchant
    d. The Host

12. This pilgrim was an Oxford student who didn't say much, didn't have a job, and just loved learning for the sake of learning.
    a. The Clerk
    b. The Squire
    c. The Franklin
    d. The Prioress/Nun

13. He seemed wise. He made a lot of money. He seemed busier than he really was.
    a. The Knight
    b. The Squire
    c. The Manciple
    d. The Sergeant at Law

Canterbury Tales Multiple Choice Questions Page 3
Prologue Page 3

14. He looked a little like Santa Claus. He liked to eat, drink and be merry. He was a country gentleman with a dagger and a silk purse.
    a. The Yeoman
    b. The Franklin
    c. The Host
    d. The Pharmacist

15. What tradesmen were there?
    a. A Minstrel, a Barrel-maker, a Tailor, and a Reeve
    b. A Merchant, a Teacher, a Lawyer, a Potter and a Weaver
    c. A Haberdasher, a Dyer, a Carpenter, a Weaver, and a Carpet-maker
    d. A Clerk, a Carpenter, a Barrel-maker, a Plowman, and a Haberdasher

16. This pilgrim was a master of the trade, had a sore on one knee, and was physically a rather disgusting character.
    a. The Plowman
    b. The Cook
    c. The Wife of Bath
    d. The Summoner

17. He was from Dartmouth, didn't ride well, and was a good navigator. He had little conscience about killing the enemy, and seemed rather like a pirate.
    a. The Miller
    b. The Knight
    c. The Reeve
    d. The Shipman

18. He knew his profession well, and took kickbacks from one in another profession. He was not particularly religious. He was dressed in red and blue-gray garments, and loved gold.
    a. The Doctor
    b. The Squire
    c. The Pharmacist
    d. The Manciple

19. This pilgrim was large and somewhat deaf, had a red complexion, wore a wide hat and spurs and had been married several times.
    a. The Host
    b. The Cook
    c. The Wife of Bath
    d. The Shipman

Canterbury Tales Multiple Choice Questions Page 4
Prologue Page 4

20. This pilgrim was truly Christ-like; patient, giving, holy and virtuous, and didn't believe in pomp or glory. He practiced what he preached.
    a. The Monk
    b. The Friar
    c. The Parson
    d. The Pardoner

21. He was the Parson's brother. He was an honest worker who paid his taxes on time.
    a. The Reeve
    b. The Plowman
    c. The Shipman
    d. The Haberdasher

22. He had a football-player build. He had a red beard, a wart on his nose, and a filthy mouth. He cheated customers and in his spare time played the bagpipes.
    a. The Miller
    b. The Cook
    c. The Clerk
    d. The Merchant

Canterbury Tales Multiple Choice Questions Page 5
Prologue Page 5

23. He was a shrewd buyer. Lawyers with all their knowledge were no match for him. He purchased well and kept the extra money for himself. He stole the lawyers blind.
    a. The Franklin
    b. The Manciple
    c. The Sergeant at Law
    d. The Merchant

24. He was old, choleric, and thin. He was a good manager and good carpenter, feared by the farm workers. He usually brought up the rear of the party, lagging behind.
    a. The Pardoner
    b. The Friar
    c. The Squire
    d. The Reeve

25. He had a red face full of sores. He ate onions and drank too much. He would take bribes. he had a garland of flowers on his head and held a cake like a shield.
    a. The Summoner
    b. The Cook
    c. The Haberdasher
    d. The Miller

26. This pilgrim sang in a strong voice, had long, yellow hair, bulging eyes, was baby-faced and carried a bunch of false relics to sell.
    a. The Friar
    b. The Monk
    c. The Pardoner
    d. The Prioress/Nun

27. His name was Harry Bailly. He was manly, good-natured, and happy.
    a. The Knight
    b. The Host
    c. The Shipman
    d. The Franklin

Canterbury Tales Multiple Choice Questions Page 6
Prologue Page 6

28. What does the host propose to the pilgrims?
    a. He proposes that they memorize Bible verses and recite them to the group each evening. The host will keep account of the number each pilgrim memorizes. The pilgrim who memorizes the most will receive a monetary reward from the rest.
    b. He proposes that they stop three times each day (morning, noon and evening) for prayers, and that a different pilgrim will lead the prayers each day.
    c. He proposes that they convert people along the way and take them on the pilgrimage. He convinces the Pardoner to offer special indulgences to the pilgrims who get converts to join them.
    d. He proposes that they each tell two stories on the way to and from their destination. The winner will get a free meal at the expense of the others. The Host will ride along and be the judge. Anyone who doesn't abide by his rule will have to pay everyone's way.

Canterbury Tales Multiple Choice Questions Page 7

The Knight's Tale
1. How did Arcita and Palamon become Theseus's prisoners?
    a. They fought against Theseus and were wounded. After the battle, they were brought to Theseus, and he declared them his prisoners forever.
    b. He found them fighting in his woods, trespassing on his lands, so he put them in his tower as prisoners.
    c. He caught them spying on Emily and sent them to the tower as punishment.
    d. They had killed King Capaneus. Theseus captured them as prisoners in revenge of the king's wrongful death.

2. About what did Arcita and Palamon argue in the tower when they were prisoners?
    a. Who would get out first
    b. Who was the braver knight
    c. Who would marry Emily
    d. Whose fault it was that they were in prison

3. Why was Arcita released from prison?
    a. He sent a note to Theseus explaining how Palamon was to blame, not him, and Theseus accepted his explanation.
    b. The Queen and Emily pleaded on his behalf to Theseus.
    c. He was sick and needed treatment.
    d. Duke Perotheus pleaded for Theseus to let him go.

4. What was the one condition of Arcita's release?
    a. Arcita would marry Emily.
    b. Arcita would never return.
    c. Arcita would not try to help Palamon escape.
    d. Arcita would remain as a servant for Theseus.

5. How and why did Arcita return to Athens?
    a. He came back with an army of knights to destroy Theseus and rescue Palamon.
    b. He came back with an army of knights to get Emily.
    c. He came back disguised as a servant so he could see Emily again.
    d. He returned with gifts to thank Duke Perotheus.

6. How did Palamon get out of prison?
    a. Theseus thought Palamon had suffered enough and let him go.
    b. Theseus's sense of justice made him feel that since Arcita had gone, Palamon should be set free too.
    c. Theseus needed another servant, so he ordered Palamon to be released as his servant.
    d. He poisoned the guard and escaped.

Canterbury Tales Multiple Choice Questions Page 8
Knight's Tale Page 2

7. Why did Theseus spare the lives of Palamon and Arcita when they were fighting in the woods?
    a. The Queen and Emily asked him to.
    b. He didn't have time to take the trouble of executing them.
    c. He didn't know who they were.
    d. He saw what good fighters they were and thought he could use them rather than destroying them.

8. What solution to the knights' problem did Theseus have?
    a. Arcita and Palamon should fight one-on-one to the death to determine who would marry Emily.
    b. They each should come back in one year with 100 knights apiece and then fight to see who would marry Emily.
    c. He decreed that neither would ever marry Emily; they should both give up and go away to live in peace.
    d. They should both marry Emily and share her as their wife.

9. Who won the contest for Emily's hand?
    a. Arcita
    b. Palamon
    c. Neither
    d. Both

10. What happened to Arcita?
    a. He was slain in the contest.
    b. He was mortally wounded in the contest and died shortly after.
    c. He fell off his horse and died from the injury.
    d. Emily poisoned him.

11. How did Palamon come to be married to Emily?
    a. He won the contest.
    b. Arcita told Theseus to marry Palamon and Emily as soon as he died, for Palamon was a noble and good knight and was most deserving.
    c. They spent the years of mourning time together and getting to know each other. Emily fell in love with Palamon. Theseus granted permission for their wedding.
    d. Theseus and his parliament decided that Palamon should marry Emily.

Canterbury Tales Multiple Choice Questions Page 9

The Miller's Tale

1. What is the Miller's condition as he begins to tell his tale?
    a. He is sleepy.
    b. He is preoccupied with his studies.
    c. He is drunk.
    d. He just awakened from a dream, which is the story he relates to the others.

2. Who is Nicholas?
    a. Parish clerk
    b. Student boarding with the carpenter and his wife
    c. The Carpenter
    d. A psychic

3. Describe the carpenter's wife, Alison.
    a. Middle aged but beautiful
    b. Of average good looks, but very provocative
    c. Exceptionally pretty, but everyone knows she is promiscuous
    d. Young and beautiful

4. How did Nicholas get the carpenter out of the way so he and Alison could sleep together?
    a. He pretended to be ill so the carpenter wouldn't suspect he and Alison were sleeping together.
    b. He pretended to have a premonition of a great flood and duped the carpenter into spending one night separated from Alison. When the carpenter fell asleep, Nicholas and Alison ran off to the bedroom together.
    c. He pretended to have a premonition. He agreed to tell the carpenter what he had seen, but insisted on their having a drink beforehand. When the carpenter got drunk, Nicholas and Alison ran off to the bedroom.
    d. Nicholas hired Absalom to pretend to be Alison's suitor to keep the carpenter's suspicions away from him.

5. Identify Absalom.
    a. Parish clerk who loves Alison
    b. Parish clerk Nicholas hires to court Alison
    c. Alison's former suitor who can't accept the fact that she married the carpenter
    d. Parish priest who lusts after Alison

Canterbury Tales Multiple Choice Questions Page 10
Miller's Tale Page 2

6. What joke did Alison and Nicholas play on Absalom?
    a. They told him a great flood was coming and left him sitting in a tub under the roof overnight.
    b. They allowed him to openly try to court Alison to keep suspicion from Nicholas.
    c. The spread the rumor that he was crazy.
    d. They fooled him into kissing Alison's behind.

7. How did Absalom get even with Alison and Nicholas?
    a. He spread rumors about their affair in the village.
    b. He told the carpenter about their affair.
    c. He burned Nicholas's behind with a hot iron.
    d. He cut down the carpenter so he would go find Nicholas and Alison together in the bedroom.

8. Why did the village people think the carpenter was crazy?
    a. Absalom told them that in hopes that they would put the carpenter away in an institution, thus eliminating him from the competition for Alison's affections.
    b. They had always thought he was crazy; this incident just proved it.
    c. He had built a crazy contraption under the roof of his house.
    d. Nicholas offered it as a plausible explanation for the carpenter's ranting.

Canterbury Tales Multiple Choice Questions Page 11

The Reeve's Tale

1. What does the Reeve vow to do through his story?
    a. Show old men still have plenty of spirit
    b. Show students aren't always as smart as the Miller thinks
    c. Get even with the Miller
    d. Win the free dinner

2. Who is Simpkin?
    a. The miller
    b. The warden
    c. Alan
    d. John

3. Identify Molly.
    a. Alan's wife
    b. The baby
    c. The miller's wife
    d. The miller's daughter

4. Why did Alan and John go to the miller's?
    a. It was their job--a part of their work at the college.
    b. They thought they could keep the miller from cheating the college.
    c. The warden was sick and asked them to go in his place.
    d. They wanted to meet Molly.

5. What did the miller do to get the best of Alan and John?
    a. Got them drunk and took 1/2 bushel of their flour
    b. Let their horse go
    c. Skimmed off about 1/2 bushel of their flour as it was being milled
    d. Stole their horse

6. Why did John and Alan stay overnight at the miller's?
    a. They wanted a chance to court Molly.
    b. They were determined to get even and figured they's have a better chance at revenge if they would stay.
    c. They were tired and wet, and it was too late to travel.
    d. The miller's wife felt sorry for them and invited them to stay before the miller had a chance to say otherwise.

Canterbury Tales Multiple Choice Questions Page 12
Reeve's Tale Page 2

7. How did the miller and his guests pass the evening?
    a. Dancing
    b. Arguing and insulting each other
    c. Playing cards
    d. Eating and drinking

8. Which did John and Alan not do to get even with the miller?
    a. Slept with his daughter
    b. Slept with his wife
    c. Took his money playing cards
    d. Got a free meal and night's lodging

9. How did Alan and John get away from the miller's house?
    a. They slipped away before the miller woke up.
    b. The miller's wife hit him on the head and knocked him out by mistake.
    c. They beat up the miller in a fist fight.
    d. Molly helped them.

Canterbury Tales Multiple Choice Questions Page 13

The Shipman's Tale

1. Which is not a main character in the Shipman's tale?
    a. A priest
    b. A merchant
    c. A merchant's wife
    d. Sir John

2. Why did the merchant go to Bruges?
    a. To see his mistress on the pretense of business
    b. To visit his cousin
    c. To do business & lend & borrow money
    d. All of the above

3. What was the merchant's wife's complaint to Sir John?
    a. The merchant abuses her
    b. The merchant doesn't give her enough money
    c. The merchant expects too much of her in bed
    d. The merchant has a mistress

4. What does the merchant's wife ask of Sir John, and what does she offer in return?
    a. To lend her 100 francs
    b. To talk to the merchant for her
    c. To help her get away
    d. To help her commit suicide

5. Why does Sir John want to borrow 100 francs from the merchant?
    a. To buy cattle
    b. To pay another debt
    c. To give to the merchant's wife
    d. To give to the monastery

6. What 'repayment' does Sir John get from the merchant's wife?
    a. She makes him a delicious dinner
    b. Nothing
    c. She has her cousin give him the money back
    d. She sleeps with him

Canterbury Tales Multiple Choice Questions Page 14
Shipman's Tale Page 2

7. Why did Sir John tell the merchant he paid back the loan to the merchant's wife?
   a. He didn't mean to; it just slipped out
   b. So he wouldn't have to pay it "out of pocket"
   c. He thought that might be the last straw that would break their marriage
   d. He was angry with the wife because she wouldn't sleep with him, and he wanted to get her in trouble.

8. What is the merchant's wife's reaction to the merchant's complaint that she didn't tell him Sir John had paid back his debt?
   a. She is furious with Sir John and tells the whole story so the merchant will get revenge.
   b. She breaks down into tears, tells the truth and begs the merchant's forgiveness.
   c. She is calm, admits John gave her money, and offers to pay the merchant back in bed.
   d. She panics and blurts out the whole story including how she was duped into sleeping with Sir John.

9. What does the merchant decide about his wife's little escapade?
   a. He asks her to be more thrifty in the future.
   b. He tells her he'll give her more money in the future.
   c. He forbids her to see Sir John again.
   d. He realizes he has neglected her and forgives her little affair with Sir John.

Canterbury Tales Multiple Choice Questions Page 15

The Prioress's Tale

1. What is the prologue to the Prioress's tale?
    a. An introduction of the tale by the Host
    b. An introduction of the Prioress
    c. A prayer
    d. A request from the Prioress to the others who are listening

2. What is the setting for this tale?
    a. A Christian town in Asia
    b. A village in England
    c. There is no specific setting; it is an unnamed, universal place.
    d. A Jewish ghetto

3. Who is the main character?
    a. A monk
    b. Mary, the Mother of Jesus
    c. There is no main character
    d. A seven year-old boy

4. What did the little boy decide to do?
    a. Become a monk
    b. Learn to sing a song honoring Mary
    c. Learn Latin
    d. Try to convert the Jews

5. What happened to the little boy?
    a. A murderer slit his throat.
    b. Some Jews beat him up in an alley.
    c. He got lost and went to the nearest abbey.
    d. He had a vision of the Blessed Mother.

6. What was unusual about the little boy's death?
    a. The Blessed Mother came for him personally and, in doing so, appeared to the Christians.
    b. Nothing was unusual about it.
    c. He kept singing even though his throat was cut.
    d. A & C

Canterbury Tales Multiple Choice Questions Page 16
Prioress's Tale Page 2

7. Where did the Christian people take the boy?
    a. Monastery
    b. Abbey
    c. Home
    d. Town square

8. What was the boy's answer when asked how he could sing with a slit throat?
    a. The Blessed Mother did it.
    b. He did not answer.
    c. It was the voice of the Blessed Mother.
    d. Christ willed it for the honor of his mother.

9. What happened when the monk took the grain of seed away?
    a. The boy disappeared.
    b. Bright lights appeared and when they left, the boy's body was gone.
    c. The boy died.
    d. The boy came fully to life, stood up, and went to his mother.

Canterbury Tales Multiple Choice Questions Page 17

The Nun's Priest's Tale

1. Identify Chanticleer and Pertelote.
    a. Pertelote is the devil disguised as a hen; she almost claims Chanticleer's soul.
    b. Chanticleer is a rooster almost eaten by Pertelote, the fox.
    c. Chanticleer is the farmer who narrates this story; Pertelote is the rooster.
    d. Chanticleer is a rooster; Pertelote is his favorite hen.

2. What was Chanticleer's dream?
    a. He dreamed that he became rich and master of the barnyard.
    b. He dreamed that he and Pertelote married and had a long and happy life together.
    c. He dreamed that an unfamiliar animal killed him.
    d. He dreamed that Pertelote took ill, but he saved her by using laxatives.

3. To what did Pertelote attribute dreams?
    a. She said he listened to too many fables told by the other animals in the barnyard.
    b. She said he must have indigestion.
    c. She said they were signs from heaven and should be taken seriously.
    d. She said he wasn't getting enough rest.

4. What was Pertelote's suggested remedy?
    a. She suggested he should sleep for two days.
    b. She suggested that he should get more exercise.
    c. She suggested that he should take a laxative.
    d. She suggested that he should pray more.

5. Explain the significance of the Latin phrase that Chanticleer tells Pertelote means "Woman is man's delight and all his bliss."
    a. Chanticleer has mistranslated. It actually means, "Woman is man's worst enemy."
    b. Chanticleer is telling her of his love, but she doesn't understand him.
    c. Chanticleer doesn't realize that he is proposing marriage, but Pertelote thinks so.
    d. It means that a man cannot live without a woman. Chanticleer doesn't really believe this.

6. To what element of the mock-heroic tone does this Latin phrase add?
    a. The supernatural element
    b. The ironic element
    c. The comic element
    d. The realistic element

Canterbury Tales Multiple Choice Questions Page 18
Nun's Priest's Tale Page 2

7. Summarize the story of the shipmates.
    a. One shipmate wanted to steal the other's fortune. They both perished in the attempt.
    b. Both shipmates loved the same woman. They fought a duel over her. In the end, she decided to marry the ship's captain instead of either of them.
    c. One shipmate had a dream that they would be killed at sea if they left port on a certain date. The other shipmate brushed off his concern. They put out to sea, and their ship did go down.
    d. A Pardoner told them that if they didn't make a large offering to the church when they returned safely from a journey, they would lose their lives and their ship on their next voyage. They didn't make the offering, and they perished when their ship went down at sea on their very next voyage.

8. State the reason for Chanticleer's stories to Pertelote.
    a. He is proposing to her in a round-about way.
    b. They are Chanticleer's way of trying to convince Pertelote that dreams should be taken seriously. They also foreshadow his own future.
    c. Chanticleer is bragging about his intelligence, trying to impress her.
    d. Chanticleer wants to scare her, so he can protect her and feel like a hero.

9. Why did the fox flatter Chanticleer?
    a. He did it to get Chanticleer to tell him where the hen house was.
    b. He did it because he wanted to be friends.
    c. He did it hoping that Chanticleer would give him Pertelote to eat.
    d. He did it to put Chanticleer at ease. As Chanticleer sang, he stretched his neck and closed his eyes, making an easy target.

10. What happened to Chanticleer?
    a. The fox hauled him away and prepared to eat him for dinner.
    b. He bit the fox on the nose and escaped.
    c. Pertelote saved him. He was grateful but embarrassed.
    d. The fox's grip on his neck caused him to lose his singing voice forever.

11. How did Chanticleer escape?
    a. He raised such a fuss that the other animals came to his rescue.
    b. He pecked the fox's eyes out and flew away.
    c. He appealed to the fox's sense of superiority and told him not to miss a chance to shout a few insults at the other animals. When the fox opened his mouth, Chanticleer got away.
    d. He pretended to be dead. The fox relaxed his grip, and Chanticleer wiggled out of his mouth.

Canterbury Tales Multiple Choice Questions Page 19

The Pardoner's Tale
1. Of what use is the bone?
    a. It could be used over and over again to make nutritious soups for devoted Christians who were too poor to afford meat.
    b. It could be used as a defense against attackers. It caused extreme pain anywhere it touched someone with evil thoughts.
    c. It brought good luck.
    d. It would cure animals' snake bites or sores. It was also a cure for jealousy.

2. For what use is the mitten and under what condition will it work?
    a. It will provide the wearer with extremely strong hands and arms if his thoughts are for good works like farming rather than evil works like murder.
    b. It will cure most illnesses if the wearer has made a pilgrimage.
    c. It will increase the yield of grain provided the wearer has made a donation to the church.
    d. It will keep the wearer from adultery if he says at least one prayer each day.

3. Describe the "trick" which has been worth a hundred marks a year to the Pardoner.
    a. The Pardoner has a bird that lights on the shoulder of someone who is about to be forgiven. In reality, the Pardoner looks over his audience, finds someone who looks rich, and signals the bird to land there. The forgiven sinners usually make a large donation.
    b. He preaches that the very sinful members of his flock cannot make an offering, but that the virtuous members may, and he will absolve them.
    c. He sells small bottles of water that he says is holy water. It is supposed to wash away the sins of the person who drinks it.
    d. He has one person in the congregation stand up and tell how much more holy his life has been and how he feels spiritually fulfilled since he gave all of his worldly goods to the church.

4. What is the Pardoner's purpose? What is he supposed to do?
    a. His real purpose is to make money. He is supposed to be concerned with saving souls.
    b. His purpose is to convert people and save their souls. That is what he does.
    c. His real purpose is to save souls. He is supposed to be collecting money for his church.
    d. His real purpose is to look for a rich wife. He is supposed to be telling people about god.

5. What is ironic about how the Pardoner gets people to repent from the sin of avarice?
    a. It is a foreshadowing.
    b. It is a metaphor.
    c. It is irony.
    d. it is onomatopoeia.

Canterbury Tales Multiple Choice Questions Page 19
Pardoner's Tale Page 2

6. What bargain or agreement did the rioters make at the tavern?
    a. They agreed to stop rioting if the Pardoner could find wives for all of them.
    b. They agreed to stop all sin within a hundred miles of the tavern.
    c. They agreed to hunt down Death.
    d. They agreed to go with the Pardoner and earn money for the church.

7. They met an old man as they began their journey. What was the old man's problem?
    a. He had been very sinful in his youth. He could not die until he had confessed each sin to a different priest or Pardoner, and made a donation to each of them.
    b. He would gain eternal life if he could find a beautiful young woman to love and marry him.
    c. He would keep getting new illnesses unless he could convert at least one person a day. Most people didn't want to listen to him, because he was so old and diseased.
    d. He had to roam the earth until he had found someone who would trade youth for age.

8. Where does the old man send the rioters?
    a. He sent them to the Holy Land.
    b. He sent them up the road to an oak tree.
    c. He sent them to a hidden cave in the forest.
    d. He sent them to the shrine at Canterbury.

9. What did they find where the old man sent them?
    a. They found three beautiful women waiting for them.
    b. They found eight bushels of gold.
    c. They found a bag full of jewels.
    d. They found jewelry and golden swords.

10. Why did they have to bring the treasure home at night?
    a. They were afraid someone would think they had stolen it.
    b. They were afraid the Pardoner would see them and demand that they turn it over to the church.
    c. They didn't want any highwaymen to rob them.
    d. It was so heavy to carry that it got them overheated in the bright sun. It was easier to carry it at night.

11. Why was one youth sent to town?
    a. He went to scout for robbers.
    b. He went to provide an alibi for the others.
    c. He went to buy food and drink so they would have something to eat while waiting.
    d. He went to buy a horse to carry the load.

12. What plan did the two other youths make to kill the one when he returned from town?
    a. They would ambush him, tie him up, and throw him in the river.
    b. They would cut off his head while he slept.
    c. They would set him on fire.
    d. One would talk to him and the other would come up from behind and stab him.

Canterbury Tales Multiple Choice Questions Page 20
Pardoner's Tale Page 3

13. What plan did the one who went to town make to kill the two others when he got back?
     a. He was going to stab them while they slept.
     b. He was going to let the horse trample them.
     c. He was going to poison them.
     d. He had hired two thugs to kill them as they brought the treasure home.

14. Who died, and how did it happen?
     a. The one died when they stabbed him.
     b. All three died. The two stabbed the one, and then they unknowingly drank the poisoned wine.
     c. Only the two died when the horse trampled them.
     d. They all died. The thugs killed the two men, then killed the one who had hired them.

Canterbury Tales Multiple Choice Questions Page 21

The Friar's Tale

1. Why did the Friar tell a story about a Summoner?
    a. It was the only story he knew well enough to tell.
    b. He was angry with the Summoner from earlier insults.
    c. It just happened to be about a Summoner; there was no foul intent.
    d. The Friar was just trying to save the Summoner's soul.

2. What did the archdeacon punish most?
    a. Lechery.
    b. Adultery.
    c. Failure to pay rents and tithes.
    d. Usury.

3. For whom did the summoner work?
    a. Himself.
    b. The archdeacon.
    c. The King.
    d. A and B.

4. Why did the summoner have informers?
    a. He could bring more of the guilty to justice.
    b. He was lazy; he got others to do his work.
    c. The more criminals he found, the more money he could make from extortion.
    d. The archdeacon had arranged it.

5. Who was the yeoman?
    a. A bailiff.
    b. A fiend from hell.
    c. A man from the north doing the same as the Summoner.
    d. Just a farmer passing by on the road.

6. Why didn't the fiend take the horses, cart and hay?
    a. He knew the farmer didn't mean his curse.
    b. He didn't want them.
    c. He was out on other business and didn't have time for such trivial wares.
    d. He didn't want to show his powers to the Summoner.

7. What had the old woman done to be summoned to court?
    a. Failed to pay her taxes.
    b. Committed adultery.
    c. Cuckolded her husband.
    d. Nothing.

8. What happened to the summoner?
    a. He kept on extorting money from people for the rest of his days.
    b. The archdeacon caught him extorting money and hanged him.
    c. After his close call with the devil, he reformed.
    d. The woman cursed him to hell, and the fiend took him there.

Canterbury Tales Multiple Choice Questions Page 22
Friar's Tale Page 2

9. What is the moral of the Friar's story?
    a. All people in public office are corrupt.
    b. Summoners should repent and quit their vices before the devil gets them
    c. The average person has no chance against the corrupt government.
    d. Beware; the devil lurks in disguise everywhere to tempt and lure even the best people to their own destruction.

Canterbury Tales Multiple Choice Questions Page 23

The Wife of Bath's Tale
1. What does the Wife of Bath think of marriage?
    a. She thinks it is the best way for a woman to protect herself.
    b. She thinks it is a necessary evil.
    c. She thinks it is enjoyable; that's why she had done it so often.
    d. She thinks it is a misery and woe.

2. How many husbands has the Wife of Bath had?
    a. The Wife of Bath has had three husbands.
    b. The Wife of Bath has had eight husbands.
    c. The Wife of Bath has had five husbands.
    d. The Wife of Bath has had two husbands.

3. The Wife of Bath talks about Solomon, Abraham, Jacob, and others from the Bible. What is her point?
    a. She is showing that men are superior, and women should be subservient.
    b. She is defending her many marriages by showing examples of how others in good stead with the church have had many marriages.
    c. She is bragging about her knowledge of the Old Testament.
    d. She is showing that family is important, even to those who are called to a higher mission by God.

4. On what commandment does the Wife of Bath like to dwell?
    a. She likes to dwell on the one that says to honor one's father and mother.
    b. She likes to dwell on the one that says not to covet thy neighbor's goods or wife.
    c. She likes to dwell on the one that says not to kill.
    d. She like to dwell on the one that says husbands should love their wives.

5-8   The Wife of Bath had many complaints about husbands. Read the following statements. Fill in circle A if the statement is one of her complaints. Fill in circle B if it is not one of her complaints.

5. If husbands would "try out" their wives before marriage, they wouldn't think the wives had hidden their "vices."
    a. This is one of her complaints.
    b. This is not one of her complaints.

6. Husbands spy on their wives because they don't trust them to handle money wisely.
    a. This is one of her complaints.
    b. This is not one of her complaints.

7. Husbands seem to forget that their valuables are common property between husband and wife.
    a. This is one of her complaints.
    b. This is not one of her complaints.

8. Husbands think wives contrive ways to make the husbands miserable.
    a. This is one of her complaints.
    b. This is not one of her complaints.

Canterbury Tales Multiple Choice Questions Page 24
Wife of Bath's Tale Page 2

9. "No empty-handed man can lure a bird," said the Wife of Bath. Explain what she meant.
    a. She would only marry a man after she had seen how much money he had.
    b. Marriage is like a cage for a woman. The only way a man can get a woman is to trap her and keep her in a cage.
    c. Her husband had to do something nice for her or bring her something before should would be nice to him or let him sleep with her.
    d. A man must be witty, intelligent, and talented in order to win a woman's love.

10. The Wife of Bath says she was her fourth husband's purgatory. Explain.
    a. Her illness made him suffer, too, out of pity.
    b. She knows she was hateful to him and that his life was miserable because of her.
    c. She was determined to convert him because he was not a Christian when she married him. She helped him see the error of his ways and repent.
    d. She took all the responsibility for his wrongdoings and sins. She wanted to suffer for him.

11. The Wife's fifth husband beat her. Why did she stay with him?
    a. She said she loved him the most.
    b. He was the richest and she wanted the money and comforts it bought.
    c. She was too afraid to leave, because he had many friends and she knew they would kill her if she did.
    d. She talked to her priest in confession and he said she had to stay because marriage was "till death."

12. Who were the Wife's confidants?
    a. The prioress and the other two nuns were the Wife's confidants.
    b. Her housekeeper and the Friar were the Wife's confidants.
    c. Her Godmother and her niece were the Wife's confidants.
    d. Her third husband's mother and sister were the Wife's confidants.

13. What lies did the Wife of Bath tell Johnny?
    a. She said she was rich and would give all of her money to him.
    b. She said she dreamed the night away thinking of him, and that as she lay there he tried to kill her.
    c. She said she loved children, wanted to have a big family, but she had never been able to bear a child full term.
    d. She said he was the most handsome, intelligent man she had ever known.

14. What book did Johnny like to read?
    a. It was The Song of Beowulf.
    b. It was the Bible.
    c. It was about a history of the world.
    d. It was a collection of stories about hateful wives.

Canterbury Tales Multiple Choice Questions Page 25
Wife of Bath's Tale Page 3

15. How did the Wife of Bath partially lose her hearing?
    a. A rock fell on her head while they were sleeping in the woods.
    b. She fell in a river, almost drowned, and then the water blocked her ear and caused deafness.
    c. Johnny hit her across her ear.
    d. She had a high fever many years ago. It damaged her hearing.

16. What was the result of the fight between the Wife of Bath and her fifth husband?
    a. They lived happily ever after.
    b. She killed him.
    c. They divorced.
    d. He was sent to prison for hurting her.

17. Why did the Friar promise to tell a tale poking fun at a Summoner?
    a. The Wife had offered him a purse full of gold to do it.
    b. After her prologue, the Summoner's insulted the Friar.
    c. He is really jealous of the Summoner's outgoing personality and easy way with women.
    d. The Monk offered the Summoner money to insult the Friar. They had been enemies for may years.

18. What did the knight do to warrant the punishment of beheading?
    a. He killed a Friar.
    b. He robbed the king's treasury and gave it to the poor.
    c. He refused to follow the king's orders.
    d. He raped a young maiden.

19. Who saved the knight, and under what condition was he let go?
    a. The King saved him, under the condition that he leave the country and never return.
    b. The priest saved him, under the condition that he enter a monastery and remain there for the rest of his life.
    c. The Queen saved him, under the condition that he would come back in one year's time and tell her the one thing women wanted above all else.
    d. The court sorcerer saved him, under the condition that he become an apprentice sorcerer.

20. What deal did he make on his way home after the year was almost ended?
    a. He met a priest who worked with the poor. The knight promised the priest he would work for a year and give everything he earned to the poor.
    b. He met an old woman who told him the answer to the queen's question and under the condition that he would grant her next request if it would be in his power to do so.
    c. He met a sorcerer who said he could erase everyone's memory of the knight's evil deed. In return, the knight would have to spend the rest of his life doing good deeds and carrying a message of peace to other knights.
    d. He met a beautiful girl and fell in love with her. She agreed to marry him after he had saved twelve other maidens from the crime which he had committed.

Canterbury Tales Multiple Choice Questions Page 26
Wife of Bath's Tale Page 4

21. What was the answer to the Queen's question?
    a. All women want to marry, regardless of the kind of man they marry.
    b. All women want to be young and beautiful forever.
    c. All women want to be happy, above all else.
    d. All women want to be masters of their husbands.

22. What did the woman ask of the knight in return for saving his life?
    a. She asked him to marry her.
    b. She asked him to give her a purse filled with gold.
    c. She asked him to return in one year to help her harvest her crops.
    d. She asked him to sacrifice his life in order that she could become young again.

23. The knight kept his word and married her, but he was miserable. What options did the old woman give him?
    a. She would release him in one year if he would devote that year to loving her.
    b. He could be unfaithful to her, but he would never be happy.
    c. He could have her old and faithful or young and perhaps not so faithful.
    d. He could leave her, but never marry again.

24. What did the knight choose?
    a. He chose to love her.
    b. He left the decision up to her.
    c. He decided to be unfaithful.
    d. He refused to choose.

25. Why did the old woman promise him both beauty and fidelity?
    a. By giving her the choice, he allowed her mastery over him.
    b. She knew he as really trying, and she cared for him.
    c. She knew she would be dead within a few years, and decided that they should both be happy during that time.
    d. She felt sorry for him.

Canterbury Tales Multiple Choice Questions Page 27

The Summoner's Tale

1. Where did the Summoner say all the friars were in hell?
    a. Hidden in the deepest, blackest pit.
    b. In the fiery dungeons.
    c. Under the devil's tail, up his behind.
    d. At the right hand of the devil.

2. What was the main objective of the friar's preaching at church at Holderness?
    a. To reform the people from their gluttonous ways.
    b. To expound upon the ill-effects of anger.
    c. To tell the tale of the Friar who went to hell and came back again.
    d. To raise money to pay for masses for the souls in purgatory.

3. What characteristic of the friars does the Summoner's story accentuate?
    a. Their asking for money and donations.
    b. Their vow of poverty.
    c. Their lack of self-control.
    d. Their insensitivity.

4. Identify Thomas.
    a. The friar.
    b. The sick man who had no money left to give.
    c. The drunken man who shot the nobleman's son with an arrow.
    d. The knight who was accused of killing his fellow knight.

5. Did the friar know about the woman's baby's death prior to her telling him about it?
    a. Yes. He had a vision and the appropriate prayers were said.
    b. Yes. In special cases friars sometimes get "inside information" of this kind because they are so Christ-like and are so close to God.
    c. No. The whole tale he told the mother was a fabrication.
    d. A and B.

6. Who did the friar use as examples showing the necessity of fasting?
    a. Judas.
    b. Moses.
    c. Aaron.
    d. Elijah.

7. Thomas says he's given all his money to various friars and now he has no more to give. What is the friar's response?
    a. Thomas is ill because he has little faith.
    b. Thomas should give more.
    c. Thomas should have given all the money to him instead of spreading it around.
    d. All of the above.

Canterbury Tales Multiple Choice Questions Page 28
Summoner's Tale Page 2

8. Why is the friar's lecture to Thomas about ire ironic?
    a. Thomas isn't an irritable man.
    b. The friar flies into a rage after receiving his "gift" and stays angry for the rest of the story.
    c. The deacon at the convent has been trying to help the friar overcome his own vice of anger.
    d. B and C.

9. What is the point of the two stories the friar uses as examples about anger?
    a. Nobility breeds ire.
    b. Wealth and ire go hand in hand.
    c. Anger makes people senseless.
    d. Anger often results in death.

10. What was Thomas's "gift" to the friar?
    a. His last gold coins he kept hidden under his covers.
    b. Since he had no money left, he promised to work with the friars when he got well.
    c. Dinner.
    d. He passed gas in the friar's hand.

11. What was the squire's solution to the problem of dividing the gift?
    a. Buy something with it that could be divided equally among the friars.
    b. Use a 12-spoked wheel to divide the gift.
    c. Have each friar visit Thomas to receive the same.
    d. There was no solution; it was just a joke.

Canterbury Tales Multiple Choice Questions Page 29

The Clerk's Tale

1. What did the Host ask of the Clerk?
    a. To pay more attention to the tales instead of studying.
    b. To tell a cheerful tale of adventure.
    c. To give the friar his seat.
    d. To tell a tale with a moral and show off his education.

2. What did the marquis' vassals want him to do?
    a. Marry someone.
    b. Pay more attention to his duties.
    c. Arrange a feast for all eligible maidens.
    d. Stop gadding about his lands in such a common manner.

3. Why did the marquis choose Griselda?
    a. Just to make the vassals angry and to test their loyalty.
    b. She was simple of heart.
    c. He just picked her by chance.
    d. He had seen she was beautiful in looks and deeds.

4. What promise did Griselda make to the marquis?
    a. To love the marquis always.
    b. To try to improve herself so she would be worthy of him.
    c. To never disobey him in actions, thoughts or words.
    d. All of the above.

5. Which was not a test?
    a. He took away the children.
    b. He sent another suitor to her bedroom.
    c. He sent her back to her father.
    d. He had her clean and decorate the castle for his new wife.

6. What was Griselda's reaction to each of the tests?
    a. Total submission and devotion to the marquis.
    b. She outwardly showed total devotion and submission, but she mourned the loss of her children.
    c. She became gloomy of heart but never showed it.
    d. She was glad when he sent her home to her father so she wouldn't be emotionally tortured anymore by his tests of her love.

7. What was Griselda's reward for keeping her promise?
    a. Her children were returned.
    b. She remained his wife.
    c. The marquis granted her three requests.
    d. A and B.

Canterbury Tales Multiple Choice Questions Page 30

<u>*The Merchant's Tale*</u>
1. Describe the Merchant's marriage.
	a. Blissful.
	b. Dull.
	c. Happy.
	d. Miserable.

2. Which was not a reason January wanted a young wife?
	a. He wanted someone who would be in awe of his age and wisdom.
	b. A beautiful, young wife would help keep him from adultery.
	c. A young woman would be more pliable and easier to handle.
	d. A young woman could bear children and give him heirs.

3. What did Placebo think of January's idea?
	a. Was very much against it.
	b. Was very much for it.
	c. Was for it, but had some reservations.
	d. Thought the whole thing was too silly to discuss, especially the part about having a young wife.

4. What was Justinus's advice?
	a. Forget the whole thing; it's a bad idea.
	b. Put if off for a few months and see if you feel the same way later.
	c. Don't be hasty; choosing a wife need careful consideration.
	d. Do it. The sooner, the better.

5. Identify May.
	a. The month in which the wedding took place.
	b. January's bride.
	c. January's servant.
	d. A symbolic nickname for all the youthful women January had had through the years.

6. Identify Damian.
	a. Another knight who loved May.
	b. One of January's squires.
	c. January's gardener.
	d. May's confidant.

7. What misfortune befell January?
	a. Damian, emboldened by his passions for May, struck January in the head and he became blind.
	b. He became an invalid.
	c. He realized Damian and his wife were lovers.
	d. He quite suddenly lost his sight.

Canterbury Tales Multiple Choice Questions Page 31
Merchant's Tale Page 2

8. How was January's handicap cured?
    a. Doctors put leeches on his eyes, which removed the blood clot causing it.
    b. He got better out of sheer determination.
    c. He and May were making love in the garden and his sight was suddenly restored.
    d. May climbed on his back to get into a tree and he was suddenly cured.

9. How did May overcome January's accusations?
    a. She told him it was just a dream.
    b. She told him his mind was playing tricks on him; he was after all, an old man.
    c. She told him his vision still wasn't good; he didn't really see what he thought he did.
    d. She told him he'd been out in the sun too long - to come and have a cool drink.

Canterbury Tales Multiple Choice Questions Page 32

The Franklin's Tale
1. Why was Dorigen so sad?
    a. She missed Arveragus.
    b. She missed Aurelius.
    c. Her husband had died when his ship crashed on a reef of rocks.
    d. She was stuck in a miserable marriage.

2. Why didn't Dorigen like the rocks?
    a. They were ugly.
    b. She was sad and angry. Rather than directing her anger at being left alone towards her friends, she vented it on the rocks.
    c. She thought they were a menace and useless, and they reminded her of accidents that could befall her husband.
    d. She longed for the green pastures in which she roamed during her childhood; instead, she had to look at the menacing rocks.

3. What unusual incident happened to Dorigen at the garden party?
    a. The garden party was a surprise party for Dorigen.
    b. She got drunk and lost her inhibitions and forgot her troubles for one evening.
    c. Aurelius professed his love for her.
    d. She and her friends found some nice men to dance and flirt with for the evening.

4. What promise did Dorigen make to Aurelius?
    a. She couldn't ever love him.
    b. She could fall in love with him given the opportunity, should anything ever happen to Arveragus.
    c. If Arveragus didn't come back in one more year, she would assume he was dead and would marry Aurelius.
    d. She would love him best if he would rid the coast of the rocks.

5. How did Aurelius get rid of the rocks?
    a. He worked day and night for three years.
    b. Hired a magician.
    c. He prayed to the gods for a high tide that would stay and cover the rocks forever, and it worked.
    d. He planted foliage so the rocks couldn't be seen.

6. What noble gesture did Arveragus make on behalf of Dorigen?
    a. He said Aurelius could borrow Dorigen for one year.
    b. He offered to kill Aurelius.
    c. He freed Dorigen so she could keep her word.
    d. B then C.

Canterbury Tales Multiple Choice Questions Page 33
Franklin's Tale Page 2

7. What was Aurelius's response when Dorigen told him she and been set free to keep her word?
    a. He praised the gods for his good fortune and they lived together ever after.
    b. After he could have Dorigen, he didn't want her anymore. The chase was done and she bored him, so he sent her away.
    c. He admired her for keeping her word and Arveragus for setting her free. He pitied them both and set Dorigen free to return to Arveragus.
    d. He set Dorigen free and then killed himself.

8. The magician also did a noble deed. What was it?
    a. Reversed the illusion.
    b. Cast a spell on Aurelius to help him forget Dorigen and fall in love with someone else.
    c. Made the illusion permanent for Dorigen so she'd never have to see the rocks again.
    d. Cancelled Aurelius's debt.

ANSWER KEY - MULTIPLE CHOICE STUDY/QUIZ QUESTIONS
The Canterbury Tales

Prologue	Miller	Pardoner	Friar	Franklin
1. C	1. C	1. D	1. B	1. A
2. B	2. B	2. C	2. A	2. C
3. D	3. D	3. B	3. D	3. C
4. A	4. B	4. A	4. C	4. D
5. B	5. A	5. C	5. B	5. B
6. C	6. D	6. C	6. A	6. C
7. A	7. C	7. D	7. D	7. C
8. D	8. D	8. B	8. D	8. D
9. B		9. B		
10. C	Reeve	10. A	Summoner	
11. C	1. C	11. C	1. C	Shipman
12. A	2. A	12. D	2. D	1. A
13. D	3. D	13. C	3. A	2. C
14. B	4. B	14. B	4. B	3. B
15. C	5. B		5. C	4. A
16. B	6. C	Wife of Bath	6. A	5. C
17. D	7. D	1. D	7. D	6. D
18. A	8. C	2. C	8. B	7. B
19. C	9. B	3. B	9. C	8. C
20. C		4. D	10. D	9. A
21. A	Prioress	5. A	11. B	
22. A	1. C	6. B		
23. B	2. A	7. A	Clerk	
24. D	3. D	8. A	1. B	
25. A	4. B	9. C	2. A	
26. C	5. A	10. B	3. D	
27. B	6. C	11. A	4. C	
28. D	7. B	12. C	5. B	
	8. D	13. B	6. A	
Knight	9. C	14. D	7. D	
1. A		15. C		
2. C	Nun's Priest	16. A	Merchant	
3. D	1. D	17. B	1. D	
4. B	2. C	18. D	2. A	
5. C	3. B	19. C	3. B	
6. D	4. C	20. B	4. C	
7. A	5. A	21. D	5. B	
8. B	6. B	22. A	6. B	
9. A	7. C	23. C	7. D	
10. C	8. B	24. B	8. D	
11. D	9. D	25. A	9. C	
	10. A			
	11. C			

PREREADING VOCABULARY WORKSHEETS

VOCABULARY - *The Canterbury Tales*

Part I: Using Prior Knowledge and Contextual Clues

Below are the sentences in which the vocabulary words appear in the text. Read the sentence. use any clues you can find in the sentence combined with your prior knowledge, and write what you think the underlined words mean in the space provided.

1. The veins are bathed in liquor of such power as brings about the engendering of the flower.

2. And plamers long to seek the stranger strands of far-off saints, hallowed in sundry lands.

3. It seems a reasonable thing to say what their condition was, the full array of each of them, as it appeared to me.

4. There was a knight, ...who from the day on which he first began to ride abroad had followed chivalry, truth, honour, generousness and courtesy.

5. In fifteen mortal battles he had been and jousted for our faith at Tramissene.

6. Just home from service, he had joined our ranks to do his pilgrimage and render thanks.

7. He'd seen some service with cavalry...and had done valiantly in little space of time, in hope to win his lady's grace.

8. Shield and sword hung at one side, and at the other slipped a jaunty dirk, spear-sharp and well equipped.

9. Her way of smiling very simple and coy.

10. She reached a hand sedately for the meat.

Part II: Determining the Meaning -- Match the vocabulary word to their definitions.

____ 1. engendering
____ 2. sundry
____ 3. array
____ 4. chivalry
____ 5. jousted
____ 6. render
____ 7. valiantly
____ 8. dirk
____ 9. coy
____ 10. sedately

A. Dignified in character or manner.
B. A combat between two mounted knights using lances.
C. Bravely.
D. Reserved, shy or modest.
E. To bring into existence.
F. The medieval system, principles, and customs of knighthood.
G. A dagger.
H. Splendid attire; finery; dress.
I. to give what is due or owed.
J. Various; miscellaneous.

Prologue Vocabulary Worksheet Page 2

11. She was so charitably <u>solicitous</u> she used to weep if she but saw a mouse caught in a trap.

12. <u>Supple</u> his boots, his horse in fine condition.

13. He was a <u>prelate</u> fit for exhibition.

14. He liked a fat swan best, and roasted whole. His <u>palfrey</u> was as brown is a berry.

15. There was a Friar, a <u>wanton</u> one and merry.

16. So <u>glib</u> with gallant phrase and well-turned speech.

17. It's a sure thing whenever gifts are given to a poor Order that a man's well <u>shriven</u>.

18. Should he give enough he knew in <u>verity</u>...for many a fellow is so hard of heart.

19. For in so <u>eminent</u> a man as he it was not fitting with dignity of his position, dealing with a scum of wretched lepers.

20. He was ever prompt to <u>arbitrate</u> disputes on settling days (for a small fee) in many helpful ways.

Part II: Determining the Meaning -- Match the vocabulary words to their definitions.

___ 11. solicitous
___ 12. supple
___ 13. prelate
___ 14. palfrey
___ 15. wanton
___ 16. glib
___ 17. shrive
___ 18. verity
___ 19. eminent
___ 20. arbitrate

A. A woman's saddle horse.
B. To act as judge, decide disputes.
C. Absolve from sins.
D. Performed with a natural, offhand ease.
E. Expressing care or concern.
F. The quality of being true, factual, or real.
G. A high-ranking member of the clergy.
H. Unrestrainedly excessive, luxuriant; frolicsome; playful.
I. Of high rank, distinguished.
J. Easily bent; pliant.

Prologue Vocabulary Worksheet Page 3

21. Wary and wise...<u>discreet</u> he was, a man to reverence. Or so he seemed, his sayings were so wise.

22. White as a daisy-petal was his beard. A <u>sanguine</u> man, high-coloured and benign.

23. He lived for pleasure and had always done...in whose opinion sensual delight was the one true <u>felicity</u> in sight.

24. Their knives were not tricked out with brass but wrought with purest silver, which <u>avouches</u>.

25. Each seemed a worthy <u>burgess</u>, fit to grace a guild-hall with a seat upon the dais.

26. To be called 'Madam' is a glorious thought...having your <u>mantle</u> carried, like a queen.

27. The cause of every <u>malady</u> you'd got he knew...he was a perfect practising physician.

28. In his own diet he observed some measure; there were no <u>superfluities</u> for pleasure. Only digestives, nutritives and such.

29. Easily on an ambling horse she sat, well <u>wimpled</u> up, and on her head a hat.

30. Who truly knew Christ's gospel and would preach it...<u>benign</u> and wonderfully diligent, and patient when adversity was sent.

Part II: Determining the meaning -- Match the vocabulary words to their definitions.

___ 21. discreet
___ 22. sanguine
___ 23. felicity
___ 24. avouches
___ 25. burgess
___ 26. mantle
___ 27. malady
___ 28. superfluities
___ 29. wimpled
___ 30. benign

A. To declare the provable truth or validity of; affirm.
B. Tactful.
C. A citizen of an English borough.
D. Illness; trouble.
E. A loose, sleeveless coat worn over outer garments; a cloak.
F. Great happiness; bliss.
G. Of a healthy, reddish color.
H. Things that are not necessary.
I. Of a kind and gentle disposition.
J. Wrinkled.

Prologue Vocabulary Worksheet Page 4

31. He did not set his <u>benefice</u> to hire...he stayed at home and watched over his fold.

32. He was a shepherd and no <u>mercenary</u>.

33. His business was to show a fair behaviour...unless indeed a man were <u>obstinate</u>.

34. As the gospel bade him, so did he, loving God best with all his heart and mind. Then his neighbour and himself, <u>repined</u>.

35. His mighty mouth was like a furnace door. A wrangler and <u>buffoon</u>, he had a store of tavern stories, filthy in the main.

36. All caterers might follow his example in buying <u>victuals</u>; he was never rash whether he bough on credit or paid cash.

37. Show him how to live on what he had debt-free...or be as <u>frugal</u> as he might desire.

38. He had been under contract to present the accounts...no one had ever caught him in <u>arrears</u>.

39. He had grown rich and had a store of treasure...yet out it came to pleasure his lord with <u>subtle</u> loans or gifts of goods.

40. A curse should put a guilty man in dread, for curses kill, as <u>shriving</u> brings, salvation.

Part II: Determining the Meaning -- Match the vocabulary words to their definitions.

___ 31. benefice
___ 32. mercenary
___ 33. obstinate
___ 34. repined
___ 35. buffoon
___ 36. victuals
___ 37. frugal
___ 38. arrears
___ 39. subtle
___ 40. shriving

A. A person given to clawing and joking.
B. Food fit for human consumption.
C. An unpaid, overdue debt.
D. Complained.
E. Not immediately obvious, operating in a hidden way.
F. Obtaining absolution for sins.
G. Thrifty.
H. Difficult to manage, control.
I. A church office endowed with fixed capital assets that provide a living.
J. One who serves or works merely for money.

Prologue Vocabulary Worksheet Page 5

41. We should beware of excommunication...as if it were a shield.

42. Thus, as he pleased, the man could bring duress.

43. By his flatteries and prevarication made monkeys of the priest and congregation.

44. He may not flinch although it were his brother, he may as well say one word as another.

45. Yet there is no scurrility in it.

46. Well, our opinion was not long deferred

47. And please don't treat my notion with disdain.

48. We promised to be ruled by his advice ... unanimously thus we set him up in judgement over us.

Part II: Determining the Meaning -- Match the vocabulary words to their definitions.

___ 41. excommunication   A. To betray pain with an involuntary gesture.
___ 42. duress   B. To treat with contempt.
___ 43. prevarication   C. Vulgar or abusive language.
___ 44. flinch   D. Being in complete harmony or accord.
___ 45. scurrility   E. Constraint by threat; coercion.
___ 46. deferred   F. Straying from or evading the truth; equivocate.
___ 47. disdain   G. Postpones; delayed.
___ 48. unanimously   H. To deprive of the right of church membership by ecclesiastical authority.

KEY: *THE PROLOGUE* PREREADING VOCABULARY WORKSHEET PART II

Page 1

E	1. engendering	A. Dignified in character or manner.
J	2. sundry	B. A combat between two mounted knights using using lances.
H	3. array	C. Bravely.
F	4. chivalry	D. Reserved, shy or modest.
B	5. jousted	E. To bring into existence.
I	6. render	F. The medieval system, principles, and customs of knighthood.
C	7. valiantly	G. A dagger.
G	8. dirk	H. Splendid attire; finery; dress.
D	9. coy	I. to give what is due or owed.
A	10. sedately	J. Various; miscellaneous.

Page 2

E	11. solicitous	A. A woman's saddle horse.
J	12. supple	B. To act as judge, decide disputes.
G	13. prelate	C. Absolve from sins.
A	14. palfrey	D. Performed with a natural, offhand ease.
H	15. wanton	E. Expressing care or concern.
D	16. glib	F. The quality of being true, factual, or real.
C	17. shrive	G. A high-ranking member of the clergy.
F	18. verity	H. Unrestrainedly excessive, luxuriant; frolicsome; playful.
I	19. eminent	I. Of high rank, distinguished.
B	20. arbitrate	J. Easily bent; pliant.

Page 3

B	21. discreet	A. To declare the provable truth or validity of; affirm.
G	22. sanguine	B. Tactful.
F	23. felicity	C. A citizen of an English borough.
A	24. avouches	D. Illness; trouble.
C	25. burgess	E. A loose, sleeveless coat worn over outer garments; a cloak.
E	26. mantle	F. Great happiness; bliss.
D	27. malady	G. Of a healthy, reddish color.
H	28. superfluities	H. Things that are not necessary.
J	29. wimpled	I. Of a kind and gentle disposition.
I	30. benign	J. Wrinkled.

Prologue Answer Key Page 2

Page 4

I	31. benefice	A. A person given to clowning and joking.
J	32. mercenary	B. Food fit for human consumption.
H	33. obstinate	C. An unpaid, overdue debt.
D	34. repined	D. Complained.
A	35. buffoon	E. Not immediately obvious, operating in a hidden way.
B	36. victuals	
G	37. frugal	F. Obtaining absolution for sins.
C	38. arrears	G. Thrifty.
E	39. subtle	H. Difficult to manage, control.
F	40. shriving	I. A church office endowed with fixed capital assets that provide a living.
		J. One who works merely for money.

Page 5

H	41. excommunication	A. To betray pain with an involuntary gesture.
E	42. duress	B. To treat with contempt.
F	43. prevarication	C. Vulgar or abusive language.
A	44. flinch	D. Being in complete harmony or accord.
C	45. scurrility	E. Constraint by threat; coercion.
G	46. deferred	F. Straying from or evading the truth; equivocate.
B	47. disdain	G. Postpones; delayed.
D	48. unanimously	H. To deprive of the right of church membership by ecclesiastical authority.

Prereading Vocabulary - *The Knight's Tale*

Part I: Using Prior Knowledge and Contextual Clues

Below are the sentences in which the vocabulary words appear in the text. Read the sentence. Use any clues you can find in the sentence combined with your prior knowledge, and write what you think the underlined words mean in the space provided.

1. Hippolyta had been besieged and taken...after the tempest that had <u>harried</u> their home-coming.

2. This Duke I mentioned...in all <u>felicity</u> and height of pride became aware that kneeling on the highway, a company of ladies were in view.

3. We in our <u>disconsolate</u> array...lost each her husband in that fatal city during the siege.

4. O alas, alas! - The Lord of Thebes, grown cruel in his age and filled with foul <u>iniquity</u> and rage, does outrage on the bodies of our dead.

5. And close by them his <u>pennon</u> of renown shown rich with gold.

6. And to the ladies he restored again the bones belonging to their husbands slain, to do, as custom was, their <u>obsequies</u>.

7. Stripping their <u>accoutrements</u> for gain, the pillagers went busily about.

8. Young Emily, that fairer was of <u>mien</u> than is the lily on its stalk of green.

9. Fortune has given us this adversity, some wicked planetary <u>dispensation</u>.

Part II: Determining the Meaning -- Match the vocabulary words to their definitions.

___ 1. harried   A. A funeral right or ceremony.
___ 2. felicity   B. Bliss; happiness.
___ 3. disconsolate   C. Harassed; bothered; disturbed.
___ 4. iniquity   D. Cheerless; gloomy.
___ 5. pennon   E. A pennant, banner, or flag.
___ 6. obsequies   F. Gross immorality or injustice; wickedness.
___ 7. accoutrements   G. An exemption or a release from an obligation or a rule.
___ 8. mien   H. Bearing or manner; appearance.
___ 9. dispensation   I. Accessories.

Knight's Tale Vocabulary Worksheet Page 2

11. O cruel Gods, whose government...writes upon an <u>adamantine</u> table all that your conclave has decreed as stable.

12. But I lie <u>languishing</u> in prison still.

13. Juno and Saturn in their jealous rage have almost <u>quelled</u> our Thebian lineage.

14. Lies there condemned to a perpetual jail, chained up in <u>fetters</u> till his dying breath.

15. On the following day Arcita <u>proffered</u> at the gate for hire. Thus they parted at the coppice-edge until the morning.

16. Consider, is it not the height of folly? What is so foolish as a man in love? Yet, in spite of that, they pose as <u>sages</u>, these devotees of love.

17. How richly decked the palace, what the place ordained for first and last upon the <u>dais.</u>

18. Mine are the maladies that kill with cold, the dark deceits, the stratagems of old; a look from me will father <u>pestilence</u>.

19. Peace must be made between you soon, I guess, although you do not share the same complexions; that is what brings these daily <u>insurrections</u>.

20. Lord on apparelled <u>coursers</u>, squires too and knights belonging to their retinue.

Part II: Determining the Meaning -- Match the vocabulary words to their definitions.

    ___ 11. adamantine   A. Ones distinguished for wisdom.
    ___ 12. languishing   B. A usually fatal epidemic disease.
    ___ 13. quelled   C. Revolts.
    ___ 14. fetters   D. A raised platform.
    ___ 15. proffered   E. Having the hardness or luster of a diamond.
    ___ 16. sages   F. Swift horses.
    ___ 17. dais   G. To put down forcibly.
    ___ 18. pestilence   H. To offer for acceptance.
    ___ 19. insurrections   I. A chain or shackle for the ankles or feet.
    ___ 20. coursers   J. Becoming weak; losing strength.

Knight's Tale Vocabulary Worksheet Page 3

21. Lord on apparelled coursers, squires too and knights belonging to their <u>retinue</u>.

22. Great Theseus was awoken out of sleep...but kept his chamber - a <u>resplendent</u> room.

23. Throned in a window giving on a pleasance sat Theseus like in a <u>panoply</u>.

24. Which of them had the advantage of his foe in <u>valiance</u>, age, degree of strength of show.

25. To stop all <u>rancour</u>, grudge and emulation, that each side was as valorous as the other.

26. Since Hector, freshly slaughtered, was <u>interred</u> in Troy.

27. He knew the <u>transmutations</u> of the world and had seen its changes as it whirled bliss upon sorrow, sorrow upon bliss.

28. This effect with wisest <u>exhortation</u>, heartening the people in their tribulation.

29. And that same Prince and Mover then, ' said he,`stablish this wretched world, appointing ways, Seasons, durations, certain length of days, to all that is engendered here, below, past which <u>predestined</u> hour none may go.

30. Arcite rose up and sought the <u>edifice</u> of fiery Mars.

31. To stop all rancour, grudge and <u>emulation</u> that each side was as valorous as the other.

Part II. Determining the Meaning - Match the vocabulary words to their definitions.

___ 21. retinue	A. Large structure or building.
___ 22. resplendent	B. To strive to equal or excel, especially through imitation.
___ 23. panoply	C. Decided in advance.
___ 24. valiance	D. Speech to incite or uplift.
___ 25. rancour	E. Buried.
___ 26. interred	F. Attendants accompanying a high-ranking person.
___ 27. transmutations	G. Deep-seated ill will.
___ 28. exhortation	H. Bravery.
___ 29. predestined	I. Changing from one form, nature, or substance into another.
___ 30. edifice	J. Splendid or dazzling in appearance.
___ 31. emulation	K. Ceremonial attire with all accessories.

Answer Key: *The Knight's Tale* Prereading Vocabulary Worksheet Part II

Page 1

C	1. harried	A. A funeral right or ceremony.
J	2. felicity	B. Bliss.
D	3. disconsolate	C. Harassed; bothered; disturbed.
F	4. iniquity	D. Cheerless; gloomy.
E	5. pennon	E. A pennant, banner, or flag.
A	6. obsequies	F. Gross immorality or injustice; wickedness.
I	7. accoutrements	G. An exemption or a release from an obligation or a rule.
H	8. mien	H. Bearing or manner; appearance.
G	9. dispensation	I. Accessories.
B	10. felicity	J. Happiness.

Page 2

E	11. adamantine	A. Ones distinguished for wisdom.
J	12. languishing	B. A usually fatal epidemic disease.
G	13. quelled	C. Revolts.
I	14. fetters	D. A raised platform.
H	15. proffered	E. Having the hardness or luster of a diamond.
A	16. sages	F. Swift horses.
D	17. dais	G. To put down forcibly.
B	18. pestilence	H. To offer for acceptance.
C	19. insurrections	I. A chain or shackle for the ankles or feet.
F	20. coursers	J. Becoming weak; losing strength.

Page 3

F	21. retinue	A. Large structure or building.
J	22. resplendent	B. To strive to equal or excel, especially through imitation.
K	23. panoply	C. Decided in advance.
H	24. valiance	D. Speech to incite or uplift.
G	25. rancour	E. Buried.
E	26. interred	F. Attendants accompanying a high-ranking person.
I	27. transmutations	G. Deep-seated ill will.
D	28. exhortation	H. Bravery.
C	29. predestined	I. Changing from one form, nature, or substance into another.
A	30. edifice	J. Splendid or dazzling in appearance.
B	31. emulation	K. Ceremonial attire with all accessories.

Vocabulary - *The Miller's Tale*

Part I: Using Prior Knowledge and Contextual Clues
    Below are the sentences in which the vocabulary words appear in the text. Read the sentence. Use any clues you can find in the sentence combined with your prior knowledge, and write what you think the underlined words mean in the space provided.

1. Some time ago there was a rich old <u>codger</u>.

2. For he was very close and sly, and took advantage of his <u>meek</u> and girlish look.

3. He rented a small chamber in the <u>kip</u> all by himself without companionship.

4. She wore a broad silk <u>fillet</u>, rather high.

5. Certainly she had a <u>lecherous</u> eye.

6. As to her song, it was as long and quick as any swallow's chirping on a <u>rick</u>.

7. He made a grab and caught her by the <u>quim</u>.

8. Then Nicholas began to plead his cause and spoke so fair in <u>proffering</u> what he could that in the end she promised him she would.

9. She put her work aside and she <u>enticed</u> the colour to her face to make her mark.

10. This Absalom, so jolly in his ways, would bear the <u>censer</u> round on holy days and cense the parish women.

Part II: Determining the Meaning -- Match the vocabulary words to their definitions.

    ___ 1. codger   A. Container holding incense.
    ___ 2. meek   B. To offer for acceptance.
    ___ 3. kip   C. Promiscuous.
    ___ 4. fillet   D. To bring out.
    ___ 5. lecherous   E. Room or bed in rooming house.
    ___ 6. rick   F. Archaic slang for vulva or vagina
    ___ 7. quim   G. A narrow of ribbon or similar material, often worn
    ___ 8. proffering   as a headband.
    ___ 9. enticed   H. Gentle, submissive.
    ___ 10. censers   I. A stack of hay or straw.
                                              J. Eccentric old man.

Miller's Tale Vocabulary Worksheet Page 2

11. He ups with his guitar and off he tours on the look-out for any paramours.

12. Larky and amorous, away he strode until he reached the carpenter's abode.

13. He lay awake all night, and all the day, wooed her by go-between and wooed by proxy.

14. Swore to page and servant to his doxy.

15. She looked upon him as her private ape and held his earnest wooing all a jape.

16. Happened just so with such another student of astronomy and he was so imprudent as to stare upwards while he crossed a field.

17. Get me a staff to prise against the floor.

18. The carpenter supposed it was despair and caught him by the shoulders mightily, shook him and shouted with asperity: `What, Nicholas! Hey! Look down!

19. Swear on your honour here not to repeat a syllable I say, for here are Christ's intentions, to betray which to a soul puts you among the lost, and vengeance for it at a bitter cost.

20. And so if good advice is to prevail I undertake with neither mast nor sail to save her yet, and save myself and you.

Part II: Determining the Meaning -- Match the vocabulary words to their definitions.

    ___ 11. paramours   A. Leverage.
    ___ 12. abode   B. Harshness of manner; ill temper or irritability.
    ___ 13. proxy   C. A person authorized to act for another; agent.
    ___ 14. doxy   D. Triumph.
    ___ 15. jape   E. Punishment in return for a wrong committed.
    ___ 16. imprudent   F. Paramour.
    ___ 17. prise   G. To joke about, make sport of.
    ___ 18. asperity   H. Unwise or indiscreet.
    ___ 19. vengeance   I. House.
    ___ 20. prevail   J. Lovers.

Miller's Tale Vocabulary Worksheet Page 3

21. The waters will <u>abate</u> and flow away.

22. Go, save our lives for us, as I <u>beseech</u> you.

23. How fancy throws us into <u>perturbation</u>!

24. Before his eyes there <u>verily</u> seemed to be the floods of Noah, wallowing like the sea

25. He groaned in sleep for <u>travail</u> of his soul

26. His <u>malady</u> was cured by this endeavour

27. No matter what the carpenter <u>asserted</u> it went for nothing, no one was converted

Part II: Determining the Meaning - Match the vocabulary words to their definitions.

    ___ 21. abate   A. Stated or expressed positively.
    ___ 22. beseech   B. Agony; anguish.
    ___ 23. perturbation   C. In truth.
    ___ 24. verily   D. The state of being irritated; bothered or annoyed.
    ___ 25. travail   E. An unwholesome condition; illness.
    ___ 26. malady   F. To request earnestly.
    ___ 27. asserted   G. To reduce in amount, degree, or intensity; lessen.

The Miller's Tale Prereading Vocabulary Worksheet Part II

Page 1

J	1. codger	A. Container holding incense.
H	2. meek	B. To offer for acceptance.
E	3. kip	C. Promiscuous.
G	4. fillet	D. To bring out.
C	5. lecherous	E. Room or bed in rooming house.
I	6. rick	F. Archaic slang for vulva or vagina
F	7. quim	G. A narrow of ribbon or similar material, often worn as a headband.
B	8. proffering	H. Gentle, submissive.
D	9. enticed	I. A stack of hay or straw.
A	10. censers	J. Eccentric old man.

Page 2

J	11. paramours	A. Leverage.
I	12. abode	B. Harshness of manner; ill temper or irritability.
C	13. proxy	C. A person authorized to act for another; agent.
F	14. doxy	D. Triumph.
G	15. jape	E. Punishment in return for a wrong committed.
H	16. imprudent	F. Paramour.
A	17. prise	G. To joke about, make sport of.
B	18. asperity	H. Unwise or indiscreet.
E	19. vengeance	I. House.
D	20. prevail	J. Lovers.

Page 3

G	21. abate	A. Stated or expressed positively.
F	22. beseech	B. Agony; anguish.
D	23. perturbation	C. In truth.
C	24. verily	D. The state of being irritated; bothered or annoyed.
B	25. travail	E. An unwholesome condition; illness.
E	26. malady	F. To request earnestly.
A	27. asserted	G. To reduce in amount, degree, or intensity; lessen.

Vocabulary - *The Reeve's Tale*

Part I: Using Prior Knowledge and Contextual Clues

Below are the sentences in which the vocabulary words appear in the text. Read the sentence. Use any clues you can find in the sentence combined with your prior knowledge, and write what you think the underlined words mean in the space provided.

1. Trenchant it was as any sword that's made.

2. This miller levied toll beyond a doubt on wheat and malt from all the land about

3. And how's your canny daughter and your wife?

4. And when he saw his chance he sidled out into the yard behind and looked about

5. Lord save us all, the Warden's palfrey's lost

6. You must be daft, bad luck to you!

7. And off ran John and Alan in dismay.

8. So back they went, John grousing all the way, towards the mill and put the horse in byre

9. They supped and talked and had a fine carouse

10. The law grants easement when things gan amiss

11. Against wor loss, I'll take the easement proffered

12. At last she gropes to where the cradle stands

13. Up started John, he needed no inciting

14. And, hoping to hit Alan, it was her fate to smite the miller on his shining pate

15. And thus the bumptious miller was well beaten

The Reeve's Tale Prereading Vocabulary Worksheet Part II

Part II: Determining the Meaning -- Match the vocabulary words to their definition.

____ 1. trenchant
____ 2. levied
____ 3. canny
____ 4. sidled
____ 5. palfrey's
____ 6. daft
____ 7. dismay
____ 8. byre
____ 9. carouse
____ 10. amiss
____ 11. proffered
____ 12. gropes
____ 13. inciting
____ 14. pate
____ 15. bumptious

A. To offer for acceptance.
B. Crudely or loudly assertive; pushy.
C. Mad; crazy; foolish; stupid.
D. Reaches about uncertainly; feel one's way.
E. to provoke and urge on.
F. Top of the head.
G. Cowshed or barn.
H. Extra post horse.
I. Boisterous, drunken merrymaking.
J. Pleasant; attractive.
K. Sharp.
L. To edge along indirectly.
M. A sudden or complete loss of courage in the face of trouble or danger.
N. Imposed or collected.
O. In an improper, defective, unfortunate, or mistaken way.

Key: *Reeve's Tale* Vocabulary Worksheet Part II

K	1. trenchant		A. To offer for acceptance.
N	2. levied		B. Crudely or loudly assertive; pushy.
J	3. canny		C. Mad; crazy; foolish; stupid.
L	4. sidled		D. Reaches about uncertainly; feel one's way.
H	5. palfrey's		E. to provoke and urge on.
C	6. daft		F. Top of the head.
M	7. dismay		G. Cowshed or barn.
G	8. byre		H. Extra post horse.
I	9. carouse		I. Boisterous, drunken merrymaking.
O	10. amiss		J. Pleasant; attractive.
A	11. proffered		K. Sharp.
D	12. gropes		L. To edge along indirectly.
E	13. inciting		M. A sudden or complete loss of courage in the face of trouble or danger.
F	14. pate		N. Imposed or collected.
B	15. bumptious		O. In an improper, defective, unfortunate, or mistaken way.

Vocabulary - *The Shipman's Tale*

Part I: Using Prior Knowledge and Contextual Clues
    Below are the sentences in which the vocabulary words appear in the text. Read the sentence. Use any clues you can find in the sentence combined with your prior knowledge, and write what you think the underlined words mean in the space provided.

1. There was a merchant in St. Denys once who being rich was held to be no <u>dunce</u>

2-4. He had a wife, unusually fair, one of a gay, companionable air, a thing which causes more <u>pecunial dearth</u> than all the <u>foppish</u> compliments are worth that menfolk offer them at feasts and dances.

5. But <u>woe</u> to him that has to pay for all!

6. It pleased the merchant's heart, and his <u>compliance</u> had furthered this unbreakable alliance

7. The merchant ... began to make arrangements for a stay somewhere near Bruges to further his affairs and buy a fresh <u>consignment</u> of his wares.

8. ... a man can keep in tune on five good hours of sleep, as I should judge, unless he is a poor old <u>pallid</u> drudge.

9. I know a wife should only speak in honour about her husband, or else <u>fie</u> upon her!

10. ... how little you <u>divine</u> of the complicated nature of affairs!

Part II: Determining the Meaning -- Match the vocabulary words to their definitions.

    ___ 1. dunce   A. Used to express distaste or disapproval.
    ___ 2. pecunial   B. Pale.
    ___ 3. dearth   C. Deep distress or misery.
    ___ 4. foppish   D. Supply of goods to sell.
    ___ 5. woe   E. To know by intuition, or reflection.
    ___ 6. compliance   F. A person regarded as stupid.
    ___ 7. consignment   G. Shortage
    ___ 8. pallid   H. To be vain; preoccupied with one's clothing; dandy.
    ___ 9. fie   I. Relating to money.
    ___ 10. divine   J. The act of complying with a wish, request, or demand; acquiescence.

Shipman's Tale Vocabulary Worksheet Page 2

11. Could you <u>contrive</u> to lend a hundred francs?

12. They drank and talked and <u>loitered</u> for a spell

13. ... to take his hundred francs and to <u>requite</u> Sir John by lying in his arms all night.

14. For he was bound by a <u>recognisance</u> for twenty thousand crowns he had to pay

15-17. Sir John was most <u>effusive</u> in his greetings and he <u>blithely</u> chatted back and told how prosperously he had bought and sold, thanks be to God, in all his merchandise, save that it was <u>incumbent</u> to devise the raising of a loan at interest ....

18. This merchant, who was wary and <u>discreet</u>, soon managed to negotiate his loan

19. And <u>wantonly</u> she gambolled for a while

20. I'm a little cross with you, my dear, though I am <u>loth</u> to be so, never fear.

21. I'll pay you readily, and as for <u>pelf</u>, if that should fail, from sunset to revally, I am your wife, so score it on my tally.

22-23. This merchant saw that there was no <u>redress</u> and that to <u>chide</u> her was but foolishness since nothing could be done

Part II: Determining the Meaning -- Match the vocabulary words to their definitions.

___ 11. contrive
___ 12. loitered
___ 13. requite
___ 14. recognisance
___ 15. effusive
___ 16. blithely
___ 17. incumbent
___ 18. discreet
___ 19. wantonly
___ 20. loth
___ 21. pelf
___ 22. redress
___ 23. chide

A. Imposed as an obligation or duty.
B. Wealth or riches.
C. Remedy.
D. Flowing out; pouring out.
E. Unrestrainedly; excessively.
F. Scold mildly; reprimand.
G. Unwilling or reluctant.
H. To stand idly about; to delay or dawdle.
I. To bring about, as by scheming; manage.
J. An obligation of record.
K. Repay.
L. Carefree and lightheartedly.
M. Showing prudence and wise self-restraint in speech and behavior.

The Shipman's Tale Prereading Vocabulary Worksheet Part II

Page 1

F	1. dunce	A. Used to express distaste or disapproval.
I	2. pecunial	B. Pale.
G	3. dearth	C. Deep distress or misery.
H	4. foppish	D. Supply of goods to sell.
C	5. woe	E. To know by intuition, or reflection.
J	6. compliance	F. A person regarded as stupid.
D	7. consignment	G. Shortage
B	8. pallid	H. To be vain; preoccupied with one's clothing; dandy.
A	9. fie	I. Relating to money.
E	10. divine	J. The act of complying with a wish, request, or demand; acquiescence.

Page 2

I	11. contrive	A. Imposed as an obligation or duty.
H	12. loitered	B. Wealth or riches.
K	13. requite	C. Remedy.
J	14. recognisance	D. Flowing out; pouring out.
D	15. effusive	E. Unrestrainedly; excessively.
L	16. blithely	F. Scold mildly; reprimand.
A	17. incumbent	G. Unwilling or reluctant.
M	18. discreet	H. To stand idly about; to delay or dawdle.
E	19. wantonly	I. To bring about, as by scheming; manage.
G	20. loth	J. An obligation of record.
B	21. pelf	K. Repay.
C	22. redress	L. Carefree and lightheartedly.
F	23. chide	M. Showing prudence and wise self-restraint in speech and behavior.

Vocabulary - *The Prioress's Tale*

Part I: Using Prior Knowledge and Contextual Clues
    Below are the sentences in which the vocabulary words appear in the text. Read the sentence. Use any clues you can find in the sentence combined with your prior knowledge, and write what you think the underlined words mean in the space provided.

1. O mother-maid, maid-mother, chaste and free!

2. For sometimes, lady, ere men pray to thee thou goest before in thy benignity

3-4. ...there were Jews, supported by the Crown for the foul lucre of their usury

5. He was so keen to know it that he went upon his knees begging the boy explain it if he please.

6. And is this anthem made to reverence Christ's mother?

7. If I may, I certainly will show my diligence to learn it off by heart for Christmas Day.

8. And twice a day ... praising Christ's mother with all his might and main.

9. Is this not something that should be redressed?

10. O cursed folk of Herod come again, of what avail your villainous intent?

Part II: Determining the Meaning -- Match the vocabulary words to their definitions

    ___ 1. chaste   A. Use.
    ___ 2. benignity   B. Eager.
    ___ 3. lucre   C. A hymn of praise or loyalty.
    ___ 4. usury   D. Marked by persevering, painstaking effort.
    ___ 5. keen   E. Money, profits.
    ___ 6. anthem   F. Physical strength.
    ___ 7. diligence   G. Gentleness and mildness.
    ___ 8. main   H. Remedied, rectified.
    ___ 9. redressed   I. Charging excessively high interest on loans.
    ___ 10. avail   J. Morally pure in thought or conduct; decent and modest.

The Prioress's Tale Vocabulary Worksheet Page 2

11. She made enquiry with a <u>piteous</u> cry of every Jew inhabiting that place

12. And his dear mother, honour of mankind, bade all the Jews be <u>fettered</u> and confined

13. They took the child with piteous <u>lamentation</u>

14. Still lay this innocent child upon his <u>bier</u>

15. This at the hour of my death <u>sufficed</u> to draw her down to me.

16. She <u>bade</u> me sing this anthem till my time of burying

17. Salt fell the abbot's tears in trickling rain, and down he fell, <u>prostrate</u>, upon the ground

18. ... in a <u>sepulchre</u> of marble clear enclosed his little body, fair and sweet, where he now is

Part II: Determining the Meaning -- Match the vocabulary words to their definitions.

___ 11. piteous
___ 12. fettered
___ 13. lamentation
___ 14. bier
___ 15. sufficed
___ 16. bade
___ 17. prostrate
___ 18. sepulchre

A. An instance of such expressed grief.
B. Lying face down, as in submission or adoration.
C. To direct; command.
D. Demanding or arousing pity.
E. A burial vault.
F. Met present needs or requirements.
G. Chained; restrained.
H. Stand on which a corpse or a coffin containing a corpse is placed before burial.

The Prioress's Tale Prereading Vocabulary Worksheet Part II

Page 1

J	1. chaste	A. Use.
G	2. benignity	B. Eager.
E	3. lucre	C. A hymn of praise or loyalty.
I	4. usury	D. Marked by persevering, painstaking effort.
B	5. keen	E. Money, profits.
C	6. anthem	F. Physical strength.
D	7. diligence	G. Gentleness and mildness.
F	8. main	H. Remedied, rectified.
H	9. redressed	I. Charging excessively high interest on loans.
A	10. avail	J. Morally pure in thought or conduct; decent and modest.

Page 2

D	11. piteous	A. An instance of such expressed grief.
G	12. fettered	B. Lying face down, as in submission or adoration.
A	13. lamentation	C. To direct; command.
H	14. bier	D. Demanding or arousing pity.
F	15. sufficed	E. A burial vault.
C	16. bade	F. Met present needs or requirements.
B	17. prostrate	G. Chained; restrained.
E	18. sepulchre	H. Stand on which a corpse or a coffin containing a corpse is placed before burial.

Vocabulary - *The Nun's Priest's Tale*

Part I: Using Prior Knowledge and Contextual Clues

Below are the sentences in which the vocabulary words appear in the text. Read the sentence. Use any clues you can find in the sentence combined with your prior knowledge, and write what you think the underlined words mean in the space provided.

1. ... there dwelt a poor old widow in a small cottage ... beside a grove and standing in a dale.

2. Repletion never left her in disquiet.

3. The equinoctial wheel and its position at each ascent he knew by intuition

4. Like azure were his legs and they were set on azure toes with nails of lily white

5. Courteous she was, discreet and debonair

6. His ears and tail were tipped with sable fur unlike the rest; he was a russet cur

7. You've forfeited my heart and lost my love

8. Dreams are engendered in the too-replete from vapours in the belly

9. You free yourself from vapours with a purge

10. Your face is choleric and shows distension

11. 'Madam,' he said, 'I thank you for your lore

12. The proof is all too manifest indeed

13. Murder's a foul, abominable treason

The Nun's Priest's Tale Vocabulary Worksheet Page 2

Part II: Determining the Meaning -- Match the vocabulary words to their definitions.

    ____ 1. dale   A. A light purplish blue.
    ____ 2. repletion   B. Purify; to induce evacuation of the bowels in individual
    ____ 3. equinoctial   C. Accumulated facts or beliefs about a particular subject
    ____ 4. azure   D. A valley
    ____ 5. discreet   E. A dog considered to be inferior or undesirable.
    ____ 6. cur   F. Thoroughly unpleasant or disagreeable.
    ____ 7. forfeited   G. Relating to the celestial equator
    ____ 8. replete   H. Filled to satiation; gorged.
    ____ 9. purge   I. Swelling.
    ____ 10. distension   J. Free from ostentation or pretension; modest.
    ____ 11. lore   K. Clearly apparent; obvious.
    ____ 12. manifest   L. Gorged; fed to escess.
    ____ 13. abominable   M. Something surrendered as punishment for a
                                            crime, an offense or an error.

Nun's Priest's Tale Vocabulary Worksheet Page 3

14. He woke and told his friend what had occurred and begged him that ;the journey be <u>deferred</u> at least a day

15. But his companion, lying there apart, began to laugh and treat him to <u>derision</u>.

16. ...many dreams ... give <u>cognizance</u> of what is to befall.

17-18. For when at night I feel your feathery side, although <u>perforce</u> I cannot take a ride because, alas, our perch was made too narrow, delight and solace fill me to the marrow and I <u>defy</u> all visions and all dreams!

19. <u>Solace</u> and revel fill my heart!

20-21. He'll say the Schools are filled with <u>altercation</u> on this vexed matter of <u>predestination</u>.

22. ... and for this he made the father lose his <u>benefice.</u>

23. Can you not <u>emulate</u> your sire and sing.

24. Their yells surpassed them all in <u>palpitating</u> fear.

25. Louder than those <u>extorted</u> from the wife of Hasdrubal.

26. A very <u>pestilence</u> upon you fall!

Nun's Priest's Tale Vocabulary Worksheet Page 4

Part II: Determining the Meaning -- Match the vocabulary words to their definitions.

___ 14. deferred
___ 15. derision
___ 16. cognizance
___ 17. perforce
___ 18. defy
___ 19. solace
___ 20. altercation
___ 21. predestination
___ 22. benefice
___ 23. emulate
___ 24. palpitating
___ 25. extorted
___ 26. pestilence

A. Conscious knowledge or recognition; awareness.
B. To resist successfully.
C. Disputes.
D. A church office endowed with fixed capital assets that provide a living.
E. To put off; postponed.
F. By force of circumstance.
G. Scoffing; ridicule.
H. A source of comfort or consolation.
I. To move with a slight tremulous motion; tremble, shake, or quiver; to beat with excessive rapidity; throb.
J. To strive to equal or excel, especially through imitation.
K. To obtain from another by coercion or intimidation.
L. A usually fatal epidemic disease.

The Nun's Priest's Tale Prereading Vocabulary Worksheet Part II

Page 1

D	1. dale	A. A light purplish blue.
L	2. repletion	B. Purify; to induce evacuation of the bowels in individual.
G	3. equinoctial	C. Accumulated facts, traditions, or beliefs about a particular subject.
A	4. azure	D. A valley.
J	5. discreet	E. A dog considered to be inferior or undesirable.
E	6. cur	F. Thoroughly unpleasant or disagreeable.
M	7. forfeited	H. Filled to satiation; gorged.
H	8. replete	I. Swelling.
B	9. purge	J. Free from ostentation or pretension; modest.
I	10. distension	K. Clearly apparent; obvious.
C	11. lore	M. Something surrendered as punishment for a crime, an offense or an error.
K	12. manifest	
F	13. abominable	

Page 2

E	14. deferred	A. Conscious knowledge or recognition; awareness.
G	15. derision	B. To resist successfully.
A	16. cognizance	C. Disputes.
F	17. perforce	D. A church office endowed with fixed capital assets that provide a living.
B	18. defy	E. To put off; postponed.
H	19. solace	F. By force of circumstance.
C	20. altercation	G. Scoffing; ridicule.
M	21. predestination	H. A source of comfort or consolation.
D	22. benefice	I. To move with a slight tremulous motion; tremble, shake, or quiver; to beat with excessive rapidity; throb.
J	23. emulate	J. To strive to equal or excel, especially through imitation.
I	24. palpitating	K. To obtain from another by coercion or intimidation.
K	25. extorted	L. A usually fatal epidemic disease.
L	26. pestilence	

Vocabulary - *The Pardoner's Tale*

Part I: Using Prior Knowledge and Contextual Clues

Below are the sentences in which the vocabulary words appear in the text. Read the sentence. Use any clues you can find in the sentence combined with your prior knowledge, and write what you think the underlined words mean in the space provided.

1. In Flanders once there was a company of youngsters haunting vice and ribaldry, riot and gambling, stews and public houses where each with harp, guitar, or lute <u>carouses</u> dancing and dicing day and night

2-3. Abominable in <u>superfluity</u> with oaths so damnable in <u>blasphemy</u> that it's a grisly thing to hear them swear.

4. . . . and girls with cakes and music, devil's gauds to kindle and blow the fires of lechery that are so close annexed to <u>gluttony</u>

5. O if we knew the <u>maladies</u> that follow on excess and gluttonies, sure we would diet

6. If we <u>contemn</u> the name, how far more filthy is the act!

7. These cooks that strain and grind and bray in mortars, <u>transubstantiate</u> God's gifts into a flavour on a plate

8. Nothing is thrown away that could delight or whet anew <u>lascivious</u> appetite

9. O drunkard, how disfigured is thy face, ... and through thy drunkenness a <u>stertorous</u> snort

10. All the most notable acts, I dare to say, ... were won in <u>abstinence</u>, were won in prayer.

11. Worse, you are <u>debased</u> in public reputation, put to shame.

Pardoner's Tale Vocabulary Worksheet Page 2

12. Again, consider King Demetrius; ... whose honour, if unable to <u>surmount</u> the vice of gambling, was of no account.

13. <u>Vengeance</u> on him and all his house shall fall that swears outrageously, or swears at all.

Part II: Determining the meaning   Match the vocabulary words and their definitions.

___ 1. carouses
___ 2. superfluity
___ 3. blasphemy
___ 4. gluttony
___ 5. maladies
___ 6. contemn
___ 7. transubstantiate
___ 8. lascivious
___ 9. stertorous
___ 10. abstinence
___ 11. debased
___ 12. surmount
___ 13. vengeance

A. The act or practice of refraining from doing something you want to do.
B. Infliction of punishment in return for a wrong committed; retribution.
C. To change (one substance) into another.
D. The vice of continually overeating.
E. Lecherous.
F. Overabundance; excess.
G. A disease, disorder, or an ailment.
H. Despise.
I. Degraded.
J. To overcome.
K. Heavy snoring sound during respiration.
L. To speak of (God or a sacred entity) in an irreverent, impious manner.
M. Drunken merrymaking.

Pardoner's Tale Vocabulary Worksheet Page 2

14. If you should meet him; you had best be <u>wary</u>, be on your guard with such an adversary

15. She has refused her grace, whence comes the <u>pallor</u> of my withered face.

16. Thou shalt rise up before the <u>hoary</u> head and honour it.

17. He isn't one to hide for all your <u>prating</u>.

18. ... there they found a pile of golden <u>florins</u> on the ground.

19. No, we must bring this treasure back by night some <u>prudent</u> way, and keep it out of sight.

20. As soon as he had gone the first sat down and thus began a <u>parley</u> with the other:

21. ... if you're for showing <u>pique</u>, I'll joke no more, not with an angry man.

Part II: Determining the Meaning -- Match the vocabulary words to their definitions.

    ___ 14. wary
    ___ 15. pallor
    ___ 16. hoary
    ___ 17. prating
    ___ 18. florins
    ___ 19. prudent
    ___ 20. parley
    ___ 21. pique

A. Gold coins.
B. A state of vexation caused by a perceived slight or indignity.
C. gray or white with or as if with age.
D. Paleness.
E. A discussion or conference.
F. To talk idly and at length; chatter.
G. Exercising good judgment or common sense.
H. On guard; watchful.

The Pardoner's Tale Prereading Vocabulary Worksheet Part II

Page 1

M	1. carouses	A. The act or practice of refraining from doing something you want to do.
F	2. superfluity	B. Infliction of punishment in return for a wrong committed; retribution.
L	3. blasphemy	C. To change (one substance) into another.
D	4. gluttony	D. The vice of continually overeating.
G	5. maladies	E. Lecherous.
H	6. contemn	F. Overabundance; excess.
C	7. transubstantiate	G. A disease, disorder, or an ailment.
E	8. lascivious	H. Despise.
K	9. stertorous	I. Degraded.
A	10. abstinence	J. To overcome.
I	11. debased	K. Heavy snoring sound during respiration.
J	12. surmount	L. To speak of (God or a sacred entity) in an irreverent, impious manner.
B	13. vengeance	M. Drunken merrymaking.

Page 2

H	14. wary	A. Gold coins.
D	15. pallor	B. A state of vexation caused by a perceived slight or indignity.
C	16. hoary	C. gray or white with or as if with age.
F	17. prating	D. Paleness.
A	18. florins	E. A discussion or conference.
G	19. prudent	F. To talk idly and at length; chatter.
E	20. parley	G. Exercising good judgment or common sense.
B	21. pique	H. On guard; watchful.

Vocabulary - *The Wife of Bath's Tale*

Part I: Using Prior Knowledge and Contextual Clues

Below are the sentences in which the vocabulary words appear in the text. Read the sentence. Use any clues you can find in the sentence combined with your prior knowledge, and write what you think the underlined words mean in the space provided.

1. The learned may rebuke me, or be loth to think it so

2-3. In that estate to which God summoned me I'll persevere; I'm not pernickety.

4. I shan't give ear to malice, I know you for a virtuous wife, Dame Alice.

5. Is there no other trouble that importunes the world and that your parables could condemn?

6. He never would have daunted me from drink.

7. We use disdain in offering our wares.

8. For she, in order he might only think of her, prepared an aphrodisiac drink

9. 'Better,' says he, 'to share your habitation with lion, dragon, or abomination than with a woman given to reproof.'

10. They are so wicked and cantankerous they hate the things their husbands like

11. I shall take gages from you to extort surrender of your body to the court.

12. Others assert we women find it sweet when we are thought dependable, discreet, and secret

13. I know indeed that such was my behest, but for God's love think of a new request

14. Are knights of his all so contemptuous?

Wife of Bath's Tale Vocabulary Worksheet Page 2

15. Christ wills we take our gentleness from Him, not from a wealth of ancestry long dim, though they <u>bequeath</u> their whole establishment by which we claim to be of high descent.

16. Poverty is, though wanting in estate, a kind of wealth that none <u>calumniate</u>.

Part II: Determining the Meaning - Match the vocabulary words to their definitions.

___ 1. rebuke
___ 2. persevere
___ 3. pernickety
___ 4. malice
___ 5. importunes
___ 6. daunted
___ 7. disdain
___ 8. aphrodisiac
___ 9. reproof
___ 10. cantankerous
___ 11. extort
___ 12. assert
___ 13. behest
___ 14. contemptuous
___ 15. bequeath
___ 16. calumniate

A. Discouraged.
B. Something, such as a drug or food arousing sexual desire.
C. Overparticular about trivial details; pretentious.
D. Reprimanded for a fault.
E. To obtain from another by coercion or intimidation.
F. Disagreeable.
G. An authoritative command.
H. A desire to harm others or to see others suffer.
I. To state or express positively.
J. To annoy; vex.
K. Manifesting or feeling contempt; scornful.
L. To pass (something) on to another; hand down.
M. To make maliciously or knowingly false statements about.
N. Steady persistence in adhering to a course of action; a belief, or a purpose.
O. To regard or treat with haughty contempt.
P. Reprimand.

The Wife of Bath's Tale Prereading Vocabulary Worksheet Part II

P	1. rebuke	A. Discouraged.
N	2. persevere	B. Something, such as a drug or food arousing sexual desire.
C	3. pernickety	C. Overparticular about trivial details; pretentious.
H	4. malice	D. Reprimanded for a fault.
J	5. importunes	E. To obtain from another by coercion or intimidation.
A	6. daunted	F. Disagreeable.
O	7. disdain	G. An authoritative command.
B	8. aphrodisiac	H. A desire to harm others or to see others suffer.
D	9. reproof	I. To state or express positively.
F	10. cantankerous	J. To annoy; vex.
E	11. extort	K. Manifesting or feeling contempt; scornful.
I	12. assert	L. To pass (something) on to another; hand down.
G	13. behest	M. To make maliciously or knowingly false statements about
K	14. contemptuous	N. Steady persistence in adhering to a course of action; a belief, or a purpose.
L	15. bequeath	O. To regard or treat with haughty contempt.
M	16. calumniate	P. Reprimand.

Vocabulary - *The Friar's Tale*

Part I: Using Prior Knowledge and Contextual Clues

Below are the sentences in which the vocabulary words appear in the text. Read the sentence. Use any clues you can find in the sentence combined with your prior knowledge, and write what you think the underlined words mean in the space provided.

1. Nothing could save them from pecunial torment.

2. On with your story, sir, and if it galls the Summoner, spare him not

3. He didn't have to show a warrant when he chose to make things hot for some obscure, uneducated sot

4. And he had wenches in his retinue

5. ... this summoner rode forth to catch his prey, a poor old fiddle of the widow-tribe from whom, on a feigned charge, he hoped a bribe.

6. 'Come out,' he said, 'you old inebriate!'

7. Twelve pence to me and I'll secure acquittal.

Part II: Determining the Meaning -- Match the vocabulary words to their definitions.

___ 1. pecunial
___ 2. galls
___ 3. obscure
___ 4. retinue
___ 5. feigned
___ 6. inebriate
___ 7. acquittal

A. To free or clear from a charge.
B. Drunk.
C. False, fabricated; made-up.
D. The retainers or attendants accompany a high-ranking person.
E. Of undistinquished or humble station or reputation; unknown
F. Causes bitterness of feeling; rancor.
G. Requiring payment of money.

The Friar's Tale Prereading Vocabulary Worksheet Part II

G	1. pecunial	A. To free or clear from a charge.
F	2. galls	B. Drunk.
E	3. obscure	C. False, fabricated; made-up.
D	4. retinue	D. The retainers or attendants who accompany a high ranking person.
	5. feigned	E. Of undistinquished or humble station or reputation; unknown
B	6. inebriate	F. Causes bitterness of feeling; rancor.
A	7. acquittal	G. Requiring payment of money.

Vocabulary - *The Summoner's Tale*

Part I: Using Prior Knowledge and Contextual Clues
Below are the sentences in which the vocabulary words appear in the text. Read the sentence. Use any clues you can find in the sentence combined with your prior knowledge, and write what you think the underlined words mean in the space provided.

1. The Summoner rose in wrath against the Friar high in his stirrups, and he quaked with <u>ire</u>.

2. God knows it's little wonder; friars and fiends are seldom far <u>asunder</u>

3. An angel led him up and down to <u>ferret</u> among the torments

4. Be quick, <u>exert</u> yourselves

5. His comrade ... bore two ivory tablets, wax-anointed, also a <u>stylus</u> elegantly pointed

6. A sturdy <u>varlet</u> followed them behind--the servant for their guests

7. And I prefer to paraphrase or <u>gloze</u>

8. ... you know these <u>curates</u> are so negligent and slow at groping consciences with tenderness

9. Dives and Lazarus lived differently, and different their <u>guerdon</u> had to be

10. When they approached the temple to renew their services and <u>supplications</u>, they refrained from drinking

Part II: Determining the Meaning - Match the vocabulary words to their definitions
___ 1. ire
___ 2. asunder
___ 3. ferret
___ 4. exert
___ 5. stylus
___ 6. varlet
___ 7. gloze
___ 8. curates
___ 9. guerdon
___ 10. supplications

A. Servant.
B. To ask earnestly and humbly.
C. A cleric, especially one who has charge of a parish
D. Too put (oneself) to strenuous effort.
E. Reward; payment.
F. Anger; wrath.
G. Apart from each other either in position or in direction
H. To uncover and bring to light by searching.
I. To minimize or underplay; gloss over; to use flattery or cajolery.
J. A sharp pointed instrument used for writing, marking or engraving.

Summoner's Tale Vocabulary Worksheet Page 2

11. ... pure, merciful, <u>austere</u>, but quick to bless though weeping often

12. <u>Fie</u> on their pomp!

13. Your own <u>inconstancy</u> has let you down

14. If you would learn or be <u>enticed</u> to learn what good there is in building churches, your namesake's life will further your researches

15. Once on a time an angry <u>potentate</u>, Seneca says, bore rule over a state

16. There's not a tile as yet or <u>tessellation</u> upon the pavement that we hope to win

17. But swear by your profession to the thing, and without fraudulence or <u>cavilling</u>

18. There never was a farm horse drawing cart that farted with a more <u>prodigious</u> sound.

19. I won't be <u>derided</u> or bidden divide what cannot be divided in equal parts

20. How the imagination of a clown had hit on this <u>conundrum</u> for the friar

Part II: Determining the Meaning -- Match the vocabulary words to their definitions.

___ 11. rancour
___ 12. fie
___ 13. inconstancy
___ 14. enticed
___ 15. potentate
___ 16. tessellation
___ 17. cavilling
___ 18. prodigious
___ 19. derided
___ 20. conundrum

A. Raising trivial objections.
B. Spoken of or treated with contempt.
C. Lured.
D. Impressively great in size, force or extent.
E. Deep-seated ill will
F. Used to express distaste or disapproval.
G. Changing or varying, especially often and without discernible patter or reason.
H. A mosaic patter, formed by small squares of stone or glass
I. One who has the power and position to rule over others
J. A riddle in which a fanciful question is answered by a pun; a paradoxical, insoluble, or difficult problem.

The Summoner's Tale Prereading Vocabulary Worksheet Part II

F	1. ire	A. Servant.
G	2. asunder	B. To ask earnestly and humbly.
H	3 ferret	C. A cleric, especially one who has charge of a parish.
D	4. exert	D. Too put (oneself) to strenuous effort.
J	5. stylus	E. Reward; payment.
A	6. varlet	F. Anger; wrath.
I	7. gloze	G. Apart from each other either in position or in direction.
C	8. curates	H. To uncover and bring to light by searching.
E	9. guerdon	I. To minimize or underplay; gloss over; to use flattery or cajolery.
B	10. supplications	J. A sharp pointed instrument used for writing, marking or engraving.

Page 2

E	11. rancour	A. Raising trivial objections.
F	12. fie	B. Spoken of or treated with contempt.
G	13. inconstancy	C. Lured.
C	14. enticed	D. Impressively great in size, force or extent.
I	15. potentate	E. Deep-seated ill will
H	16. tessellation	F. Used to express distaste or disapproval.
A	17. cavilling	G. Changing or varying, especially often and without discernible patter or reason.
D	18. prodigious	H. A mosaic patter, formed by small squares of stone or glass.
B	19. derided	I. One who has the power and position to rule over others.
J	20. conundrum	J. A riddle in which a fanciful question is answered by a pun; a paradoxical, insoluble, or difficult problem.

Vocabulary - *The Clerk's Tale*

Part I: Using Prior Knowledge and Contextual Clues

Below are the sentences in which the vocabulary words appear in the text. Read the sentence. Use any clues you can find in the sentence combined with your prior knowledge, and write what you think the underlined words mean in the space provided.

1. This is no time for <u>abstruse</u> meditation

2. This worthy cleric left the land of nod and said <u>benignly</u>, 'Sir, I kiss the rod!'

3. Let me say first he starts it by <u>enditing</u> a preface in the highest style of writing

4. Then, sir let not your <u>clemency</u> withhold a hearing to our pitiful petition

5. Scarce can imagine thoughts that could be voiced to lap us round in more <u>felicity</u>

6. Leave me alone to choose myself a wife, that is my burden, my <u>prerogative</u>

7. With fostering love and reverent <u>constancy</u> her poor old father in his poverty she tended

8. The royal marquis ... rode off ... towards the little thorpe I spoke about and by the shortest road, in <u>sumptuous</u> rout.

9. Leading the way with joyful heart he let her be brought in triumph, and the day had end in <u>revel</u> till they saw the sun descend

10. ... men held him to have been a <u>prudent</u> man, and that is seldom seen.

Part II: Determining the Meaning -- Match the vocabulary words to their definitions.

___ 1. abstruse   A. Kindly; mildly.
___ 2. benignly   B. Exercising good judgment or common sense.
___ 3. enditing   C. Of a size or splendidity suggesting great expense; lavish
___ 4. clemency   D. Loyalty, faithfulness.
___ 5. felicity   E. Difficulty to understand
___ 6. prerogative   F. A disposition to show mercy.
___ 7. constancy   G. Great happiness; bliss.
___ 8. sumptuous   H. Festivities; celebration
___ 9. revel   I. Writing
___ 10. prudent   J. An exclusive right or privilege held by a person or group

Clerk's Tale Vocabulary Worksheet Page 2

11. There was no <u>rancour</u>, no discordant mood in all that country that she did not ease

12. ... if the nobles of the land fell into <u>enmity</u> she made their peace

13. The marquis ... longed to expose her <u>constancy</u> to test.

14. He could not throw the thought away or rest, having a marvelous passion to <u>assay</u> her

15. I will do nothing, but it is for you to <u>acquiesce</u> and show no discontent.

16. And surely had I had the <u>prescience</u> to know your will before you told it me I had performed it without negligence

17. What patience to endure the law of my <u>caprices</u>

18. I say he ordered them to counterfeit a papal bull declaring <u>approbation</u> of a divorce

19. And all the people ran to see the sight of so much <u>opulence</u> and rich array

20. O stormy people, frivolous and <u>fickle</u>, void of true judgement, turning like a vane

Part II: determining the Meaning -- Match the vocabulary words to their definitions.

___ 11. rancour
___ 12. enmity
___ 13. constancy
___ 14. assay
___ 15. acquiesce
___ 16. prescience
___ 17. caprices
___ 18. approbation
___ 19. opulence
___ 20. fickle

A. Characterized by changeableness or instability.
B. Luxury, showing great wealth.
C. Knowledge of actions or events before they occur.
D. Official approval.
E. Whims.
F. Consent; give in; agree.
G. Deep-seated, often mutual hatred.
H. Loyalty or faithfulness.
I. Bitter, long-lasting resentment; deep-seated ill will.
J. Qualitative or quantitative analysis of a substance.

The Clerk's Tale Prereading Vocabulary Worksheet Part II

Page 1

E	1. abstruse	A. Kindly; mildly.
A	2. benignly	B. Exercising good judgment or common sense.
I	3. enditing	C. Of a size or splendidity suggesting great expense; lavish.
F	4. clemency	D. Loyalty, faithfulness.
G	5. felicity	E. Difficulty to understand.
J	6. prerogative	F. A disposition to show mercy.
D	7. constancy	G. Great happiness; bliss.
C	8. sumptuous	H. Festivities; celebration.
H	9. revel	I. Writing
B	10. prudent	J. An exclusive right or privilege held by a person or group.

Page 2

I	11. rancour	A. Characterized by changeableness or instability.
G	12. enmity	B. Luxury, showing great wealth.
H	13. constancy	C. Knowledge of actions or events before they occur.
J	14. assay	D. Official approval.
F	15. acquiesce	E. Whims.
C	16. prescience	F. Consent; give in; agree.
E	17. caprices	G. Deep-seated, often mutual hatred.
D	18. approbation	H. Loyalty or faithfulness.
B	19. opulence	I. Bitter, long-lasting resentment; deep-seated ill will.
A	20. fickle	J. Qualitative or quantitative analysis of a substance.

Vocabulary - *The Merchant's Tale*

Part I: Using Prior Knowledge and Contextual Clues
Below are the sentences in which the vocabulary words appear in the text. Read the sentence. Use any clues you can find in the sentence combined with your prior knowledge, and write what you think the underlined words mean in the space provided.

1. I have a wife, the worst that there could be.... She's a <u>shrew</u> in all.

2. Yet I believe no bachelor alive, ... could tell of so much grief as I could tell you of; beyond belief, the curst <u>malignity</u> I get from her!

3. A wife is <u>verily</u> the gift of God.

4. That woman is man's helper, his resort, his earthly paradise and his disport. So <u>pliant</u> and virtuous is she they cannot but abide in unity.

5. There is no <u>superlative</u> that ranks in life, says Seneca, above a humble wife

6. You may <u>discern</u> more readily than I where it would most befit me to ally.

7. The woman must on no account be old, certainly under twenty, and <u>demure</u>.

8. I know the reason why one ought to wed, though I could specify many who <u>prate</u> of it

9. ... but to curb lechery, which he could <u>eschew</u>

10. You have no need ... to take advice from anybody here, save they your <u>sapience</u> after meditation, would prudently resist the inclination to set aside the word of Solomon

Part II: Determining the Meaning -- Match the vocabulary words to their definitions.

_____ 1. shrew   A. Easily altered or modified to fit conditions; adaptable
_____ 2. malignity   B. Something of the highest possible excellence.
_____ 3. verily   C. Chatter
_____ 4. pliant   D. Great wisdom and discernment.
_____ 5. superlative   E. To recognize or comprehend mentally.
_____ 6. discern   F. To avoid; shun.
_____ 7. demure   G. Shy, modest, or reserved.
_____ 8. prate   H. A woman with a violent, scolding, or nagging temperament
_____ 9. eschew   I. In truth; in fact.
_____ 10. sapience   J. Intense ill will or hatred.

Merchant's Tale Vocabulary Worksheet Page 2

11. He says it's always better to think twice before you give away estate or <u>pelf</u>

12. Yet there's so perfect a <u>felicity</u> in marriage, so much pleasure, so few tears

13. And at the wedding-banquet he and she sat with their worthier guests upon the <u>dias</u>

14. The night his arms would strain her with the <u>ardour</u> that Paris showed for Helen

15. And homeward each <u>convivially</u> seeks to undertake such business as will keep him happy

16. Lest I offend the <u>precious</u>, I will go no further into what he did

17. Thou has <u>bereft</u> him of his sight, his eye is dark, and in his grief he longs to die

18. He took in patience his adversity, save that the <u>ineradicable</u> sting of jealousy embittered everything

19. ... what might it thee <u>avail</u> though thou couldst see as far as ship can sail?

20. He made a temple for false gods as well, and what could be more <u>reprehensible</u>?

Part II: Determining the Meaning -- Match the vocabulary words to their definitions.

___ 11. pelf
___ 12. felicity
___ 13. dias
___ 14. ardour
___ 15. convivially
___ 16. precious
___ 17. bereft
___ 18. ineradicable
___ 19. avail
___ 20. reprehensible

A. Great happiness; bliss.
B. Benefit.
C. Deserving rebuke or censure; blameworthy.
D. Fiery intensity of feeling.
E. Indelible, can't be erased or removed; permanent.
F. Dainty or overrefined.
G. Deprived of something.
H. A raised platform.
I. Merrily.
J. Wealth or riches, especially when dishonestly acquired; loot.

The Merchant's Tale Prereading Vocabulary Worksheet Part II

Page 1

H	1. shrew	A. Easily altered or modified to fit conditions; adaptable.
J	2. malignity	B. Something of the highest possible excellence.
I	3. verily	C. Chatter
A	4. pliant	D. Great wisdom and discernment.
B	5. superlative	E. To recognize or comprehend mentally.
E	6. discern	F. To avoid; shun.
G	7. demure	G. Shy, modest, or reserved.
C	8. prate	H. A woman with a violent, scolding, or nagging temperament.
F	9. eschew	I. In truth; in fact.
D	10. sapience	J. Intense ill will or hatred.

Page 2

J	11. pelf	A. Great happiness; bliss.
A	12. felicity	B. Benefit.
H	13. dias	C. Deserving rebuke or censure; blameworthy.
D	14. ardour	D. Fiery intensity of feeling.
I	15. convivially	E. Indelible, can't be erased or removed; permanent.
F	16. precious	F. Dainty or overrefined.
G	17. bereft	G. Deprived of something.
E	18. ineradicable	H. A raised platform.
B	19. avail	I. Merrily.
C	20. reprehensible	J. Wealth or riches, especially when dishonestly acquired loot.

Vocabulary - *The Franklin's Tale*

Part I: Using Prior Knowledge and Contextual Clues
   Below are the sentences in which the vocabulary words appear in the text. Read the sentence. Use any clues you can find in the sentence combined with your prior knowledge, and write what you think the underlined words mean in the space provided.

1. ... there was a knight enthralled to love

2. He scarce had the temerity of mind to tell her of his longing and distress

3. Why answer back at every angry speech? No, learn forbearance

4. And there they lived in amity unharried.

5. Through hope and reason, and her long prostration turned to recovery

6. I leave the learned to their disquisition

7. They went into a garden near at hand where they had staged a picnic and supplied victuals enough and other things beside

8. It well may be would linger on her face beseechingly, as is the common case

9. She looked at him with closer scrutiny

10. Lord Phoebus, have compassion, grant my boon!

Part II: Determining the Meaning -- Match the vocabulary words to their definitions.
   ___ 1. enthralled   A. Addressing an earnest or urgent request.
   ___ 2. temerity   B. Peaceful relations.
   ___ 3. forbearance   C. A formal discourse on a subject.
   ___ 4. amity   D. The ability to refrain from; resist.
   ___ 5. prostration   E. Held spellbound; captivated; enslaved.
   ___ 6. disquisition   F. Total exhaustion or weakness; collapse.
   ___ 7. victuals   that expresses deference or homage.
   ___ 8. beseechingly   G. Careful examination or study .
   ___ 9. scrutiny   H. Foolhardy disregard of danger; recklessness.
   ___ 10. boon   I. A benefit bestowed, especially one bestowed
                                 in response to a request.
                              J. Food fit for human consumption.

Franklin's Tale Vocabulary Worksheet Page 2

11. No comfort during all that time he found except his brother, who had been a scholar, and who knew all about his woes and <u>dolour</u>

12. This subtle <u>sage</u> had pity on the man

13. With terror in his heart, and humbled face, he made <u>obeisance</u> to her sovereign grace.

14. You know what you have promised to <u>requite</u>

15. Why, to the garden, as my husband bade to keep my <u>plighted</u> word, alas, alas!

16. If not I'll have to sell my <u>patrimony</u>; there's no more to tell.

Part II: Determining the Meaning -- Match the vocabulary words to their definitions.

___ 11. dolour
___ 12. sage
___ 13. obeisance
___ 14. requite
___ 15. plighted
___ 16. patrimony

A. A gesture or movement of the body that expresses deference or homage.
B. An inheritance or a legacy; heritage.
C. Promised.
D. Sorrow; grief.
E. Wise person.
F. To make repayment or return of.

The Franklin's Tale Prereading Vocabulary Worksheet Part II

Page 1

E	1. enthralled	A. Addressing and earnest or urgent request.
H	2. temerity	B. Peaceful relations.
D	3. forbearance	C. A formal discourse on a subject.
B	4. amity	D. The ability to refrain from; resist.
F	5. prostration	E. Held spellbound; captivated; enslaved.
C	6. disquisition	F. Total exhaustion or weakness; collapse.
J	7. victuals	that expresses deference or homage.
A	8. beseechingly	G. Careful examination or study.
G	9. scrutiny	H. Foolhardy disregard of danger; recklessness.
I	10. boon	I. A benefit bestowed, especially one bestowed in response to a request.
		J. Food fit for human consumption.

Page 2

D	11. dolour	
E	12. sage	A. A gesture or movement of the body that expresses deference or homage.
A	13. obeisance	B. An inheritance or a legacy; heritage.
F	14. requite	C. Promised.
C	15. plighted	D. Sorrow; grief.
B	16. patrimony	E. Wise person.
		F. To make repayment or return of.

DAILY LESSONS

LESSON ONE

Objectives
1. To distribute the materials which will be used in the unit
2. To explain the small group project students will do in this unit
3. To do the prereading vocabulary work for the Prologue

Activity #1
Distribute the materials which will be used in this unit. Explain in detail how students are to use these materials.

Study Guides Students should read the study guide questions for each tale as homework the night before each tale is to be done in class to get a feeling for what events and ideas are important in the tale. After reading the section, students will as a class answer the questions to review the important events and ideas from that tale. Students should keep the study guides as study materials for the unit test.

Vocabulary Prior to listening to or reading each tale, students will do vocabulary work related to each tale. Following the completion of the reading of the text, there will be a vocabulary review of all the words used in the vocabulary assignments. Students should keep their vocabulary work as study materials for the unit test.

Reading Assignment Sheet You need to fill in the reading assignment sheet to let students know by when their presentations have to be completed. You can either write the assignment sheet up on a side blackboard or bulletinboard and leave it there for students to see each day, or you can make copies for each student to have. In either case, you should advise students to become very familiar with the reading assignments so they know what is expected of them.

Extra Activities Center The unit resource portion of this unit contains suggestions for an extra library of related plays and articles in your classroom as well as crossword and word search puzzles. Make an extra activities center in your room where you will keep these materials for students to use. (Bring the books and articles in from the library and keep several copies of the puzzles on hand.) Explain to students that these materials are available for students to use when they finish reading assignments or other class work early or as extra review/study materials.

Nonfiction Assignment Sheet Explain to students that they each are to read at least one non-fiction piece from the in-class library at some time during the unit. Suggest that students do this assignment in conjunction with the background research they will have to do for their presentations. Students will fill out a nonfiction assignment sheet after completing the reading to help you evaluate their reading experiences and to help the students think about and evaluate their own reading experiences.

Books Each school has its own rules and regulations regarding student use of school books. Advise students of the procedures that are normal for your school.

Activity #2

Distribute the Project Assignment Sheet. Discuss the directions in detail, and make sure everyone understands what is expected. Divide your class into pairs and assign the tales.

Tale/Assignment	Character	Background
Historical Background	-------- -------- --------	
Chaucer's Life	-------- -------- --------	
Knight's Tale		
Miller's Tale		
Reeve's Tale		
Shipman's Tale		
Prioress's Tale		
Nun's Priest's Tale		
Pardoner's Tale		
Wife of Bath's Tale		
Friar's Tale		
Summoner's Tale		
Clerk's Tale		
Merchant's Tale		
Franklin's Tale		

The way this project is set up, some students may not have to read any of the tales. You may wish to tell students that they all have to read all of the tales covered in class, or that those who do the general background research and are not connected with a tale must read one of the tales not covered in class and give a short summary of the tale orally. The actual reading requirements other than the ones dictated by the project are left totally up to you, the teacher. There is room on the third page of the project assignment for you to type in any additional requirements you might have for your classes.

NOTE: A fun thing to do is to offer a prize to the group with the best presentation; that also helps to connect the project to the tales.

Activity #3

Tell students that prior to your next class period, they should have completed the prereading work for the Prologue to the tales.

PROJECT ASSIGNMENT - *The Canterbury Tales*

PROMPT

The Canterbury Tales is a collection of stories told by a group of travellers on their way to Canterbury. Each traveller was supposed to tell two tales on the way to Canterbury and two tales on the return trip. However, Chaucer died before he was able to compete all of the tales, so what you will be reading during the next several weeks is the collection of tales he was able to complete. Each of the storytellers was in competition with the others; the prize for the best story was a free dinner at the Tabbard Inn at the end of the trip. Anyone who wouldn't cooperate with the Host, who acts as the judge and referee on the trip, would have to pay the way of all of the other travelers. So, you see, these tales were told orally for amusement to pass the time on the trip, and each traveler was trying to outdo the others by telling the best story. Chaucer used this framework in which to expose a cross-section of his society and to express many opinions about not only topics of his era but also about life and people in general.

Chaucer wrote these tales in the late 1300's--quite a long time ago! Life in England in the late 1300's was quite different from our lives today, so not only do we need to read the tales, we need to have some background to better understand the tales. These are the main purposes of this assignment: to read the tales and to have ample background information to make the tales meaningful.

THE ASSIGNMENT

You will be assigned to one of three different assignments. You will either be a) a character and have to read your tale to the class, b) a background person and have to prepare the appropriate background for your partner's (a character's) tale, or you will be c) a background person who prepares either a historical background for the play or background information about Chaucer's life.

The Character Assignment

If you are assigned to be a character, you must find out everything you can about your character so you can become that character in looks and actions while making your presentation of your tale to the class. Your requirements are:

1. Dress and act as the character while giving your presentation.
2. Act as your character while listening to others present their tales.
3. Read your tale to the class.
4. Help your partner identify names of gods or people or places mentioned in your tale, and together with your partner create a reference sheet of these names and their identifications.
5. As you are reading the tale, pause when you come to the names on your list and give your background partner a moment to briefly identify the name before you continue.

Canterbury Tales Project Assignment Page 2

The Character Background Assignment

If you are assigned to do the background for a character and the character's tale, these are your requirements:
1. Dress and act appropriately during the presentation. If you are related to the *Knight's Tale*, for example, you could dress as a squire. If you are related to the *Prioress's Tale*, you could dress as a nun or monk, and so on.
2. Research and find out who your character was in the 1300's. You won't have a specific name to look up, but you should find information about what the life of your character was like, what his/her job was, what social status he/she held, the kind of place he/she probably lived in, and so on.
3. Give a short presentation (less than 5 minutes) about your character as an introduction to him/her before the tale begins.
4. Help your partner identify names of gods or people or places mentioned in your tale, and together with your partner create a reference sheet of these names and their identities.
5. Your partner will pause when he/she comes upon the names on your reference sheet in the text. When he/she pauses, quickly give a short (1-2 sentence) identification of the name.

The General Background Assignment

If you are assigned to give the general background of the era, your requirements are:
1. Dress appropriately, in the costume of the era, for your presentation.
2. Make a brief timeline history of what had happened in the world prior to and then shortly after this time to put the tales in proper historical perspective.
3. Give an explanation of church and state and their influences on the people.
4. Give a brief explanation of daily life in the 1300's.
5. Give a brief summary of the influences of the elements and gods on people in the 1300s.
6. Do numbers 2-5 in a presentation to the class that will last about 1/2 of a class period.

If you are assigned to give the general background for Chaucer's life, your requirement are:
1. One member of the group should dress as Chaucer would have dressed, and give a presentation as if he/she is Chaucer talking about his life.
2. Many of the finer details of Chaucer's life are unknown because, let's face it, he lived about 700 years ago! Still, find as much information as you can about his heritage, his personal life, the positions he held, his writing, and the main events in his life.
4. A second person from the group should discuss what other people (critics?!) have said about Chaucer and his writing, especially *The Canterbury Tales*.
5. Your oral presentation to the class should last a total of about 1/2 of a class period.

The members of these groups should divide the work equitably among themselves. Assign one topic to each group member for research, do the research and then get back together to pool your information.

The Canterbury Tales Project Assignment Page 3

REQUIREMENTS FOR THE WHOLE CLASS
1. During this project, you must complete the prereading vocabulary worksheets for each of the tales as homework on the evening prior to the day the tale is scheduled to be presented.
2. During this project, you must preview the study guide questions for each of the tales as homework on the evening prior to the day the tale is scheduled to be presented.
3. You will be given a grade for your contributions to the presentations.
4. You will be given a grade for your attentiveness to the other tale-tellers' presentations.
5. You are responsible for understanding the chosen vocabulary words.

NONFICTION ASSIGNMENT SHEET - *The Canterbury Tales*
(To be completed after reading the required nonfiction article)

Name _____ Date _____

Title of Nonfiction Read _____

Written By _____ Publication Date _____

I. Factual Summary: Write a short summary of the piece you read.

II. Vocabulary
    1. With which vocabulary words in the piece did you encounter some degree of difficulty?

    2. How did you resolve your lack of understanding with these words?

III. Interpretation: What was the main point the author wanted you to get from reading his work?

IV. Criticism
    1. With which points of the piece did you agree or find easy to accept? Why?

    2. With which points of the piece did you disagree or find difficult to believe? Why?

V. Personal Response: What do you think about this piece? OR How does this piece influence your ideas?

LESSON TWO

Objectives
1. To begin reading *The Canterbury Tales* by reading the Prologue
2. To introduce the students to the characters they will be working with in the project

Activity #1

Have students read the Prologue to the tales orally in class. Students may take turns reading, you could read it to them, or if you have a favorite recording of the Prologue, you might want to use that.

Activity #2

After students have completed reading the Prologue, give them a few minutes to look at the study questions and formulate answers, then discuss the answers to the study questions in detail.

LESSONS THREE AND FOUR

Objectives
1. To give students access to the library's resources for their project research
2. To give students practice using the library's resources
3. To have students gather background information for the tales

Activity

Take students to the library. Those who need to find background information should do so. Students who have been assigned to be characters and to read their tales to the class should skim through their tales and compile a list of names for their reference sheets. After this list is compiled, they should divide the list in half (part for themselves and part for their partners) and begin looking up the information. When the partner is finished finding background information about the character, he/she should find information about the names on his/her half of the list.

LESSON FIVE

<u>Objectives</u>
    1. To give students practice writing to inform
    2. To help students doing background research organize and plan their presentations
    3. To evaluate students' research
    4. To give the teacher the opportunity to evaluate students' writing skills

<u>Activity</u>
    Distribute Writing Assignment #1. Discuss the directions in detail and give students ample time to complete the assignment.

Follow up with a writing conference in Lesson Twenty-two as directed.

WRITING ASSIGNMENT #1 - *The Canterbury Tales*

PROMPT

You have been reading lots of factual information about the 1300s, gods, goddesses, people and places. Take a few minutes today to organize your information and begin planning your presentation. To this end, you are to write a composition in which you inform me what you have learned through your research.

PREWRITING

You have done most of your prewriting by taking notes while you were doing your research. Look at your notes now and think about the information you have gathered. Categorize the information you have, then organize your categories in a logical (chronological, alphabetical, or some other) order.

DRAFTING

Write an introductory paragraph in which you generally explain what you have been researching.

In the body of your composition, write a paragraph about each of the categories you made in the prewriting stage. Use the information you gathered within each category to fill out your paragraphs.

Write a paragraph in which you state any conclusions to which you may have come as a result of collecting this data and in which you bring your composition to a close.

PROMPT

When you finish the rough draft of your paper, ask a student who sits near you to read it. After reading your rough draft, he/she should tell you what he/she liked best about your work, which parts were difficult to understand, and ways in which your work could be improved. Reread your paper considering your critic's comments, and make the corrections you think are necessary.

PROOFREADING

Do a final proofreading of your paper double-checking your grammar, spelling, organization, and the clarity of your ideas.

LESSON SIX

Objectives
    1. To give the entire class background information about Chaucer's era and Chaucer himself
    2. To give students the opportunity to practice public speaking

Activity
    Use this class period for students to give their presentations about Chaucer and his times.

Remind students that prior to the next class period they should have previewed the study questions and have done the prereading vocabulary worksheet for *The Knight's Tale*.

LESSONS SEVEN THROUGH TWENTY

Objectives
    1. To read *The Canterbury Tales*
    2. To evaluate students' project work
    3. To review the main ideas and events from each of the tales
    4. To expose students to the ideas and way of life in a different era

Activity
    Use these class periods for students to give their project presentations. In the first five minutes of the presentation, the person responsible for the background information should introduce the character by giving the information from his/her research. That should be followed by the character giving his/her presentation of the tale. After the tale has been told, give students a few minutes to formulate answers to the study guide questions. Then discuss the answers to the questions in detail as a review of the facts of the story. Students should do the prereading work for the next story as homework.

NOTE: Because some tales are longer than others, and because your students will have different reading ability levels, some tales may take a couple of days to be told while others may only take a half of a class period. When you finish with one tale, do the study questions, and move on to the next tale. The Unit Outline at the beginning of this unit is just a rough guideline for the telling of the tales. There are too many variables to give an accurate schedule (fire drills not withstanding!); just go at a pace that is comfortable for you and your students, and have students be prepared to tell their tales when the tale prior to theirs is done.

ORAL READING EVALUATION - *The Canterbury Tales*

Name _____ Class_____ Date _____

SKILL	EXCELLENT	GOOD	AVERAGE	FAIR	POOR
Fluency	5	4	3	2	1
Clarity	5	4	3	2	1
Audibility	5	4	3	2	1
Pronunciation	5	4	3	2	1
_____	5	4	3	2	1
_____	5	4	3	2	1

Total _____ Grade _____

Comments:

LESSON TWENTY-ONE

Objectives
    1. To review all of the tales
    2. To give students the opportunity to express their personal opinions in writing
    3. To choose a winner for the tales

Activity #1

    Have each group give a short (1-minute or less) summary of the facts of its tale. If you have required any students to read tales other than those covered in this unit, now is the time for them to tell the summaries of their tales as well.

NOTE: If you are offering a prize for the best presentation, you may wish to alter the writing assignment to say, "Write a composition in which you give your own personal opinions about which group presentation was the best."

Activity #2

    Distribute Writing Assignment #2. Discuss the directions in detail and give students ample time to complete the assignment.

While students are doing the writing assignment, call students to your desk or some other private area to have individual writing conferences using Writing Assignment #1 as the basis of your discussion. Have students revise their first writing assignments taking your comments into consideration. Tell students when their revisions will be due. Students who finish Writing Assignment #2 before the end of the class period may use the remaining time to work on their revisions. When grading the revisions, you may wish to consider using an A-C-E scale (A=all corrections done well, C= some corrections done, E= no corrections done or all done poorly) to help speed grading and yet still give students the appropriate credit for their efforts.

WRITING ASSIGNMENT #2 - *The Canterbury Tales*

PROMPT
You have listened to all the tales and all the presentations made by all the groups. Now pretend you are the Host and you have to make a decision about which one will win the dinner at the Tabbard Inn. Write a composition in which you express your personal opinions about which tale was the best.

PREWRITING
You have just heard a summary of all the tales we did in class. Which tale did you like the best? Write down three reasons why you liked it the best. Next to each reason, give specific examples from the story or the presentation supporting that reason.

DRAFTING
Write one paragraph in which you introduce the idea that you think the ----------'s tale was the best one.

In the body of your composition, write one paragraph for each of the reasons you thought the ----------'s tale was the best. Fill out each paragraph with specific examples to support your reason.

Write a concluding paragraph in which you give your final thoughts and bring your composition to a close.

PROMPT
When you finish the rough draft of your paper, ask a student who sits near you to read it. After reading your rough draft, he/she should tell you what he/she liked best about your work, which parts were difficult to understand, and ways in which your work could be improved. Reread your paper considering your critic's comments, and make the corrections you think are necessary.

PROOFREADING
Do a final proofreading of your paper double-checking your grammar, spelling, organization, and the clarity of your ideas.

WRITING EVALUATION FORM - *The Canterbury Tales*

Name _____ Date _____

Writing Assignment #1 for *The Canterbury Tales* unit Grade _____

Circle One For Each Item:

Grammar: correct   errors noted on paper

Spelling: correct   errors noted on paper

Punctuation: correct   errors noted on paper

Legibility: excellent   good   fair   poor

Strengths:

Weaknesses:

Comments/Suggestions:

LESSON TWENTY-TWO

Objective

    To review the vocabulary words chosen for this unit

Activity

    Choose one of the vocabulary review activities listed below and spend your class time as directed. Some of the materials for these review activities are located in the Vocabulary Resource Materials section in this unit.

VOCABULARY REVIEW ACTIVITIES

1. Divide your class into two teams and have an old-fashioned spelling or definition bee.

2. Give each of your students (or students in groups of two, three or four) a *Canterbury Tales* Vocabulary Word Search Puzzle. The person (group) to find all of the vocabulary words in the puzzle first wins.

3. Give students a *Canterbury Tales* Vocabulary Word Search Puzzle without the word list. The person or group to find the most vocabulary words in the puzzle wins.

4. Use a *Canterbury Tales* Vocabulary Crossword Puzzle. Put the puzzle onto a transparency on the overhead projector (so everyone can see it), and do the puzzle together as a class.

5. Give students a *Canterbury Tales* Vocabulary Matching Worksheet to do.

6. Divide your class into two teams. Use the *Canterbury Tales* vocabulary words with their letters jumbled as a word list. Student 1 from Team A faces off against Student 1 from Team B. You write the first jumbled word on the board. The first student (1A or 1B) to unscramble the word wins the chance for his/her team to score points. If 1A wins the jumble, go to student 2A and give him/her a definition. He/she must give you the correct spelling of the vocabulary word which fits that definition. If he/she does, Team A scores a point, and you give student 3A a definition for which you expect a correctly spelled matching vocabulary word. Continue giving Team A definitions until some team member makes an incorrect response. An incorrect response sends the game back to the jumbled-word face off, this time with students 2A and 2B. Instead of repeating giving definitions to the first few students of each team, continue with the student after the one who gave the last incorrect response on the team. For example, if Team B wins the jumbled-word face-off, and student 5B gave the last incorrect answer for Team B, you would start this round of definition questions with student 6B, and so on. The team with the most points wins!

7. Have students write a story in which they correctly use as many vocabulary words as possible. Have students read their compositions orally! Post the most original compositions on your bulletin board!

VOCABULARY LIST - *The Canterbury Tales*
For definitions to the words, see the Vocabulary Sheet in the Vocabulary Resource section.

Benign	Carouses
Obstinate	Gluttony
Sundry	Pallor
Coy	Prating
Eminent	Daunted
Felicity	Aphrodisiac
Languishing	Extort
Retinue	Bequeath
Exhortation	Obscure
Lecher	Feigned
Proffering	Inebriate
Paramours	Acquittal
Beseech	Ire
Trenchant	Supplications
Frugality	Prodigious
Amiss	Conundrum
Inciting	Prerogative
Woe	Constancy
Contrive	Acquiesce
Blithely	Caprices
Chide	Demure
Usury	Eschew
Diligence	Pelf
Redressed	Dais
Avail	Reprehensible
Repletion	Insinuations
Discreet	Revel
Abominable	Verily
Derision	Enthralled
Predestination	Victuals
	Sage
	Requite

LESSONS TWENTY-THREE AND TWENTY-FOUR

Objectives
> To discuss *The Canterbury Tales* on interpretive and critical levels

Activity
> Choose the questions from the Extra Discussion Questions/Writing Assignments which seem most appropriate for your students. A class discussion of these questions is most effective if students have been given the opportunity to formulate answers to the questions prior to the discussion. To this end, you may either have all the students formulate answers to all the questions, divide your class into groups and assign one or more questions to each group, or you could assign one question to each student in your class. The option you choose will make a difference in the amount of class time needed for this activity.

> After students have had ample time to formulate answers to the questions, begin your class discussion of the questions and the ideas presented by the questions. Be sure students take notes during the discussion so they have information to study for the unit test.

LESSON TWENTY-FIVE

Objectives
> 1. To give students the opportunity to practice writing to persuade
> 2. To help students review the main ideas from the *Canterbury Tales*

Activity
> Distribute Writing Assignment #3. Discuss the directions in detail and give students ample time to complete the assignment.

LESSON TWENTY-SIX

Objective
> To review the main ideas presented in *The Canterbury Tales*

Activity #1
> Choose one of the review games/activities included in the packet and spend your class period as outlined there. Some materials for these activities are located in the unit resource section of this unit.

Activity #2
> Remind students that the Unit Test will be in the next class meeting. Stress the review of the Study Guides and their class notes as a last minute, brush-up review for homework.

EXTRA WRITING ASSIGNMENTS/DISCUSSION QUESTIONS - *The Canterbury Tales*

<u>Interpretation</u>

1. From what point of view is the frame of *The Canterbury Tales* written? What effect does this have on the total work?

2. What does the setting of *The Canterbury Tales* contribute to the story?

3. Does the work *The Canterbury Tales* have a climax? If so, where? If not, explain why not..

4. Is the frame for the tales believable? Why or why not?

5. Are the characters in *The Canterbury Tales* stereotypes? If so, explain why Geoffrey Chaucer used stereotypes. If not, explain how the characters merit individuality.

<u>Critical</u>

6. Evaluate Geoffrey Chaucer's style of writing. How does it contribute to the value of the work?

7. What is "mock heroic epic"? Do any of the tales fit this description? If so, which ones and why?

8. Compare and contrast the Friar and the Parson.

9. What function does the character of Bailly serve in the tales?

10. Explain how Chaucer gave us a personal look at life in the 1300s through *The Canterbury Tales*.

11. Discuss the theme of faithfulness throughout the tales. Give specific examples.

12. Discuss the theme of extortion/greed throughout the tales. Give specific examples.

13. Discuss the theme of corruption throughout the tales. Give specific examples.

14. Discuss the theme of love throughout the tales. Give specific examples.

15. Discuss the treatment of women in *The Canterbury Tales*. Give specific examples.

16. Discuss Chaucer's use of references to other people, places and gods to give depth to his tales.

17. Discuss the significance of the physical appearance of each of the main characters.

18. Give a synopsis of the fourteenth-century view of the world based on *The Canterbury Tales*.

Canterbury Tales Extra Discussion Questions Page 2

Personal Response

19. Did you enjoy reading *The Canterbury Tales*? Why or why not?

20. Had the story been framed from the Wife of Bath's (or any other individual character other than Bailly's) point of view, would we have been given as good of a portrait of fourteenth-century people? Why or why not?

21. The Parson gets sidetracked talking about free will in his tale. The question he poses is that if God knows all things (including the future), does man still have free will or is everything already decided? What is your answer to that question?

22. Chanticleer believed in the meaning of dreams. Do you? Why or why not?

23. Are there pilgrims today? Who are they, where do they live, and to where are their pilgrimages?

24. Would you have liked living in fourteenth-century England? Why or why not?

25. Suppose the Queen in the Wife of Bath's tale would ask you, "What do women most desire?" What would be your answer?

26. Define fable. Which of the tales could be considered a fable?

WRITING ASSIGNMENT #3 - *The Canterbury Tales*

PROMPT
The Canterbury Tales contain some of the most vile, lecherous, contemptuous, gluttonous, greedy and generally disgusting characters in all literature. Consider all the tales we heard in class. Choose the one character you think is the most vile of all and convince me that your choice is the best one.

PREWRITING
Review your class notes and study guides to refresh your memory about the characters and the tales. As you review, jot down the names/identities of some of the worst "bad guys" as you come across them. When you are finished, go back and look at your little list. Which one was the rottenest of the whole bunch? Jot down three reasons why he/she was rotten. Next to those three reasons, jot down some specific examples or notes of explanation.

DRAFTING
Write a paragraph of introduction, in which you lead up to the idea that ----- was the most vile character in all of the tales.

In the body of your composition, write one paragraph for each of the reasons you noted in the prewriting stage above. Fill out each of the paragraphs with specific examples or further explanations to support your reasons.

Write a paragraph in which you conclude your thoughts and bring your composition to a close.

PROMPT
When you finish the rough draft of your paper, ask a student who sits near you to read it. After reading your rough draft, he/she should tell you what he/she liked best about your work, which parts were difficult to understand, and ways in which your work could be improved. Reread your paper considering your critic's comments, and make the corrections you think are necessary.

PROOFREADING
Do a final proofreading of your paper double-checking your grammar, spelling, organization, and the clarity of your ideas.

REVIEW GAMES/ACTIVITIES - *The Canterbury Tales*

1. Ask the class to make up a unit test for *The Canterbury Tales*. The test should have 4 sections: matching, true/false, short answer, and essay. Students may use 1/2 period to make the test and then swap papers and use the other 1/2 class period to take a test a classmate has devised. (open book) You may want to use the unit test included in this packet or take questions from the students' unit tests to formulate your own test.

2. Take 1/2 period for students to make up true and false questions (including the answers). Collect the papers and divide the class into two teams. Draw a big tic-tac-toe board on the chalk board. Make one team X and one team O. Ask questions to each side, giving each student one turn. If the question is answered correctly, that students' team's letter (X or O) is placed in the box. If the answer is incorrect, no mark is placed in the box. The object is to get three marks in a row like tic-tac-toe. You may want to keep track of the number of games won for each team.

3. Take 1/2 period for students to make up questions (true/false and short answer). Collect the questions. Divide the class into two teams. You'll alternate asking questions to individual members of teams A & B (like in a spelling bee). The question keeps going from A to B until it is correctly answered, then a new question is asked. A correct answer does not allow the team to get another question. Correct answers are +2 points; incorrect answers are -1 point.

4. Have students pair up and quiz each other from their study guides and class notes.

5. Give students a *Canterbury Tales* crossword puzzle to complete.

6.. Divide your class into two teams. Use the *Canterbury Tales* crossword words with their letters jumbled as a word list. Student 1 from Team A faces off against Student 1 from Team B. You write the first jumbled word on the board. The first student (1A or 1B) to unscramble the word wins the chance for his/her team to score points. If 1A wins the jumble, go to student 2A and give him/her a clue. He/she must give you the correct word which matches that clue. If he/she does, Team A scores a point, and you give student 3A a clue for which you expect another correct response. Continue giving Team A clues until some team member makes an incorrect response. An incorrect response sends the game back to the jumbled-word face off, this time with students 2A and 2B. Instead of repeating giving clues to the first few students of each team, continue with the student after the one who gave the last incorrect response on the team. For example, if Team B wins the jumbled-word face-off, and student 5B gave the last incorrect answer for Team B, you would start this round of clue questions with student 6B, and so on. The team with the most points wins!

UNIT TESTS

SHORT ANSWER UNIT TEST 1 - *The Canterbury Tales*

I. Matching/Identify: Prologue

____ 1. Knight A. Bald and fat, didn't like hard work

____ 2. Squire B. Had five husbands

____ 3. Yeoman C. Liked to eat, drink and be merry

____ 4. Prioress D. Host

____ 5. Monk E. Garland of flowers on head, insulted Friar

____ 6. Friar F. Squire's servant

____ 7. Merchant G. Aristocratic, takes bribes for easy penance

____ 8. Clerk H. Sells false relics, bulging eyes, long yellow hair

____ 9. Sergeant At Law I. Had been in many battles, was a gentleman

____ 10. Franklin J. Dainty, pleasant, sensitive, medieval beauty

____ 11. Cook K. Good navigator, didn't ride well, from Dartmouth

____ 12. Shipman L. Loved to learn for the sake of learning

____ 13. Physician M. Son of the Knight

____ 14. Wife of Bath N. Old, thin, brought up the rear, good manager

____ 15. Parson O. Seemed busier than he actually was

____ 16. Pardoner P. Forked beard, good negotiator, always told his opinions

____ 17. Miller Q. Master chef, sores on his knee

____ 18. Manciple R. Christ-like, patient, giving, holy, virtuous

____ 19. Reeve S. Not religious, loved gold, dressed in red and blue-grey

____ 20. Summoner T. Football-player build, cheated customers, played bagpipes

____ 21. Bailly U. Stole from lawyers, shrewd buyer

The Canterbury Tales Short Answer Unit Test 1 Page 2

II. Short Answer

1. How did Arcita and Palamon become Theseus's prisoners?

2. How did Palamon come to be married to Emily?

3. How did Nicholas get the carpenter out of the way so he and Alison could sleep together?

4. How did Absalom get even with Alison and Nicholas?

5. What did the miller do to get the best of Alan and John?

6. How did John and Alan get even with the miller?

7. Why did Sir John tell the merchant he paid back the loan to the merchant's wife?

Canterbury Tales Short Answer Unit Test 1 Page 2

8. What happened to the little boy in the Prioress's Tale?

9. Explain the significance of the Latin phrase that Chanticleer tells Pertelote means "Woman is man's delight and all his bliss."

10. What happened to the three rioters (youths) who went looking for Death?

11. What happened to the summoner in the Friar's tale?

12. "No empty-handed man can lure a bird," said the Wife of Bath. Explain what she meant.

13. What was the answer to the Queen's question? What do all women want most of all (according to the tale)?

14. What characteristic of the friars does the Summoner's story accentuate?

Canterbury Tales Short Answer Unit Test 1 Page 3

15. Why is the friar's lecture to Thomas about ire ironic?

16. What promise did Griselda make to the marquis?

17. How did the marquis test Griselda's faithfulness to him?

18. What was Griselda's reward for keeping her promise?

19. How was January's handicap cured?

20. What promise did Dorigen make to Aurelius?

21. What was Aurelius's response when Dorigen told him she and been set free to keep her word?

The Canterbury Tales Short Answer Unit Test 1 Page 4

III. Composition

    Explain how *The Canterbury Tales* is a profile of fourteenth century life. Use specific examples from the text.

Canterbury Tales Short Answer Unit Test 1 Page 5

IV. Vocabulary

Listen to the vocabulary words and spell them. After you have spelled all the words, go back and write down the definitions.

1.

2.

3.

4.

5.

6.

7.

8.

9.

10.

KEY: SHORT ANSWER UNIT TEST #1 - *The Canterbury Tales*

I. Matching/Identify

_I_	1. Knight	A.	Bald and fat, didn't like hard work
_M_	2. Squire	B.	Had five husbands
_F_	3. Yeoman	C.	Liked to eat, drink and be merry
_J_	4. Prioress	D.	Host
_A_	5. Monk	E.	Garland of flowers on head, insulted Friar
_G_	6. Friar	F.	Squire's servant
_P_	7. Merchant	G.	Aristocratic, takes bribes for easy penance
_L_	8. Clerk	H.	Sells false relics, bulging eyes, long yellow hair
_O_	9. Sergeant At Law	I.	Had been in many battles, was a gentleman
_C_	10. Franklin	J.	Dainty, pleasant, sensitive, medieval beauty
_Q_	11. Cook	K.	Good navigator, didn't ride well, from Dartmouth
_K_	12. Shipman	L.	Loved to learn for the sake of learning
_S_	13. Physician	M.	Son of the Knight
_B_	14. Wife of Bath	N.	Old, thin, brought up the rear, good manager
_R_	15. Parson	O.	Seemed busier than he actually was
_H_	16. Pardoner	P.	Forked beard, good negotiator, always told his opinions
_T_	17. Miller	Q.	Master chef, sores on his knee
_U_	18. Manciple	R.	Christ-like, patient, giving, holy, virtuous
_N_	19. Reeve	S.	Not religious, loved gold, dressed in red and blue-grey
_E_	20. Summoner	T.	Football-player build, cheated customers, played bagpipes
_D_	21. Bailly	U.	Stole from lawyers, shrewd buyer

II. Short Answer

1. How did Arcita and Palamon become Theseus's prisoners?

    Theseus went to slay Creon at Thebes. After he had won and conquered the city, pillagers found Arcita and Palamon, knights who had fought against Theseus. They were wounded, so the pillagers took them to Theseus's tent. He ordered that they would be kept perpetual prisoners.

2. How did Palamon come to be married to Emily?

    After a sufficient period of mourning, a certain number of years, Theseus sent for Palamon. Theseus and his parliament gave permission for Palamon to marry Emily, and they lived happily ever after.

3. How did Nicholas get the carpenter out of the way so he and Alison could sleep together?

    He pretended to have had a premonition of a second great flood that would destroy the world, and he convinced the carpenter to make preparations to save the three of them. The carpenter was to get three tubs and hang them under the roof. On the night the flood was to happen, the three would spend the night in the separate tubs. They did so, and when the carpenter fell asleep, Alison and Nicholas climbed out of their tubs and ran off to the bedroom.

4. How did Absalom get even with Alison and Nicholas?

    He went to the blacksmith's shop and borrowed a hot iron. When he came back for another kiss, he put the hot iron on the bare behind that was stuck out of the window.

5. What did the miller do to get the best of Alan and John?

    He let their horse go, and when they went to find it, he took 1/2 bushel of their flour.

6. How did John and Alan get even with the miller?

    Alan slept with Molly; John tricked the miller's wife into sleeping with him. In the morning, they took their flour and the cake that had been made with part of it, and left. They had slept with both women, had a free meal, had a free night's lodging, and left with all of their goods.

7. Why did Sir John tell the merchant he paid back the loan to the merchant's wife?

    This way he didn't have to have any money out of pocket. He used the merchant's 100 francs to loan to the merchant's wife and then claimed that he had paid back his loan to the merchant's wife. The merchant had been duped into, in effect, giving his wife 100 francs for clothes. The wife had slept with Sir John for nothing; he hadn't really lent her any money at all.

8. What happened to the little boy in the Prioress's Tale?
    The Jewish people hired a murderer who slit the boy's throat.

9. Explain the significance of the Latin phrase that Chanticleer tells Pertelote means "Woman is man's delight and all his bliss."
    Chanticleer has not translated this properly. It actually means, "woman is man's worst enemy." This mistranslation is ironic because Pertelote, in brushing off Chanticleer's concern, actually is helping to lead to Chanticleer's downfall. Also the mistranslation adds to the comic element of the mock-heroic tone.

10. What happened to the three rioters (youths) who went looking for Death?
    They met an old man who told them death was under the oak tree. They found bushels of gold there. Because of their greed, the two stabbed the one, and then they unknowingly drank the poisoned wine. All three died.

11. What happened to the summoner in the Friar's tale?
    The old woman cursed him to hell, and the fiend took him there.

12. "No empty-handed man can lure a bird," said the Wife of Bath. Explain what she meant.
    Her husband had to do something nice for her or bring her something before she would be nice to him or let him sleep with her.

13. What was the answer to the Queen's question? What do all women want most of all (according to the tale)?
    The knight told the Queen that all women want to be masters of their husbands and lovers.

14. What characteristic of the friars does the Summoner's story accentuate?
    It accentuated their asking for money and charitable donations for their cause(s).

15. Why is the friar's lecture to Thomas about ire ironic?
    After Thomas gives the friar his "gift" for the friar to share with others at the convent, the friar is furious and spends the rest of the story ranting and raving in anger.

16. What promise did Griselda make to the marquis?
    "And here I promise never willingly
    To disobey in deed or thought or breath"

17. How did the Marquis test Griselda's faithfulness to him?
    Over a period of years, he took both children away and then threw her out of the castle back home to her father empty-handed. He then asked her to come back and clean and decorate his home for his new wife.

18. What was Griselda's reward for keeping her promise?
    Both children were brought back, she remained the wife of the Marquis, and they lived happily ever after.

19. How was January's handicap cured?
    When May stepped on his back to climb into the pear tree to meet Damian, January regained his sight just in time to catch May and Damian in the act.

20. What promise did Dorigen make to Aurelius?
    If he would clear the coasts of all those dreadful rocks, she would love him most.

21. What was Aurelius's response when Dorigen told him she and been set free to keep her word?
    He gave her back her freedom and allowed her to be with her husband.

IV. Vocabulary - Choose ten words from the vocabulary list. Read them orally so your students can write them down for part IV of the test.

SHORT ANSWER UNIT TEST 2 - *The Canterbury Tales*

I. Matching

____ 1. Knight   A. Stole from lawyers, shrewd buyer

____ 2. Squire   B. Bald and fat, didn't like hard work

____ 3. Yeoman   C. Had five husbands

____ 4. Prioress   D. Liked to eat, drink and be merry

____ 5. Monk   E. Host

____ 6. Friar   F. Garland of flowers on head, insulted Friar

____ 7. Merchant   G. Squire's servant

____ 8. Clerk   H. Aristocratic, takes bribes for easy penance

____ 9. Sergeant At Law I. Sells false relics, bulging eyes, long yellow hair

____ 10. Franklin   J. Had been in many battles, was a gentleman

____ 11. Cook   K. Dainty, pleasant, sensitive, medieval beauty

____ 12. Shipman   L. Good navigator, didn't ride well, from Dartmouth

____ 13. Physician   M. Loved to learn for the sake of learning

____ 14. Wife of Bath   N. Son of the Knight

____ 15. Parson   O. Old, thin, brought up the rear, good manager

____ 16. Pardoner   P. Seemed busier than he actually was

____ 17. Miller   Q. Forked beard, good negotiator, always told his opinions

____ 18. Manciple   R. Master chef, sores on his knee

____ 19. Reeve   S. Christ-like, patient, giving, holy, virtuous

____ 20. Summoner   T. Not religious, loved gold, dressed in red and blue-grey

____ 21. Bailly   U. Football-player build, cheated customers, played bagpipes

Canterbury Tales Short Answer Unit Test 2 Page 2

II. Short Answer

1. About what did Arcita and Palamon argue in the tower when they were prisoners?

2. What happened to Arcita?

3. What joke did Alison and Nicholas play on Absalom?

4. Why did the village people think the carpenter was crazy?

5. Why did Alan and John go to the miller's? Were they successful? How?

6. What does the merchant's wife ask of Sir John, and what does she offer in return?

Canterbury Tales Short Answer Unit Test 2 Page 3

7. Why did Sir John tell the merchant he paid back the loan to the merchant's wife?

8. What was unusual about the little boy in the Prioress's tale?

9. Identify Chanticleer and Pertelote.

10. What happened to Chanticleer?

11. What is the Pardoner's purpose? What is he supposed to do?

12. What is ironic about how the Pardoner gets people to repent from the sin of avarice?

13. Why did the Friar tell a story about a Summoner?

Canterbury Tales Short Answer Unit Test 2 Page 4

14. Why did the summoner have informers?

15. What is the Wife of Bath's complaint about husbands?

16. What deal did the knight in the Wife of Bath's Tale make on his way home after his year was almost ended?

17. Thomas says he's given all his money to various friars and now he has no more to give. What is the friar's response?

18. What was Griselda's reward for keeping her promise?

19. Identify Damian.

20. How did May overcome January's accusations?

21. Why was Dorigen so sad?

22. What promise did Dorigen make to Aurelius?

23. How did Aurelius get rid of the rocks?

The Canterbury Tales Short Answer Unit Test 2 Page 5

III. Composition
   Characterize Chaucer's treatment of women in *The Canterbury Tales*. Use specific examples from the text.

Canterbury Tales Short Answer Unit Test 2 Page 6

IV. Vocabulary

Listen to the vocabulary word and spell it. After you have spelled all the words, go back and write down the definition.

1.

2.

3.

4.

5.

6.

7.

8.

9.

10.

KEY: SHORT ANSWER UNIT TEST 2 *The Canterbury Tales*

I. Matching (Use this matching key also for the Advanced Short Answer Unit Test)

__J__ 1. Knight	A.	Stole from lawyers, shrewd buyer
__N__ 2. Squire	B.	Bald and fat, didn't like hard work
__G__ 3. Yeoman	C.	Had five husbands
__K__ 4. Prioress	D.	Liked to eat, drink and be merry
__B__ 5. Monk	E.	Host
__H__ 6. Friar	F.	Garland of flowers on head, insulted Friar
__Q__ 7. Merchant	G.	Squire's servant
__M__ 8. Clerk	H.	Aristocratic, takes bribes for easy penance
__P__ 9. Sergeant At Law	I.	Sells false relics, bulging eyes, long yellow hair
__D__ 10. Franklin	J.	Had been in many battles, was a gentleman
__R__ 11. Cook	K.	Dainty, pleasant, sensitive, medieval beauty
__L__ 12. Shipman	L.	Good navigator, didn't ride well, from Dartmouth
__T__ 13. Physician	M.	Loved to learn for the sake of learning
__C__ 14. Wife of Bath	N.	Son of the Knight
__S__ 15. Parson	O.	Old, thin, brought up the rear, good manager
__I__ 16. Pardoner	P.	Seemed busier than he actually was
__U__ 17. Miller	Q.	Forked beard, good negotiator, always told his opinions
__A__ 18. Manciple	R.	Master chef, sores on his knee
__O__ 19. Reeve	S.	Christ-like, patient, giving, holy, virtuous
__F__ 20. Summoner	T.	Not religious, loved gold, dressed in red and blue-grey
__E__ 21. Bailly	U.	Football-player build, cheated customers, played bagpipes

II. Short Answer

1. About what did Arcita and Palamon argue in the tower when they were prisoners?
    Each one had seen and fallen in love with Emily, the Queen's sister. They argued about which of them first saw Emily and could claim her for his own.

2. What happened to Arcita?
    There was an earth tremor as he was taking his victory round. His horse stepped and stumbled, and Arcita was thrown out of the saddle upon his head with his breast shattered by the saddle bow. He later died.

3. What joke did Alison and Nicholas play on Absalom?
    When Absalom came to Alison's window pleading for a kiss, she agreed. She opened her window and stuck out her behind, which unsuspecting Absalom kissed.

4. Why did the village people think the carpenter was crazy?
    When Nicholas's behind got burned, he began yelling, "Help! Water!" The carpenter, thinking the flood had come, cut the ropes holding the tub and fell to the floor. People came to see what the commotion was all about, and they saw the carpenter (broken arm and all) in a tub ranting about a flood. Nicholas pretended not to know what the carpenter was talking about, and brushed him off as having gone crazy, an explanation the people easily accepted and joked about.

5. Why did Alan and John go to the miller's? Were they successful? How?
    They were taking corn from the college to be milled. The Warden was tired of being cheated and these two students thought they could outwit the miller. At first it appeared as if the miller was going to get the best of them by letting the horse go and stealing their flour while they were looking for the horse, but the boys stayed overnight and got even with the miller by sleeping with his wife and daughter, getting a free meal and night's lodging, and taking back the flour the miller had stolen from them.

6. What does the merchant's wife ask of Sir John, and what does she offer in return?
    She asks for 100 francs to buy clothes with and promises to repay him and do "some little task" he might want.

7. Why did Sir John tell the merchant he paid back the loan to the merchant's wife?
    This way he didn't have to have any money out of pocket. He used the merchant's 100 francs to loan to the merchant's wife and then claimed that he had paid back his loan to the merchant's wife. The merchant had been duped into, in effect, giving his wife 100 francs for clothes. The wife had slept with Sir John for nothing; he hadn't really lent her any money at all.

8. What was unusual about the little boy's in the Prioress's tale?
    He kept singing the song to the Blessed Mother even though his throat had been cut.

9. Identify Chanticleer and Pertelote.
   Chanticleer is a rooster who dreams that he is killed by a strange animal. Pertelote is his favorite hen who tells him to ignore the dream and take a laxative.

10. What happened to Chanticleer?
    The fox hauled him away and prepared to make a meal of him, but he outsmarted the fox and flew away when the fox opened its mouth to shout some insults at the other animals.

11. What is the Pardoner's purpose? What is he supposed to do?
    He does everything he can to make money. He is supposed to be saving souls.

12. What is ironic about how the Pardoner gets people to repent from the sin of avarice?
    The Pardoner is very guilty of the sin of avarice himself. He uses ways of getting people to repent from avarice as a means for acquiring more money for the church.

13. Why did the Friar tell a story about a Summoner?
    He was mad at the Summoner for reprimanding him during the Wife of Bath's turn.

14. Why did the summoner have informers?
    He wasn't interested in bringing the guilty to justice and reformation; he wanted to extort money from them. Therefore, the more guilty people he could find, the more money he would make. Informers helped him find guilty people.

15. What is the Wife of Bath's complaint about husbands?
    She had many complaints which basically involve husbands' complaints about their wives and how their complaints are unfounded or the husbands' own fault. For instance, she says if husbands would "try out" their wives before marriage, they wouldn't think the wives had hidden their "vices." Husbands, she says, don't trust their wives; they have to spy on them all the time for fear of infidelity. Husbands "hide the keys of coffer doors" and seem to forget that their valuables are common property between man and wife. She says husbands think women contrive ways to make their husbands miserable.

16. What deal did the knight in the Wife of Bath's Tale make on his way home after his year was almost ended?
    He met an old woman who told him the answer to the Queen's question under the condition that he would grant her next request if it would be in his power to do so.

17. Thomas says he's given all his money to various friars and now he has no more to give. What is the friar's response?
    Thomas is ill because he has so little faith; he should give more. He should have given all his donations to him instead of spreading the money about.

18. What was Griselda's reward for keeping her promise?
    Both children were brought back, she remained the wife of the marquis, and they lived happily ever after.

19. Identify Damian.
   Damian was one of January's squires. He lusted after May, gave her a note, and they contrived a way to get together.

20. How did May overcome January's accusations?
   She just kept telling him over and over that he really didn't see what he thought he saw. His vision was still a bit fuzzy.

21. Why was Dorigen so sad?
   She missed Arveragus, who had gone off to do his knightly work for two years.

22. What promise did Dorigen make to Aurelius?
   If he would clear the coasts of all those dreadful rocks, she would love him most.

23. How did Aurelius get rid of the rocks?
   He hired a magician to perform an optical illusion.

IV. Vocabulary: See Short Answer Unit Test 1 Part IV for directions.

ADVANCED SHORT ANSWER UNIT TEST - *The Canterbury Tales*

I. Matching

_____ 1. Knight   A. Stole from lawyers, shrewd buyer

_____ 2. Squire   B. Bald and fat, didn't like hard work

_____ 3. Yeoman   C. Had five husbands

_____ 4. Prioress   D. Liked to eat, drink and be merry

_____ 5. Monk   E. Host

_____ 6. Friar   F. Garland of flowers on head, insulted Friar

_____ 7. Merchant   G. Squire's servant

_____ 8. Clerk   H. Aristocratic, takes bribes for easy penance

_____ 9. Sergeant At Law   I. Sells false relics, bulging eyes, long yellow hair

_____ 10. Franklin   J. Had been in many battles, was a gentleman

_____ 11. Cook   K. Dainty, pleasant, sensitive, medieval beauty

_____ 12. Shipman   L. Good navigator, didn't ride well, from Dartmouth

_____ 13. Physician   M. Loved to learn for the sake of learning

_____ 14. Wife of Bath   N. Son of the Knight

_____ 15. Parson   O. Old, thin, brought up the rear, good manager

_____ 16. Pardoner   P. Seemed busier than he actually was

_____ 17. Miller   Q. Forked beard, good negotiator, always told his opinions

_____ 18. Manciple   R. Master chef, sores on his knee

_____ 19. Reeve   S. Christ-like, patient, giving, holy, virtuous

_____ 20. Summoner   T. Not religious, loved gold, dressed in red and blue-grey

_____ 21. Bailly   U. Football-player build, cheated customers, played bagpipes

The Canterbury Tales Advanced Short Answer Unit Test Page 2

II. Short Answer

1-3. Choose three of the tales that were about fidelity/faithfulness and explain why that theme applies to each.

1.

2.

3.

The Canterbury Tales Advanced Short Answer Unit Test Page 3

4-5. Choose two tales that were about greed/avarice and explain how that theme applies to them.

4.

5.

The Canterbury Tales Advanced Short Answer Unit Test Page 4

6. Choose any two characters from any tales we heard and tell how they are alike.

7. Choose two characters from any tales we heard and explain how they are opposites.

8. Which tale is a fable?

9. How do the tales reflect life in the 1300s?

10. Explain the importance of the character of Harry Bailly.

The Canterbury Tales Advanced Short Answer Unit Test Page 5

III. Composition
    Describe the portrait of the clergy as painted by Chaucer in *The Canterbury Tales*. Was it an accurate picture?

The Canterbury Tales Advanced Short Answer Unit Test Page 6

IV. Vocabulary

Listen to the vocabulary words and write them down. Go back later and write a composition in which you use all the words. The composition should relate in some way to *The Canterbury Tales*.

Multiple Choice Unit Test 1 - *The Canterbury Tales*

I. Matching

____ 1. Knight   A. Host

____ 2. Squire   B. Had five husbands

____ 3. Yeoman   C. Liked to eat, drink and be merry

____ 4. Prioress   D. Squire's servant

____ 5. Monk   E. Christ-like, patient, giving, holy, virtuous

____ 6. Friar   F. Bald and fat, didn't like hard work

____ 7. Merchant   G. Aristocratic, takes bribes for easy penance

____ 8. Clerk   H. Sells false relics, bulging eyes, long yellow hair

____ 9. Sergeant At Law I. Had been in many battles, was a gentleman

____ 10. Franklin   J. Master chef, sores on his knee

____ 11. Cook   K. Old, thin, brought up the rear, good manager

____ 12. Shipman   L. Football-player build, cheated customers, played bagpipes

____ 13. Physician   M. Son of the Knight

____ 14. Wife of Bath   N. Dainty, pleasant, sensitive, medieval beauty

____ 15. Parson   O. Seemed busier than he actually was

____ 16. Pardoner   P. Forked beard, good negotiator, always told his opinions

____ 17. Miller   Q. Good navigator, didn't ride well, from Dartmouth

____ 18. Manciple   R. Garland of flowers on head, insulted Friar

____ 19. Reeve   S. Stole from lawyers, shrewd buyer

____ 20. Summoner   T. Loved to learn for the sake of learning

____ 21. Bailly   U. Not religious, loved gold, dressed in red and blue-grey

The Canterbury Tales Multiple Choice Unit Test 1 Page 2

II. Matching/Identify: Tales

____ 1. Molly   A. He didn't give his wife enough money

____ 2. Nicholas   B. He kissed Alison's behind by mistake

____ 3. Yeoman   C. He hit the Wife of Bath and made her deaf

____ 4. Arveragus   D. He lived happily ever after with Emily

____ 5. Arcita   E. January's wife

____ 6. May   F. He dreamed a strange animal killed him

____ 7. John   G. Miller's daughter

____ 8. Thomas   H. She was totally loyal and obedient to the marquis

____ 9. Absalom   I. He let Alan's horse go

____ 10. Old Woman   J. He set Arcita free without ransom

____ 11. Chanticleer   K. The merchant's wife slept with him to repay her debt

____ 12. Aurelius   L. He was a fiend from hell in disguise

____ 13. Palamon   M. He fell off his horse and died from the injury

____ 14. Sir John   N. She told the knight the answer to the Queen's question

____ 15. Miller   O. Tricked the miller's wife into sleeping with him

____ 16. Johnny   P. He had to find a way to make the rocks disappear

____ 17. January   Q. His behind got branded with a hot iron

____ 18. Theseus   R. Dorigen's husband

____ 19. Merchant   S. He gave a friar an unusual gift

____ 20. Griselda   T. He regained his sight in time to catch his wife in a pear tree with her lover

The Canterbury Tales Multiple Choice Unit Test 1 Page 3

II. Multiple Choice: Identify the Speaker
A = Griselda   **B** = Palamon   **C** = Alan   **D** = Arcite   **E** = Merchant's Wife   **F** = Clerk

G = Nicholas   **H** = Pertelote   **I** = Knight in Wife of Bath's Tale   **J** = Queen   **L** = Thomas

M = Friar   **N** = Summoner   **O** = Chanticleer   **P** = May   **Q** = Aurelius   **R** = Old Woman

1. My lady and my love, my dearest wife,
   I leave the matter to your wise decision.
   You make the choice yourself . . . .

2. Alas, O Death! Alas, my Emily!
   Alas the parting of our company!

3. Help! Water! Water! Help! For Heaven's love!

4. 'Well, now,' he said, 'there's something I can give
   Your holy convent, if I am to live.
   And you shall have it in your hand to own

5. Only to you, the only one on earth,
   This much I'll say. God help me, he's not worth
   A fly upon the wall! In no respect.
   But his worst fault is niggardly neglect!

6. . . . if you discern
   The force of these examples, you may learn
   One never should be careless about dreams,
   For, undeniably, I say it seems
   That many are a sign of trouble breeding.

7. Yet you are little likely, all your life
   To stand in grace with her; no more shall I.
   You know yourself, too well, that here we lie
   Condemned to prison both of us, no doubt
   Perpetually. No ransom buys us out.

8. I keep my word of honour to a brother,
   As I have sworn, and so shall each to other;
   True brothers we shall be; the bargain's made

9. . . . Well, Simon, lad, how's things?
   And how's your canny daughter and your wife?

10. 'Nor is there anything, as God may save
    My soul, that pleasing you displeases me,
    Nor is there anything that I could crave
    To have, or dread to lose, but you,' said she.

The Canterbury Tales Multiple Choice Unit Test 1 Page 4

III. Composition
    In one sentence state what you think is the most important thing Chaucer shows in *The Canterbury Tales*. List under that one sentence three reasons why you think that thing is the most important.

The Canterbury Tales Multiple Choice Unit Test 1 Page 5

IV. Vocabulary   Match the correct definitions to the vocabulary words.

____ 1. INEBRIATE   A. Even; indeed

____ 2. PREROGATIVE   B. Deserving condemnation; despicable

____ 3. INCITING   C. To get revenge for

____ 4. ACQUIESCE   D. Extreme paleness

____ 5. FEIGNED   E. Artificial; counterfeited; faked

____ 6. AVAIL   F. Reserved in manner; shy; modest

____ 7. DEMURE   G. Agree; consent

____ 8. PRATING   H. Chattering; jabbering

____ 9. REDRESSED   I. The right to command or decide

____ 10. ENTHRALLED   J. Lovers

____ 11. DERISION   K. Mockery; ridicule

____ 12. OBSTINATE   L. Usefulness

____ 13. REPREHENSIBLE   M. Stirring to action

____ 14. VERILY   N. Full to or beyond satisfaction

____ 15. ABOMINABLE   O. Drunk

____ 16. PALLOR   P. A drug or food having the effect of arousing sexual desire

____ 17. USURY   Q. Stubborn

____ 18. APHRODISIAC   R. Enchanted; fascinated

____ 19. PARAMOURS   S. Lending money & charging outrageously high interest

____ 20. REPLETION   T. Hateful; horrid; awful

MULTIPLE CHOICE UNIT TEST 2 - *The Canterbury Tales*

I. Matching

____ 1. Knight   A. Forked beard, good negotiator, always told his opinions

____ 2. Squire   B. Bald and fat, didn't like hard work

____ 3. Yeoman   C. Old, thin, brought up the rear, good manager

____ 4. Prioress   D. Seemed busier than he actually was

____ 5. Monk   E. Christ-like, patient, giving, holy, virtuous

____ 6. Friar   F. Had five husbands

____ 7. Merchant   G. Stole from lawyers, shrewd buyer

____ 8. Clerk   H. Sells false relics, bulging eyes, long yellow hair

____ 9. Sergeant At Law   I. Not religious, loved gold, dressed in red and blue-grey

____ 10. Franklin   J. Master chef, sores on his knee

____ 11. Cook   K. Liked to eat, drink and be merry

____ 12. Shipman   L. Football-player build, cheated customers, played bagpipes

____ 13. Physician   M. Loved to learn for the sake of learning

____ 14. Wife of Bath   N. Dainty, pleasant, sensitive, medieval beauty

____ 15. Parson   O. Squire's servant

____ 16. Pardoner   P. Host

____ 17. Miller   Q. Good navigator, didn't ride well, from Dartmouth

____ 18. Manciple   R. Garland of flowers on head, insulted Friar

____ 19. Reeve   S. Aristocratic, takes bribes for easy penance

____ 20. Summoner   T. Son of the Knight

____ 21. Bailly   U. Had been in many battles, was a gentleman

The Canterbury Tales Multiple Choice Unit Test 2 Page 2

II. Matching/Identify: Tales

_____ 1. Molly   A. He set Arcita free without ransom

_____ 2. Nicholas   B. The merchant's wife slept with him to repay her debt

_____ 3. Yeoman   C. She told the knight the answer to the Queen's question

_____ 4. Arveragus   D. He lived happily ever after with Emily

_____ 5. Arcita   E. He was a fiend from hell in disguise

_____ 6. May   F. He dreamed a strange animal killed him

_____ 7. John   G. Tricked the miller's wife into sleeping with him

_____ 8. Thomas   H. She was totally loyal and obedient to the marquis

_____ 9. Absalom   I. He let Alan's horse go

_____ 10. Old Woman   J. He didn't give his wife enough money

_____ 11. Chanticleer   K. He kissed Alison's behind by mistake

_____ 12. Aurelius   L. January's wife

_____ 13. Palamon   M. He had to find a way to make the rocks disappear

_____ 14. Sir John   N. He hit the Wife of Bath and made her deaf

_____ 15. Miller   O. Miller's daughter

_____ 16. Johnny   P. He fell off his horse and died from the injury

_____ 17. January   Q. He gave a friar an unusual gift

_____ 18. Theseus   R. Dorigen's husband

_____ 19. Merchant   S. His behind got branded with a hot iron

_____ 20. Griselda   T. He regained his sight in time to catch his wife in a pear tree with her lover

The Canterbury Tales Multiple Choice Unit Test 2 Page 3

II. Multiple Choice: Identify the Speaker
A = Alan   **B** = Arcite   **C** = Griselda   **D** = Chanticleer   **E** = Pertelote   **F** = Clerk

G = Summoner   **H** = Merchant's Wife   **I** = Thomas   **J** = Queen   **L** = Aurelius   **M** = Friar

N = Nicholas   **O** = Palamon   **P** = May   **Q** = Knight in Wife of Bath's Tale   **R** = Old Woman

1. Help! Water! Water! Help! For Heaven's love!

2. Yet you are little likely, all your life
   To stand in grace with her; no more shall I.
   You know yourself, too well, that here we lie
   Condemned to prison both of us, no doubt
   Perpetually. No ransom buys us out.

3. 'Nor is there anything, as God may save
   My soul, that pleasing you displeases me,
   Nor is there anything that I could crave
   To have, or dread to lose, but you,' said she.

4. 'Well, now,' he said, 'there's something I can give
   Your holy convent, if I am to live.
   And you shall have it in your hand to own

5. I keep my word of honour to a brother,
   As I have sworn, and so shall each to other;
   True brothers we shall be; the bargain's made

6. . . . if you discern
   The force of these examples, you may learn
   One never should be careless about dreams,
   For, undeniably, I say it seems
   That many are a sign of trouble breeding.

7. Alas, O Death! Alas, my Emily!
   Alas the parting of our company!

8. Only to you, the only one on earth,
   This much I'll say. God help me, he's not worth
   A fly upon the wall! In no respect.
   But his worst fault is niggardly neglect!

9. . . . Well, Simon, lad, how's things?
   And how's your canny daughter and your wife?

10. My lady and my love, my dearest wife,
    I leave the matter to your wise decision.
    You make the choice yourself . . . .

The Canterbury Tales Multiple Choice Unit Test 2 Page 4

III. Composition

On the rear cover of the Penguin Classic edition of the tales, the author writes, "With their astonishing diversity of tone and subject-matter, *The Canterbury Tales* have become one of the touchstones of medieval literature." Explain how the tales have a "diversity of tone and subject matter" using examples from the tales we have read in class.

The Canterbury Tales Multiple Choice Unit Test 2 Page 5

IV. Vocabulary   Match the correct definitions to the vocabulary words.

____ 1. DAIS   A. Mockery; ridicule

____ 2. DERISION   B. Stirring to action

____ 3. PALLOR   C. Wrong; awry

____ 4. FRUGALITY   D. To leave material goods by will

____ 5. FELICITY   E. Usefulness

____ 6. BEQUEATH   F. Extreme paleness

____ 7. BENIGN   G. A raised platform

____ 8. USURY   H. Full to or beyond satisfaction

____ 9. REPLETION   I. Faithfulness; fidelity

____ 10. PELF   J. Speech that incites

____ 11. INCITING   K. Chattering; jabbering

____ 12. ESCHEW   L. Loot; goods seized unlawfully

____ 13. AMISS   M. Happiness; bliss

____ 14. AVAIL   N. To stay away from

____ 15. ABOMINABLE   O. Thriftiness; careful use of material goods

____ 16. CONSTANCY   P. Steady attention and effort

____ 17. PRATING   Q. Hateful; horrid; awful

____ 18. DILIGENCE   R. Group of attendants or followers

____ 19. EXHORTATION   S. Kindhearted, considerate

____ 20. RETINUE   T. Lending money & charging outrageously high interest

ANSWER SHEET - *The Canterbury Tales*
Multiple Choice Unit Tests

I. Matching/Prologue
1. ___
2. ___
3. ___
4. ___
5. ___
6. ___
7. ___
8. ___
9. ___
10. ___
11. ___
12. ___
13. ___
14. ___
15. ___
16. ___
17. ___
18. ___
19. ___
20. ___
21. ___

II. Matching/Tales
1. ___
2. ___
3. ___
4. ___
5. ___
6. ___
7. ___
8. ___
9. ___
10. ___
11. ___
12. ___
13. ___
14. ___
15. ___
16. ___
17. ___
18. ___
19. ___
20. ___

II. Multiple Choice/Quotations
1. ___
2. ___
3. ___
4. ___
5. ___
6. ___
7. ___
8. ___
9. ___
10. ___

IV. Vocabulary
1. ___
2. ___
3. ___
4. ___
5. ___
6. ___
7. ___
8. ___
9. ___
10. ___
11. ___
12. ___
13. ___
14. ___
15. ___
16. ___
17. ___
18. ___
19. ___
20. ___

ANSWER SHEET KEY - *The Canterbury Tales*
Multiple Choice Unit Test 1

I. Matching/Prologue
1. I
2. M
3. F
4. J
5. A
6. G
7. P
8. L
9. O
10. C
11. Q
12. K
13. S
14. B
15. R
16. H
17. T
18. U
19. N
20. E
21. D

II. Matching/Tales
1. G
2. Q
3. L
4. R
5. M
6. E
7. O
8. S
9. B
10. N
11. F
12. P
13. D
14. K
15. I
16. C
17. T
18. J
19. A
20. H

II. Multiple Choice/Quotations
1. I
2. D
3. G
4. L
5. E
6. O
7. D
8. N
9. C
10. A

IV. Vocabulary
1. O
2. I
3. M
4. G
5. E
6. L
7. F
8. H
9. C
10. R
11. K
12. Q
13. B
14. A
15. T
16. D
17. S
18. P
19. J
20. N

ANSWER SHEET KEY - *The Canterbury Tales*
Multiple Choice Unit Test 2

I. Matching/Prologue
1. U
2. T
3. O
4. N
5. B
6. S
7. A
8. M
9. D
10. K
11. J
12. Q
13. I
14. F
15. E
16. H
17. L
18. G
19. C
20. R
21. P

II. Matching/Tales
1. O
2. S
3. E
4. R
5. P
6. L
7. G
8. Q
9. K
10. C
11. F
12. M
13. D
14. B
15. I
16. N
17. T
18. A
19. J
20. H

III. Multiple Choice/Quotations
1. N
2. B
3. C
4. I
5. G
6. D
7. B
8. H
9. A
10. Q

IV. Vocabulary
1. G
2. A
3. F
4. O
5. M
6. D
7. S
8. T
9. H
10. L
11. B
12. N
13. C
14. E
15. Q
16. I
17. K
18. P
19. J
20. R

UNIT RESOURCE MATERIALS

BULLETIN BOARD IDEAS - *The Canterbury Tales*

1. Leave a portion of the bulletin board for the students' best writing assignments.

2. Write out some of the significant quotes from the text on colorful construction paper. Cut out letters to title the board Chaucer's *Canterbury Tales*.

3. Take one of the word search puzzles and draw it (enlarged) on the bulletin board. Write the clue words to find to one side. Invite students to take pens and find and circle the words in the time before and after class (or perhaps if they finish their work early).

4. Take snapshots of the students in their costumes (or have the newspaper or yearbook staff take them.) Post the pictures on the bulletin board. Keep the pictures from year to year and pretty soon you'll have a lot of material for a fun bulletin board!

5. Enlarge and post articles about *The Canterbury Tales*.

6. Get together with your art teacher and have some students draw portraits of some of the pilgrims described in the Prologue.

7. Make a bulletin board about careers today related to the occupations of the pilgrims.

8. Write a biography of Chaucer in the middle of the board. Around it, make little "books" out of construction paper. Title each one with the name of a tale and write a little summary of the tale inside.

9. Post a huge map of England as it was in the 1300s.

10. Take time after Lesson Four for each student to write on the board one thing he/she learned from his/her research.

EXTRA ACTIVITIES - *The Canterbury Tales*

One of the difficulties in teaching literature is that all students don't read at the same speed. One student who likes to read may take the book home and finish it in a day or two. Sometimes a few students finish the in-class assignments early. The problem, then, is finding suitable extra activities for students.

The best thing I've found is to keep a little library in the classroom. For this unit on *The Canterbury Tales,* you might check out from the school library other related books and articles about castles, history of the period, pilgrimages, the occupations mentioned in the text, or the history of the Church in England. Also, you might include other works by Chaucer (either in original text or simplified versions) and articles of criticism about *The Canterbury Tales*.

Other things you may keep on hand are puzzles. We have made some relating directly to *The Canterbury Tales* for you. Feel free to duplicate them for your class.

Some students may like to draw. You might devise a contest or allow some extra-credit grade for students who draw characters or scenes from *The Canterbury Tales*. Note, too, that if the students do not want to keep their drawings you may pick up some extra bulletin board materials this way. If you have a contest and you supply the prize (a CD or something like that perhaps), you could, possibly, make the drawing itself a non-refundable entry fee.

The pages which follow contain games, puzzles and worksheets. The keys, when appropriate, immediately follow the puzzle or worksheet. There are two main groups of activities: one group for the unit; that is, generally relating to *The Canterbury Tales* text, and another group of activities related strictly to *The Canterbury Tales* vocabulary.

Directions for these games, puzzles and worksheets are self-explanatory. The object here is to provide you with extra materials you may use in any way you choose.

MORE ACTIVITIES - *The Canterbury Tales*

1. Have students design a book cover for *The Canterbury Tales.*

2. Have students design a bulletin board (ready to be put up; not just sketched) for *The Canterbury Tales.*

3. Use some of the related topics (noted earlier for an in-class library) as topics for research, reports or written papers, or as topics for guest speakers.

4. Have students choose a character from the Prologue and write another tale that person may have told on the way back from Canterbury.

5. Have students write a story imitating one of the literary forms used in *The Canterbury Tales.* (for example, a mock-heroic tale or a fable)

6. Hold a Medieval England Day in your class. Have students all wear their costumes from their presentations. Decorate the room as a medieval castle, have whatever light refreshments medieval people would have had at such a gathering, etc. Students could research various elements in preparation.

7. Have students write a description of someone they know using Chaucer's style from the Prologue.

8. Divide your class into groups of five students. Have each group design and build a medieval castle.

9. Take a day or two to discuss England: Past and Present.

10. Have a travel agent come in to show pictures or film clips of England today.

WORD SEARCH - *The Clerk's Tale*

All words in this list are associated with The Clerk's Tale. The words are placed backwards, forward, diagonally, up and down. The clues below the word searches can help you find the words.

```
J C Q A D L E S I R G B C D D D V R
X M Z V W X H N A L U C I N A J P X
Q F A P Y A L U G L D E C O R A T E
K C N R B N L X N L U C B W D T B L
C P F Y Q K W T R T Y Z I P G O V H
V R E X I U G R E I I F Z H L I J O
D P O T C H I L D R E N B O Y K R T
F E A S R F R S J R W H G R R A S L
S L E D S A Q W U O T N R E N Z S S
Y N Y D E C R T R F A A L A L L R S
M F G V S G N C X F M C P W A B G K
S L Q S S E M F H S V Z Q S G V O W
H Y Y Q V N X G M B B D S B F X H N
O B E D I E N C E W H A B F H K Q K
N S A N K F W T F W V R V X Y Q C Z
```

Countess of ----; marquis' sister
Griselda placed this sign on each child's head
Griselda remained the Walter's ----
Griselda was not of --- birth
Lord Panaro
Marquis' pasttime activity
One was placed on Griselda's head
Region where the marquis lived
The ----' Tale is about a marquis and his new bride
The host wanted the clerk to tell a tale of ---
The marquis had to choose someone to -----
The source of the clerk's tale
Walter brought the --- back to Griselda

Griselda agreed to obey him
Griselda promised total ----- to the marquis
Griselda was beautiful in looks and ---
Griselda's father
Marquis' new wife
Marquis' sister lived there
One who will inherit
Setting for the clerk's tale
The first child was a ---
The marquis
The second child was a ---
They wanted the marquis to get married
What Walter wanted Griselda to do; clean & ---- the home

WORD SEARCH - *The Franklin's Tale*

All words in this list are associated with The Franklin's Tale. The words are placed backwards, forward, diagonally, up and down. The clues below the word searches can help you find the words.

```
S Q U I R E F I W H O N O R L N Y H
J P M H C T D R J Z K R O W W R V T
V F L V Y O Y L A J Y C R S R L Q T
A R V E R A G U S N K J U A F F D L
D V F I S M W F X S K I M J B L T W
R L G P Y C R D M M L L R C W P Q Y
J E A M P D D Z N E A R I B X B D S
N T M M Q Q R N R A A G V N Y W Z R
V D W J E D S U E E S K I R W X H L
D N N L Z N A D P D C U L C G W C X
K R K A A S T P X S R U O O I L B J
P I F E B K A E M T D A A H V A P P
R E L E A S E D D K N I G H T E N M
C R F L I W U B R S H Q J W C P T M
O M Z D S E A H P R O L O G U E F L
```

Arveragus to Dorigen
Arveragus was one
Aurelius --- Dorigen from her promise
Author
Dorigen agrees to ---- Arveragus
Dorigen to Arveragus
He loved Dorigen and tried to rid the coast of rocks for her
Magician's fee; a ---- pounds
Place where Aurelius and his brother found the magician
She misses Arveragus
The knight Dorigen agrees to marry
The rocks appeared to do this

Arveragus tried to help save Dorigen's
Arveragus's castle was near the ---
Aurelius was one
Dorigen ---- her husband's absence
Dorigen contemplated ---ing herself
Feeling between Dorigen & Arveragus
He performed an illusion making the rocks disappear
Number of years Arveragus was gone
Place where Aurelius professed his love to Dorigen
The ---'s Tale
The part before the tale begins
They were a menace and of no use, and Dorigen wanted them gone

WORD SEARCH - *The Friar's Tale*

All words in this list are associated with The Friar's Tale. The words are placed backwards, forward, diagonally, up and down. The clues below the word searches can help you find the words.

```
M V S H K W Y S C W L P S B T G F X
N R T G A H M R B J I S S E R K K F
X W L Z T R L T G J H D Y H S I Q T
K W Y R E H C E L N A M O E Y R B G
P A L B V Y R H O W A S W W E V O E
H K Z C A V F I D T T F T N S W R H
N O R T H I T G R E E N O W T Y R Y
S B D J E R L A H T A M V N E A N E
G R A N O Q C I K P M C A Z I L U M
C Z D T H E L L F U W M O R J G V W
V U X L H Y K H S F R Q F N O N T E
F E R M G F D R G O V M F L P T P K
H B B S S S Q N F D B J O Q L C T P
S H A P E S T N V F G R E C U A H C
L Y M N Q L I Z N N P Q T G Y J S R
```

Author
Color of Yeoman's garments
Direction of Yeoman's home
Fiends take different ---- to catch their prey
He has to referee between the Friar and the Summoner
His tale is about a Summoner
How the Summoner makes his profits
It was in the cart
Money paid to the Summoner to keep him from making an arrest
One who tells on someone who is being bad
She cursed the Summoner to hell
Sum Summoner wanted from the widow; ---- pence
Summoner meets him on the road

The Archdeacon punishes this vice the most
The Friar enjoyed the Wife of ---'s tale but cautioned her not to preach
The Friar is --- with the Summoner over insults
The Summoner's boss
The farmer cursed the hay, horses & this all to hell
The farmer didn't mean his, but the widow did
The main character in the Friar's tale
The part before the tale starts
They finally pulled the cart out of the mud
What the Yeoman and Summoner profess to be
Yeoman's true home
Yeoman's true identity

WORD SEARCH - *The Knight's Tale*

All words in this list are associated with The Knight's Tale. The words are placed backwards, forward, diagonally, up and down. The clues below the word searches can help you find the words.

```
D H H L M T Y T H E D H A J D W R Z
G R Q I G M O V N X S R S R F T B S
T L W Q P Y E W P D K R O I C T N J
N N B T K P C R E O N B O W K I Y S
R M E R J Y O V C R Z O T H S R T V
T X N M M F O L H Y I W M U R V U A
S H B N I L Z D Y X T F O A S F M T
T M E K C L U J W T D C M N L K P Z
T V C S J K R K C O A F E Y Y A Q J
S H B S E R V A N T O H B L H T P T
H H E Q C U B G P I T D P S H D Y C
D B I B G X S X R A G S S G C H H K
B F S E E M I L Y Z Y H I B K H S S
Z W B B L S J R W R N N T D S D V M
N K N Y T D S G Q H K Q S S L F Z N
```

Arcita fell off of his

Arcita had a ----- bow

Both Arcita and Palamon wanted to ---- Emily

He married Emily after his cousin died

He won the contest for Emily's hand

It was used to fend off blows from the enemy

Place where Arcita and Palamon first physically fought over Emily

Place where Theseus lived

Relationship between Arcita and Palamon

The king Theseus killed

The queen and Emily pleaded for ---- from Theseus towards the knights

Theseus's title

What Arcita and Palamon both were; their position

Arcita fell onto this and broke his breast

Arcita's body was burned in this

Both knights truly ---- Emily

He put Arcita and Palamon in prison in his tower

Long, sharp fighting instrument

Place where Arcita and Palamon were from

Place where Arcita and Palamon were held captive

The ----'s Tale

The queen

The queen's sister

Theseus and his ---- decided Palamon should marry Emily

What Arcita pretended to be

WORD SEARCH - *The Merchant's Tale*

All words in this list are associated with The Merchant's Tale. The words are placed backwards, forward, diagonally, up and down. The clues below the word searches can help you find the words.

```
J U S T I N U S M N V J Q R T W P J
J F F Y W W M H Q E K L D Q B K X B
F R D J S F I V V P R T L N I M Y J
D C V P V V T F P W M C B N I K H Q
S E N E C A T R E C U A H C T L S B
N Q V F Z V O R H H S E D A U W B Y
L B U N V L H D Q H R C D F N Z O Y
A P W I O S F Q N I U E S T P T K J
P D N G R T D K T E B S B I H K A K
W L U B P E E A F M I M B L X N B K
W E A L K E N S I L D F F A U T P F
M A Y C T C A L B D A M I A N M Y R
P F S P E E C R V D L Z R L Z D H Y
B Q N J V B R N P P R Y W W P S P M
Y O U N G J O Y Z G P K K S F H V T
```

A young wife would help keep January from committing this sin

Author

Damian's relationship to January

He agrees with everything January says

January is over -- years old

January wants his wife to be -----

January's misfortune

January's wife

May claimed to desperately want one of this kind of fruit

May should be true to January out of love of Christ, to honor herself & to get this

The bachelor January expects married life to be

The merchant says his wife could overmatch one

The old knight

Amount of time the merchant has been married; --- months

Damian and May exchange these to communicate

He thinks January should not get married in haste

January wants to take a ---; to get married

January's relationship to May

May did this on January to get up into the tree

May meets him in the tree

Straw for ----

The ---- Tale is about an old knight and his new bride

The merchant thinks his wife is one

The part before the tale begins

WORD SEARCH - *The Miller's Tale*

All words in this list are associated with The Miller's Tale. The words are placed backwards, forward, diagonally, up and down. The clues below the word searches can help you find the words.

```
T N C X Y A B D H Q D E K W I E C Y
Q G T F R E R M W A J N C N C R D D
W I F E H T I M S M R S S I K J O W
R T T I F L I A O E T P R N V O B N
B A N V L N L L T O N O U E L D N C
W D J E D O A N N X U R T F D S A M
P N R S H S E E L Q D N B U Z D Y B
V Q F C B P D B I R E X A B B L A M
T Y I A R Y Z L O D C L E R K S O L
X N V A Z W P P U A I R B F O O Y J
X T C A Y B E T V S R W Q H R O T W
P C R X B C S Q O G B D H D F D F V
L C L J V S Y N B P S N E Q W Z W C
N G H X Y B N R J Q T B D R D F N C
A S T R O N O M Y V R J G Z Y P L G
```

Absalom chewed this to get rid of his bad breath
Alison agreed to do this to Absalom to make him go away
Alison's relationship to the carpenter
Condition of the Miller as he told the tale
He and Alison are newlyweds
He told this tale about the carpenter, his wife and the student boarder
Musical instrument played by Nicholas
Nicholas warned of the coming of a great one
One who rents a room
Out of Sight is also Out of ____
Place Nicholas and Alison ran off to when the carpenter fell asleep
The carpenter broke his when he fell
The tubs were hung just under there
The village people thought the carpenter was this
When the carpenter hit the axe against this, his tub fell
Who takes ____ shall never fare the worse

Absalom's job
Alison threatened to throw one at Absalom
Carpenters wife
From whom Absalom borrowed the iron
Hobby/interest of Nicholas
It branded Nicholas
Nicholas is one; one who studies
Nicholas yelled for it when his behind got burned
Parish clerk who lusts after Alison
Student boarder with the carpenter and Alison
The carpenter built these to provide access to the hanging tubs
They were hung under the roof to serve as boats
Where Absalom kissed Alison

WORD SEARCH - *The Pardoner's Tale*

All words in this list are associated with The Pardoner's Tale. The words are placed backwards, forward, diagonally, up and down. The clues below the word searches can help you find the words.

```
D P S D E C N G G T S W J J L S R K
O Y R A C E H T O P A D I E D E P Z
L F L E T T R A K L R V T S N L W R
H S F T A T P T U U D I E O T I O Z
V L I E H C E O N C R R D R G A W C
G M D G R C H K I C E R I N N Y B N
M L I X I I E E O S A R I N Q N T H
X N U R G N N P S P O R T J K W T S
K S A T N B Y G R R A N E G Y S Z K
T V W E T H D N Q E E A F J Q X W R
A T S J C O K J W V L L N W S Y K L
D S T L D D N S Y O L I B D L N M B
V G T V R D F Y U X N Z C M N C F K
C Q G Z V D D S W W Y R K S A M K W
P Y Z X D B Y Y Y N L Y K J J G V J
```

Author
He forgives people's sins (for a small fee!)
It was under the tree
It would multiply grain
One must be made to receive a pardon
Pardoner sells them as remedies
Stilbon refused to ally with these
old man sent the young men to an oak ----
The older youths planned to do this to the
    youngest upon his return
The three young men met an --- man
The youngest planned to --- the other two youths
The youngest was sent back for food and ---
Vice warned against in the third commandment
Where the young man got the poison

Beverage in which the poison was put
He tried to smooth things over between the
    Host and the pardoner
Lust is bred of wine and this
Overindulgence in food
Pardoner's vice
The bone could cure everything from sores The
    to this
The pardoner does this to advise people to
    mend their ways
The three young men went to find and
    conquer it
Three young rioters were sitting in a -----
What happened to all three youths
Word to describe the pardoner

WORD SEARCH - *The Nun's Priest's Tale*

All words in this list are associated with The Nun's Priest's Tale. The words are placed backwards, forward, diagonally, up and down. The clues below the word searches can help you find the words.

```
F L A T T E R E R S T Q X R N Y L S
P F M L R X M D M Y F T B S X H C N
R E D F X E J D P S G H R F N H O Y
M R R X Q N C D D Z K Y Y G A I M Y
L K K T L N X U T F D L X N T V E N
P T H D I K L K A G S O T A V L E C
B G R N K L V M Q H F I N K A H K Q
W O M A N Y O T A C C I L T C E M T
K G E R C N Q T T L T X B A V A Q X
V P T K E T N T E S Y H M I E W N S
S K P Y K V S E E G S O T R X N P T
E L B I B E R D P M R I D N U N Y R
G Y M X I T E I N D X V N F H B N Q
H T E R N R H E N A W K F G C V B M
J M P S P S H A L V D Q F N D P K Q
```

--- is man's delight and all his bliss
-----'s Priest's Tale
Author
Be on guard against the ----- of this world
Belief that one's fate is already decided
Chanticleer closed his when he began to sing
Chanticleer escaped when the fox opened its mouth to ---
Chanticleer had one that scared him
Chanticleer quoted from this Book relating stories about dreams
He said, 'Take no account of dreams'
Hector's wife who warned him not to go to battle
It came to kill Chanticleer
It sank, drowning all on board
Nun's ----'s Tale
Nun's Priest's ---
Pertilote recommended this remedy
Pertilote, for example
The cock
The fox said he came to hear Chanticleer do this
The hen
The man's friend was murdered for his ---
Where the man's friend's body was hidden

WORD SEARCH - *The Prioress's Tale*

All words in this list are associated with The Prioress's Tale. The words are placed backwards, forward, diagonally, up and down. The clues below the word searches can help you find the words.

```
K L Q Z M D T N D Z F T H R O A T B
P L A V R S K W T S M D E S B S K T
L N D L D J C Z J Q Q Y S W I P L F
R A W Y L N H B M A E O R D Y X Y
C S T R E E T O O R R D H A S I A K
G H E I E D Y N P O I C I E B O Z B
S I R U N H K N I W L Y E E A B N M
B E Q I B L T R L J G D R L D L E G
T H A B S J P O G V E E V A P R M Y
L R B R D T H M M N R W G F M O S A
C J N K C X I N W E Q X S M B K E L
S Y G J M H H A D B C F S S L L S P
Y V P Q N V E R N C Q P Q D Z J T S
H T Z H P F U D N S Y Z Y D J V V W
T H P L T M N P V G P R F S L J W B
```

Hail ____
He sang
He took the grain of seed from the boy's mouth
It was His will that the boy should sing to honor His mother
Language of the song
O ---- Redemptoris
Person hired to kill the boy
Place the boy was attacked
Place where the boy walked to and from each day
Place where they took the boy
Setting of Prioress's Tale
She searched for the boy
The ------'s Tale
The Christian --- gathered to hear the boy sing
The Prioress refers to the Blessed Mother as _____
The boy passed by the Jewish --- on his way to and from school
The boy sang a ----
The boy's mother was a ---
The boy's was cut
The child lay upon one
The monk took it from the boy's mouth
The prologue to the Prioress's Tale is a ---
These people gathered to see the boy singing in the alley
They hired a murderer to kill the boy
What happened to the boy in the end
What the boy's mother did when he did not come home

WORD SEARCH - *The Reeve's Tale*

All words in this list are associated with The Reeve's Tale. The words are placed backwards, forward, diagonally, up and down. The clues below the word searches can help you find the words.

```
C O R N C A M B R I D G E F L O U R
R A H Z A G T Q U X N L C V C B Q Z
Z O K P P L M E G L A S Z J E F M P
J D L E M B A F S Q L G D M J E Y Q
T R U M P I N G T O N Y O C H N R Z
M R G X R D L K N Y N L W O O E L L
R B H A H R E L W M L P H I S Q A V
R E L L C V L K E Y C O T J Z E J D
V O P M N C S K C R V A D H P G F G
S T V P L G R J Q I C R W G K G N P
Z D G N U L E A M U R P S A I I K G
K P N U N S T U D E N T S W R N N S
K C N B R R H E C L I T T O K D G K
M T M O H C M N R C E D N S K Q E L
K X H L M Y R X K L Q S I M P K I N
```

--- Hall
A place to stay overnight
Alan bashed the miller in the ---
Alcoholic drink
Dinner
Dinner meat at the miller's house
He gave permission for Alan & John to go to the miller's
He slept with the miller's daughter
He tricked the miller's wife into sleeping with him
John & Alan were --- at the college
John ---- the miller's wife into sleeping with him
Molly received her ---- at the nunnery
Product after milling grain
Simpkin's daughter
Simpkin's occupation

The ---'s tale is about two students who trick a greedy miller
The baby was in one
The miller
The miller untied it and let it go
The miller's wife mistakenly hit him with one
Town near the mill
Town where the college was located
What Alan & John brought to have ground
What the miller's family was doing to keep Alan & John awake
What the miller's wife made with the stolen flour
Where the miller's wife hit him
Women who educated Molly
Word describing the miller

WORD SEARCH - *The Shipman's Tale*

All words in this list are associated with The Shipman's Tale. The words are placed backwards, forward, diagonally, up and down. The clues below the word searches can help you find the words.

```
P N Q Q H G X B L T P S C W M Z T V
S V P Z F B S J R T B G J O N Z F F
W K F C B I T Y K L M E J H U R L T
I N T E R E S T R S B E D M A S S H
S L L A L O L N E T R E Y N H C I L
R A P V M T W H Y B N E C I N H T N
T I S S J O T N F Y W E P A J A T C
V Y C L T O M A S S T M R A B O O P
C Y Z H L M P E C M A F S B Y M H L
M E R C H A N T Y N J X O S P B Q N
M C V P T N Z C T V M T E L S M L C
Y D W B V L S G B R Q G A W Y C D B
G X Y F Y V L W D M U I L T S T K B
T H W R D F M Q Y R N G K P D L H Z
Y S T G W K T D B T P K F M J F B G
```

Amount owing
Bruges or St. Denys, for example
Country of setting of Shipman's story
Double ----
Fee for lending money
Friendly nickname between merchant and monk
Having lots of money
He gave permission for Sir John to go to St. Denys
Pay back
Place of merchant's first business trip
Place where Sir John lived
The --- Tale
The Shipman's ____
The loan amount: 100 ---
The merchant needed 20,000 of these for a business deal
The merchant's wife asked for a loan from Sir John
    while the merch. was counting his ---
The merchant's wife asked for one from Sir John
The merchant's wife told her --- to Sir John
The monk and he were best friends
The monk; Sir ---
They all went there and prayed before dinner
Town where merchant lived; St. ---
What Sir John said he wanted a loan to buy
What the merchant's wife wanted to buy with her loan money
Where the merchant's wife promised to pay the merchant back

WORD SEARCH - *The Summoner's Tale*

All words in this list are associated with The Summoner's Tale. The words are placed backwards, forward, diagonally, up and down. The clues below the word searches can help you find the words.

```
M T L A J H V X H P H G S Z G W Y T
Y V M S R T M X Q C U Z G Q X Z V Q
H J V Y S R T J Y S V R R S U B P Z
G Z B Q H E O E R Q S A G P F I M R
C A T J O H N W G N I T S A F S R Y
B D S T P O H R O L Q R I T T T N E
M D K P M E K M E K S T E B H O F Y
L C N H E H R N P D H U H W T J R C
V O V L B E E J I R L C M T C S B Y
S B K S S Q Y L Z G O O U M E Y H S
T R E N T A L S L S H L H D O V J D
T F H T Q Z K C E R G T O G F N E S
W A K Y Y Q S L P K L S G V W E N
K R I Y D Y O R K S H I R E U F D R
H Y H L T M U N D I V I D E D E G J
```

An ---- thing is stronger than when it is scattered
Anger
Going without food
He fasted before getting the commandments
He thought of a solution to the problem of dividing the gift
Masses for the souls in purgatory
Place where souls go between heaven and hell
Place where the friar went in the prologue
Place where the friars were hidden in hell; under the devil's ----
The ----'s Tale is about a friar
The Summoner wants to get --- with the Friar
The boy was shot with one
The friar
The friar called the summoner this
The friar told Thomas he had to little of it
The friar wanted the people to give ---- to pay for the trentals
The marshy district
The noble man's --- was killed
The part before the tale begins
The squire suggested a twelve-spoked ---- to divide the gift
The woman's --- had died
Thomas's gift to the friar
Three of them were sentenced to be killed by an angry judge
Vice of overeating
What the friar preaches
Where the marshy district lies

WORD SEARCH - *The Wife of Bath's Tale*

All words in this list are associated with The Wife of Bath's Tale. The words are placed backwards, forward, diagonally, up and down. The clues below the word searches can help you find the words.

```
P R O V E R B S R G N R Y X D D Y D
J O H N N Y N W T Y Q K R O Z G Z P
G L S L U F H T I A F M R J U D P Q
T E Z N D P C S N F L W O S R N Q P
L T N H P R O M I S E L T N E G G V
X F T T Z Q H F Y V S G O S E C G F
N C H C L F A T I K M I A R L Y S J
M A R R Y E I F N H S A K I E V O L
B J M V D N N O R I E O S R R T B C
M A K O I P S E C A O R I T M R A P
J Q T G W M C E S B E S C F E V A W
V Z R H A U D A J S E Y H U I R V M
K I K S A C D V Z D B J F Q L F Y F
V Q W H W I X D J Q L L Y L P E T T
X B C R M N N K J L X F B W B Y S H
```

--- is he that does a ---- deed
--- of Bath
Author
He grew ass's ears
His wife cut off his hair and he lost his strength
His wife tricked him into setting himself on fire
It is a misery and a woe
It is not 'annexed in nature to possessions'
Johnny hit his wife for tearing pages out of his ----
Johnny would look for these in the Bible
Midas's wife told her secret to it
Number of husbands the Wife of Bath had
The Wife of ---
The Wife of Bath loved this husband best
The clout Johnny gave her made the wife of bath ----; suffer loss of hearing
The fifth husband; the boy from Oxford

The knight and his wife were --- to each other
The knight had one --- and one day to find an answer
The knight had to --- to do the first thing the old woman asked of him
The knight had to ---- the old woman
The knight left the final --- to the old woman
The knight was to find the thing that women most ----
The old --- gave the knight the right answer
The old woman became ---- and beautiful
Topic of the first part of the prologue
What women most desire is -- over husbands & lovers
Wife of Bath married Johnny for this, not money
Wife of Bath married first husbands for this, not love

WORD SEARCH - *The Canterbury Tales*

All words in this list are associated with The Canterbury Tales. The words are placed backwards, forward, diagonally, up and down. The clues on the next page can help you find the words.

```
B O W C L E R K N U R D R H E N I C H O L A S Y
S P Z I K E I E N A D E I H J V A R H P R U K X
J H A A Y S R P E I I S W E C M E M E A G T C F
H T C A S D R Y M L G M E O D J O E O A U A Q R
A U R E L I U S E O C H A A T N U N R E H C R M
B P E I O K T U J L L I T D D R I E K T Y A E M
N D H R G A G S O F L L T I S L V K I B I J R R
E C E I B O Y T S T M A Y N A R E M P R B E D Y
M S N M L A H S R H B A L E A F S S F M L V F L
S K R O G E I Z X B I L D I N H T F I L I I Y J
B P R U S R N L E Q Y P W U S O C E I R V S H W
T P A J C G E Y L I M E M H L O M M R E G F G S
K H O L O X O L O Y B E T A E T N A V I N N O J
N H R J A H C L I B D A R Y N E E O N F U D V X
N Q N O C M N O D C B O R C L P L R F O I Q N X
A S T A A H O N O R S E R C H B M O Y R S S S F
D Z P U R T A N Y K T L B I I A Y W O S A R F Z
T V T L B L P F G S F D N I G T N N T T K N A K
J M O L A S B A A K Y Z H R R E A T J P V Y C P
V A L I S O N M D E S I R E Y B N S H A P E S S
```

WORD SEARCH CLUES - *The Canterbury Tales*

----'s Priest's Tale
A young wife would help January from committing this sin
Alison agreed to do this to Absalom to make him go away
Anger
Arcita fell onto his and broke his breast
Aristocratic, takes bribes for easy penance
Arveragus tried to help save Dorigen's
Arveragus's castle was near the ---
Author
Bald & fat, didn't like work
Carpenter broke his when he fell
Carpenter's wife
Christ-like, patient, giving, holy, virtuous
Condition of the Miller as he told his tale
Dainty, pleasant, sensitive, medieval beauty
Dorigen's husband
Fiends take different ones to catch their prey
Football-player build, cheated customers, plays bagpipes
Forked beard, good negotiator, always told his opinions
From whom Absalom borrowed an iron
Good navigator, didn't ride well, from Dartmouth
Griselda was beautiful in looks and ----
Had been in many battles, was a gentleman
Had sores, master chef
He married Emily after his cousin died
He sang
He slept with the miller's daughter
He tricked the miller's wife into sleeping with him
He tried to rid the coast of rocks for Dorigen
He won the contest for Emily's hand
Host
It branded Nicholas
It came to kill Chanticleer
It was under the tree
January's wife
Loved to learn for the sake of learning
Marquis' new wife
May claimed to desperately want one of this fruit
May meets him in a tree
Money paid to the summoner to keep him from making an arrest
Number of husbands the Wife of Bath had
Old, thin, brought up the rear, good manager

Pardoner sells them as remedies
Parish clerk who lusts after Alison
Pertelote, for example
Place where Theseus kept Arcita and Palamon
Place where the friars were hidden in hell
Place where the singing boy was attacked
Place where they took the singing boy
She missed Arveragus
Simpkin's daughter
Son of the knight
Squire's servant
Squire's suggestion as to how to divide the gift
Student boarder with Alison and the carpenter
The Wife of Bath married Johnny for this, not money
The boy's was cut
The cock
The farmer didn't mean his, but the widow did
The fifth husband of the Wife of Bath
The friar told Thomas he had too little of it
The friar wanted the people to give --- to pay for trentals
The knight had one -- and one day to find an answer
The knight was sent to find the thing women most
The knight's old woman wife became --- and beautiful
The loan amount: 100 ---
The miller
The monk took this from the boy's mouth
The older youths planned to do this to the youngest upon his return
The part that comes before the story
The prologue to the Prioress's Tale is a ---
The queen's sister; two knights loved her
The yeoman's true identity
They were hung under the roof to serve as boats
Walter brought the --- back to Griselda
What happened to all three youths who found Death
What the merchant's wife wanted to buy with her loan
What the miller's wife made from the flour he took from A & J
What women most desire is --- over husbands
Where the merchant's wife was going to pay him back
Wife of ---

KEY: WORD SEARCH - *The Clerk's Tale*

PANARO	MARQUIS
CROSS	OBEDIENCE
WIFE	DEEDS
NOBLE	JANICULA
EARL	GRISELDA
HUNTING	BOLOGNA
SALUZZO	HEIR
CLERK	ITALY
ADVENTURE	GIRL
MARRY	WALTER
PETRARCH	BOY
CHILDREN	VASSALS
	DECORATE

KEY: WORD SEARCH - *The Franklin's Tale*

HUSBAND	HONOR
KNIGHT	SEA
RELEASED	SQUIRE
CHAUCER	LAMENTED
MARRY	KILL
WIFE	LOVE
AURELIUS	MAGICIAN
THOUSAND	TWO
ORLEANS	GARDEN
DORIGEN	FRANKLIN
ARVERAGUS	PROLOGUE
DISAPPEAR	ROCKS

KEY: WORD SEARCH - *The Friar's Tale*

CHAUCER	GREEN
NORTH	SHAPES
HOST	FRIAR
EXTORTION	HAY
BRIBE	INFORMANT
WIDOW	TWELVE
YEOMAN	LECHERY
BATH	ANGRY
ARCHDEACON	CART
CURSE	SUMMONER
PROLOGUE	HORSES
BAILIFF	HELL
FIEND	

KEY: WORD SEARCH - *The Knight's Tale*

HORSE	BOW
TURKISH	FIRE
MARRY	LOVED
PALAMON	THESEUS
SHIELD	SWORD
ARCITA	THEBES
WOODS	TOWER
ATHENS	KNIGHT
COUSINS	HIPPOLYTA
CREON	EMILY
MERCY	PARLIAMENT
DUKE	SERVANT
KNIGHTS	

KEY: WORD SEARCH - *The Merchant's Tale*

ADULTERY	TWO
CHAUCER	NOTES
SQUIRE	JUSTINUS
PLACEBO	WIFE
SIXTY	HUSBAND
YOUNG	CLIMBED
BLIND	DAMIAN
MAY	SENECA
PEAR	MERCHANT
INHERITANCE	SHREW
BLISSFUL	PROLOGUE
FIEND	
JANUARY	

KEY: WORD SEARCH - *The Miller's Tale*

LIQUORICE	CLERK
KISS	STONE
WIFE	ALISON
DRUNK	ASTRONOMY
CARPENTER	IRON
MILLER	STUDENT
HARP	WATER
FLOOD	ABSALOM
BOARDER	LADDERS
MIND	TUBS
BEDROOM	BEHIND
ARM	ADVICE
ROOF	NICHOLAS
CRAZY	
ROPE	

KEY: WORD SEARCH - *The Pardoner's Tale*

CHAUCER	WINE
PARDONER	KNIGHT
MITTEN	DRUNKENNESS
OFFERING	GLUTTONY
RELICS	AVARICE
GAMBLERS	JEALOUSY
TREE	PREACHES
STAB	DEATH
OLD	TAVERN
POISON	DIED
DRINK	HYPOCRITE
SWEARING	
APOTHECARY	

KEY: WORD SEARCH - *The Nun's Priest's Tale*

WOMAN	NUN
CHAUCER	FLATTERERS
PREDESTINATION	
SPEAK	DREAM
CATO	ANDROMACHE
FOX	SHIP
PRIEST	LAXATIVE
HEN	EYES
SING	PERTELOTE
MONEY	CART
CHANTICLEER	

KEY: WORD SEARCH - *The Prioress's Tale*

MARY	BOY
MONK	CHRIST
LATIN	ALMA
MURDERER	ALLEY
SCHOOL	ABBEY
ASIA	MOTHER
PRIORESS	PEOPLE
QUEEN	STREET
SONG	WIDOW
THROAT	BIER
SEED	PRAYER
CHRISTIANS	JEWS
DIED	SEARCHED

KEY: WORD SEARCH - *The Reeve's Tale*

```
       C  O  R  N  C  A  M  B  R  I  D  G  E     F  L  O  U  R
          A        H           A           U        L     V
          O        K           A           E     L  A        E
    J        E  M        A  S           L  A  L  G     M        E
    T  R  U  M  P  I  N  G  T  O  N        Y  O        H  N  R
                R  D           L              N  L     O  O     E
       R        A        E  L                    L     I  S     A        D
       E        L           K     E  Y        O  T        E              D  G
       O        P              C        C  R  I  A        D        N
    S              P        R        I  C        W  G        I              N
                      U  N     E  A  U  R        S  A  I     N        G
                N  U  N  S  T  U  D  E  N  T  S        R  N        G
                      R              E     L  I              O  D     G  E
                      O                    C           E              N
                      H              K           S  I  M  P  K  I  N
```

SOLAR   LODGING
NOSE   ALE
SUPPER   GOOSE
WARDEN   ALAN
JOHN   STUDENTS
TRICKED   EDUCATION
FLOUR   MOLLY
MILLER   REEVE
CRADLE   SIMPKIN
HORSE   STICK
TRUMPINGTON   CAMBRIDGE
CORN   SNORING
CAKE   HEAD
NUNS   BULLY

KEY: WORD SEARCH - *The Shipman's Tale*

```
                            T        C
                   S        B        O        F
             C  I  Y        E        U  R
    I  N  T  E  R  E  S  T  R  S  B  E  D  M  A  S  S
          L  A  L  O  N  E  T  R  E     N  H  C  I
    R  A  P     M  T  W  H     N  E  C  I  N        N
    T  I     C     O  T  N     Y     E  P  A  J  A     C
             H     T  O  N  A  S        M  R  A  B  O  O
             L     E  C     A  F        B  Y  M  H  L
    M  E  R  C  H  A  N  T  Y  N        O  S  P        N
                               T        E  L
                               G        A
                               U
                               R        I
                            B  T        N
```

DEBT   TOWN
FRANCE   ENTRY
INTEREST   COUSIN
RICH   ABBOT
REPAY   BRUGES
PARIS   SHIPMAN
FRANCS   CROWNS
MONEY   LOAN
COMPLAINT   MERCHANT
JOHN   MASS
DENYS   CATTLE
CLOTHES   BED
TALE

KEY: WORD SEARCH - *The Summoner's Tale*

```
                A                       P              S
                S     R                 U        Q
                Y     S  R  E  O  E     Y        R  R     U
       G     B        J  O  H  N  W  G  N  I  T  S  A  F     R  Y
       B  A  S        O  H  R  O  L        R  I        E     T     N  E
                         M  E  K  M  E     S  T  E              O     R
             N        E  H  R  N  P  D  H  U        M              T        Y
       O        L     E  E        I  R  L        M  T                    Y
    S           S              L     G  O  O  U  M  E
    T  R  E  N  T  A  L  S  L  S  H  L  H        O  V                 E
       T                    E        G  T     O        N  E           R
       A                       S              S  G        E  N        R
                      I        Y  O  R  K  S  H  I  R  E  U              R
                         L  M  U  N  D  I  V  I  D  E  D  E
```

UNDIVIDED   IRE
FASTING   MOSES
SQUIRE   TRENTALS
PURGATORY   HELL
TAIL   SUMMONER
EVEN   ARROW
JOHN   LIAR
FAITH   MONEY
HOLDERNESS   SON
PROLOGUE   WHEEL
BABY   GAS
KNIGHTS   GLUTTONY
SERMONS   YORKSHIRE

KEY: WORD SEARCH - *The Wife of Bath's Tale*

```
P R O V E R B S           Y                GENTLE      WIFE
J O H N N Y   W             O              CHAUCER     MIDAS
G     L U F H T I A F M     U              SAMPSON     HERCULES
  E           F     O   N                  MARRIAGE    GENTLENESS
    N   P R O M I S E L T N E G G          BOOK        PROVERBS
      T     F Y V   G O   E                WATER       FIVE
N       L A T I   M I A R   Y              FIFTH       DEAF
M A R R Y E I F N H S A K I E V O L        JOHNNY      FAITHFUL
B   M   D N N O R I E O S R R T            YEAR        PROMISE
  A   O I   S E C A O R I T   R A          MARRY       DECISION
    T G W M C E S B E S C F E   A W        DESIRE      WOMAN
    R H A U D A   S E Y   U I R   M        YOUNG       VIRGINITY
    I   S A   D     D       L F Y          MASTERY     LOVE
V     H   I                   E T          MONEY       BATH
      C   M                     S H
```

KEY: *The Canterbury Tales*

```
        B O W C L E R K N U R D   H E N I C H O L A S
          I K E I E N A   E I     V A R H       U
          A A Y S R P E I I S W E   M E M E A G
        T C A S D R Y M L G M E O D   O E O A U A
      A U R E L I U S E O C H A A T N U N R E H C R
        P E I O   T U J L L I T D D   I E K T Y A E M
        D H R G A G   O   L L T I   L V K I     I R R
      E C E I B O Y T S   M A Y N A R E M P R B E D F
      S N   L A H     H B A L E A F S S F M L   F
    S K R O   E I     B I   D I N H   F I L I I
      P R U S R   L E     P W U S O C E I R V S
    T P A J C G E Y L I M E M H L O M M R E G F G
      H O L O   O L O Y   E T A E T N A V I N N O
      H R   A H C L I B D A R Y N E E O N   U D   X
    N     O   M N O D C B O R C   P L R F O I Q
        S T A A H O N O R S E R C H   M O Y R S   S
            U   T A N Y K T   B I I A     O   A R
                B L       S       I G T N N     N A
          M O L A S B A A         R E A T       C P
          A L I S O N M D E S I R E   B N S H A P E S S
```

If you are stuck for an answer to a clue, see the *Canterbury Tales* Word Sheet in the Unit Resource Section. It has all of the words and all of the clues for the unit.

CROSSWORD - *The Clerk's Tale*

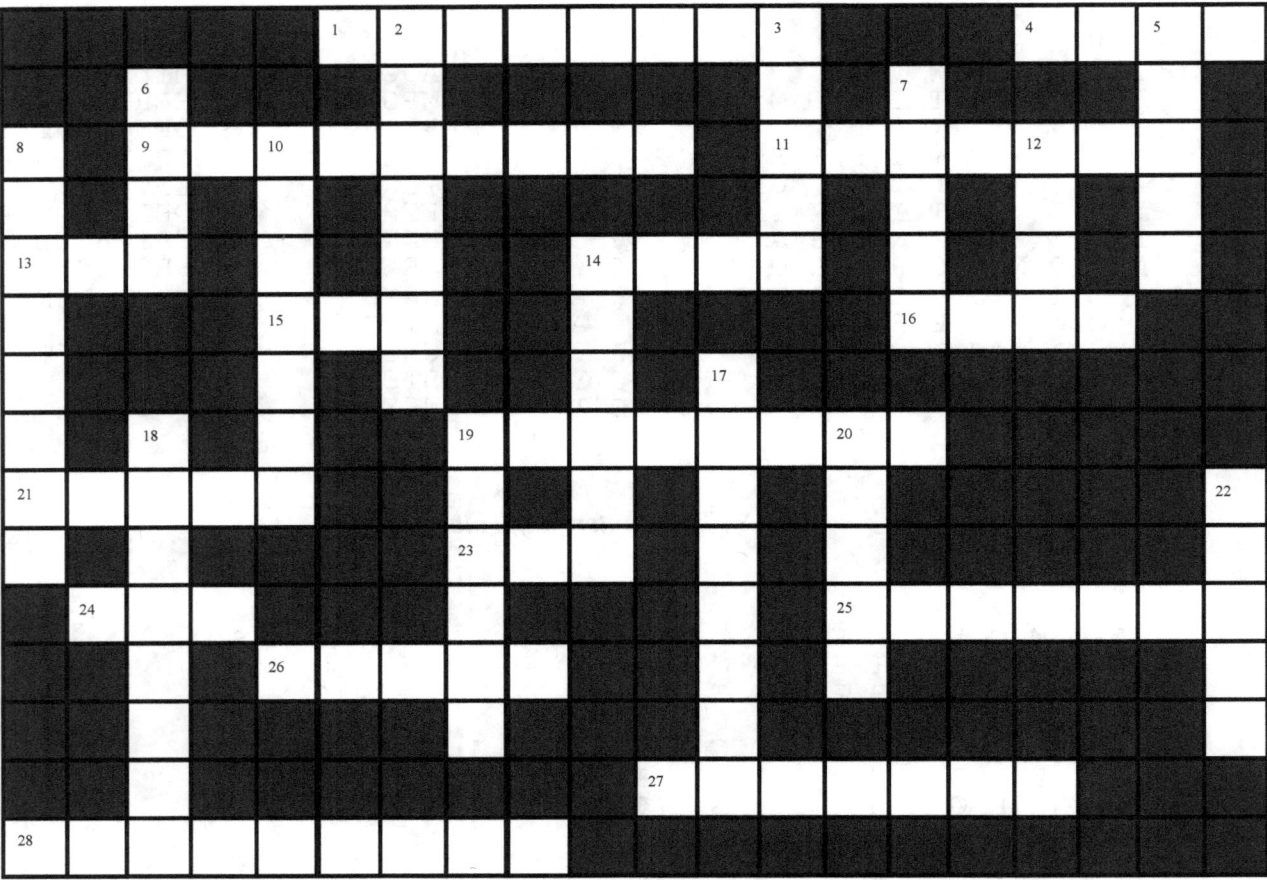

ACROSS
1. Walter brought the --- back to Griselda
4. One who will inherit
9. The host wanted the clerk to tell a tale of ---
11. Marquis' sister lived there
13. Sick
14. Griselda remained the Walter's ----
15. The boy child's relation to the marquis
16. Griselda thought the marquis would --- the children
19. The source of the clerk's tale
21. Griselda was beautiful in looks and ---
23. Neither's partner
24. The second child was a ---
25. Region where the marquis lived
26. The marquis had to choose someone to -----
27. Griselda agreed to obey him
28. Griselda promised total ----- to the marquis

DOWN
2. Marquis' pastime activity
3. Griselda was not of --- birth
5. Setting for the clerk's tale
6. Lord Panaro
7. The ----' Tale is about a marquis and his new bride
8. Marquis' new wife
10. They wanted the marquis to get married
12. The first child was a ---
14. The marquis
17. Griselda's father
18. What Walter wanted Griselda to do; clean & ---- the home
19. Countess of ----; marquis' sister
20. Griselda placed this sign on each child's head
22. One was placed on Griselda's head

CROSSWORD ANSWER KEY - *The Clerk's Tale*

CROSSWORD - The Franklin's Tale

ACROSS
3. Dorigen agrees to ---- Arveragus
5. ... learn --- or you will be taught it whether you will or not
8. Arveragus tried to help save Dorigen's
10. Coordinating conjunction
11. Place where Aurelius professed his love to Dorigen
12. Dorigen contemplated ---ing herself
14. Number of years Arveragus was gone
15. Arveragus to Dorigen
17. He performed an illusion making the rocks disappear
19. Distress signal a ship would give
20. Negative reply
21. The knight Dorigen agrees to marry
25. Arveragus's freeing Dorigen was an --- act
27. The part before the tale begins
28. She misses Arveragus
29. Dorigen to Arveragus

DOWN
1. Arveragus's castle was near the ---
2. Arveragus was one
4. He loved Dorigen and tried to rid the coast of rocks for her
5. The ---'s Tale
6. They were a menace and of no use, and Dorigen wanted them gone
7. Feeling between Dorigen & Arveragus or from Aurelius towards Dorigen
9. Place where Aurelius and his brother found the magician
13. Dorigen ---- her husband's absence
16. The rocks appeared to do this
18. Author
22. Make a mistake
23. Dorigen wanted Aurelius to remove --- the rocks; every one
24. Aurelius was one
26. Unusual
27. A kind of servant; also that upon which words are written in a book

CROSSWORD ANSWER KEY - *The Franklin's Tale*

				S				K			M	A	R	R	Y			
F	O	R	B	E	A	R	A	N	C	E		U						L
R				A				O			I		R		H	O	N	O	R
A	N	D					C		G	A	R	D	E	N		R		V
N						K		H			L		L			E
K	I	L	L			S		T	W	O		I				E
L		A									H	U	S	B	A	N	D
I		M	A	G	I	C	I	A	N			S				N		I
N		E				H									S	O		S
		N	O		A	R	V	E	R	A	G	U	S					A
		T				U			R		L		Q					P
		H	E	R	O	I	C		P	R	O	L	O	G	U	E		P
			D		D		E		A						I			E
					D	O	R	I	G	E	N				R			A
							E			W	I	F	E					R

215

CROSSWORD - *The Friar's Tale*

ACROSS
4. What the Yeoman and Summoner profess to be
8. The farmer cursed the hay, horses & this all to hell
9. It was in the cart
10. Direction of Yeoman's home
11. The Friar enjoyed the Wife of ---'s tale but cautioned her not to preach
12. A thought
13. The Archdeacon punishes this vice the most
17. Color of Yeoman's garments
19. The Friar is --- with the Summoner over insults
20. Promises; the Summoner ---- to stay with his 'brother'
22. She cursed the Summoner to hell
23. Sum Summoner wanted from the widow; ---- pence
25. He has to referee between the Friar and the Summoner
26. Contraction for 'it is'
27. The main character in the Friar's tale
29. Fiends take different ---- to catch their prey
30. Coordinating conjunction

DOWN
1. Yeoman's true identity
2. The farmer didn't mean his, but the widow did
3. Money paid to the Summoner to keep him from making an arrest
5. The Summoner's boss
6. His tale is about a Summoner
7. One who tells on someone who is being bad
8. Author
9. Yeoman's true home
14. How the Summoner makes his profits
15. They finally pulled the cart out of the mud
16. The part before the tale starts
18. Opposite of old
21. Summoner meets him on the road
24. For----; a very long time; always
28. Definite article; --- Friar's Tale

CROSSWORD ANSWER KEY - *The Friar's Tale*

														F	
					C		B	B	A	I	L	I	F	F	
			I	U	C	A	R	T	R			E		R
H	A	Y	N	O	R	T	H	I		C		N		1
E			F	S	A	B	A	T	H	I	D	E	A	
L			O	E	U	E			D				R
L	E	C	H	E	R	Y		C		E		P		
	X	O	M	G	R	E	E	N	A	N	G	R	Y	
	T	R	A		R	E		C		O				
V	O	W	S	N	Y	W	I	D	O	W	L			
	R	E	T	W	E	L	V	E		N	H	O	S	T
I	T	'	S	O		V				G				
	I	S	U	M	M	O	N	E	R	T		U		
	O		A		R	S	H	A	P	E	S			
	N		A	N	D			E						

217

CROSSWORD - *The Knight's Tale*

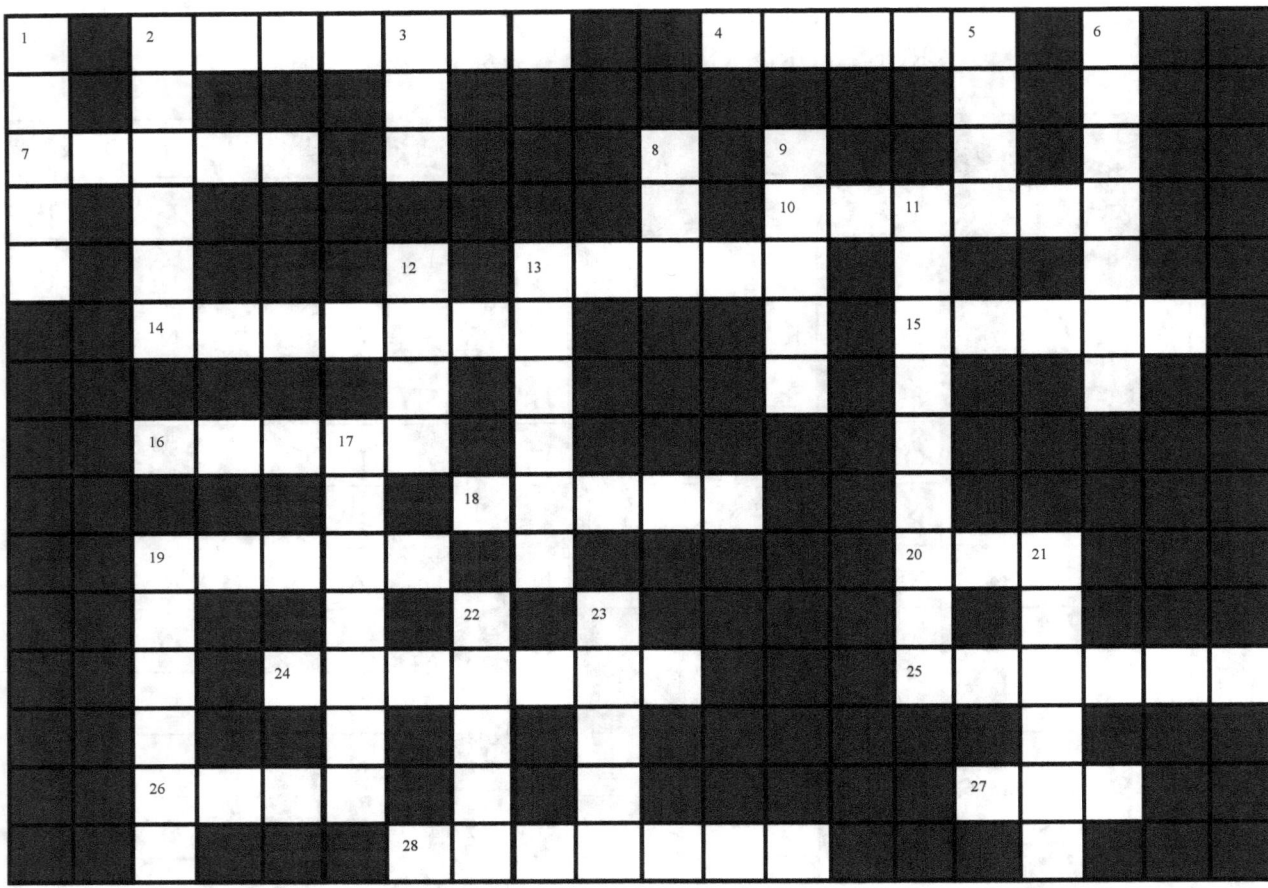

ACROSS
2. What Arcita and Palamon both were; their position
4. Both knights truly ---- Emily
7. The queen's sister
10. Place where Theseus lived
13. Place where Arcita and Palamon were held captive
14. Arcita had a ----- bow
15. The end of a dagger has a sharp one
16. Arcita fell off of his
18. The queen and Emily pleaded for ---- from Theseus towards the knights
19. Long, sharp fighting instrument
20. Palamon's answer to Theseus's proposal
24. He married Emily after his cousin died
25. He won the contest for Emily's hand
26. Arcita did it first; went away
27. Coordinating conjunction
28. He put Arcita and Palamon in prison in his tower

DOWN
1. The king Theseus killed
2. The ----'s Tale
3. Belonging to him
5. Theseus's title
6. Relationship between Arcita and Palamon
8. Arcita fell onto this and broke his breast
9. Both Arcita and Palamon wanted to ---- Emily
11. The queen
12. Arcita's body was burned in this
13. Arcita and Palamon were from there
17. What Arcita pretended to be
19. It was used to fend off blows from the enemy
21. Palamon was Emily's --- husband; number two
22. Arcita and Palamon would --- Emily from their cell window; look at
23. Place where Arcita and Palamon first physically fought over Emily

CROSSWORD ANSWER KEY - *The Knight's Tale*

	C		K	N	I	G	H	T	S			L	O	V	E	D		C	
	R		N				I						U				O		
	E	M	I	L	Y		S			B		M		K			U		
	O		G							O		A	T	H	E	N	S		
	N		H			F		T	O	W	E	R		I			I		
			T	U	R	K	I	S	H			R		P	O	I	N	T	
					R		E					Y		P			S		
			H	O	R	S	E		B					O					
					E		M	E	R	C	Y			L					
			S	W	O	R	D		S					Y	E	S			
			H		V		W		W					T		E			
			I		P	A	L	A	M	O	N			A	R	C	I	T	A
			E		N		T		O							O			
			L	E	F	T		C		D				A	N	D			
			D			H	E	S	E	U	S					D			

CROSSWORD - *The Merchant's Tale*

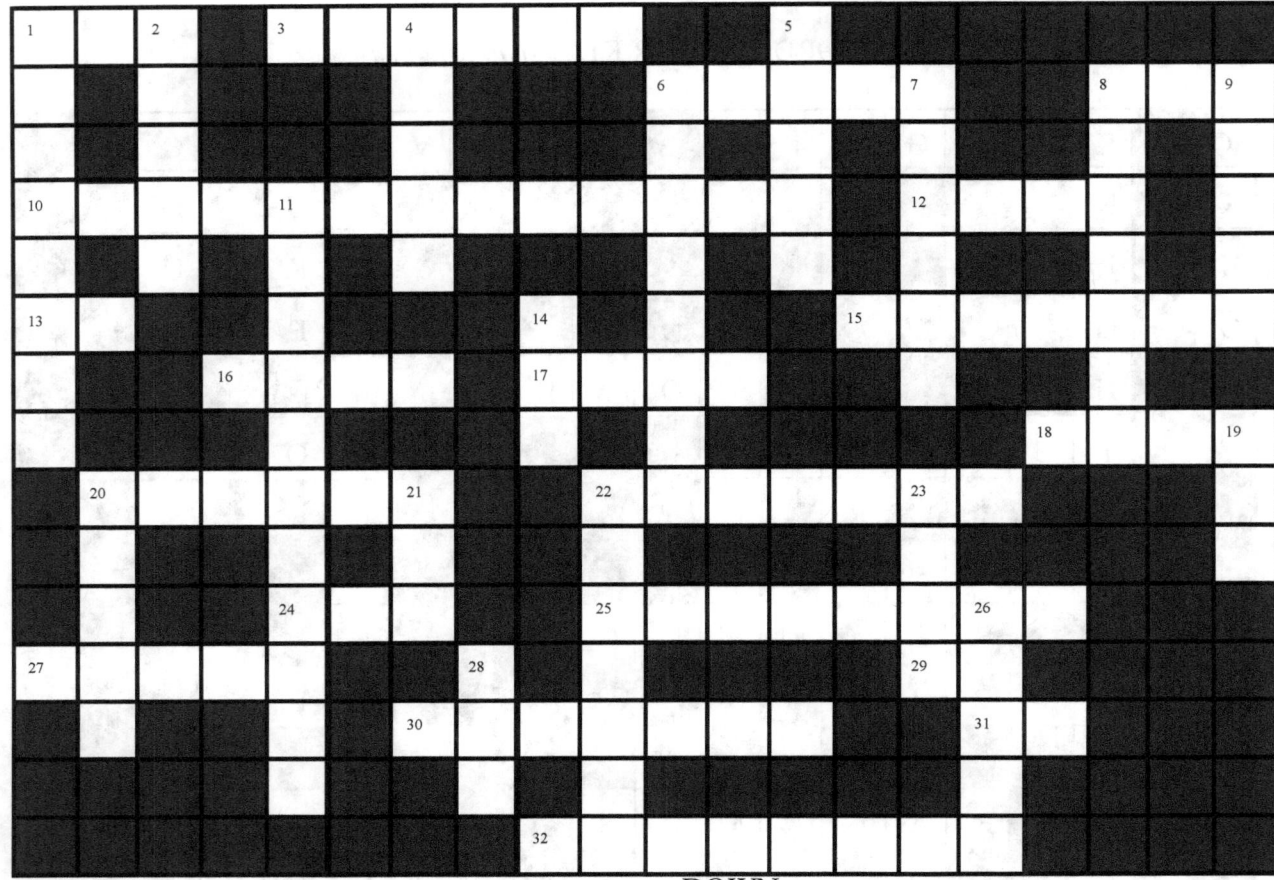

ACROSS
1. January's wife
3. Straw for ----
6. January's misfortune
8. Belonging to him
10. Justinus thinks when choosing a wife one should use careful ----
12. Title for unmarried woman
13. Indefinite article
15. The old knight
16. May claimed to desperately want one of this kind of fruit
17. January wants to take a ---; to get married
18. Revise one's writing
20. Damian's relationship to January
22. May did this on January to get up into the tree
24. Coordinating conjunction
25. A young wife would help keep January from commiting this sin
27. Start
29. Coordinating conjunction
30. He agrees with everything January says
31. May climbed on January's back to -- up the tree
32. The part before the tale begins

DOWN
1. The ---- Tale is about an old knight and his new bride
2. January wants his wife to be -----
4. Damian and May exchange these to communicate
5. The merchant says his wife could overmatch one
6. The bachelor January expects married life to be ----
7. May meets him in the tree
8. January's relationship to May
9. January is over -- years old
11. May should be true to January out of love of Christ, to honor herself & to get this
14. Amount of time the merchant has been married; --- months
19. Also
20. The merchant thinks his wife is one
21. The closing; there is no more; the ---
22. Author
23. January's didn't work temporarily
26. Unprincipled, deceitful person; scoundrel; Damian, for example
28. January was this; not young

CROSSWORD ANSWER KEY - *The Merchant's Tale*

CROSSWORD - *The Miller's Tale*

ACROSS
1. Where Absalom kissed Alison
6. When the carpenter hit the axe against this, his tub fell
9. He and Alison are newlyweds
10. The carpenter broke his when he fell
12. It branded Nicholas
13. Possess
14. Nicholas was Alison's ---- against Absalom; partner; friend; one on your side
15. Parish clerk who lusts after Alison
17. Nicholas warned of the coming of a great one
19. Alison agreed to do this to Absalom to make him go away
21. Out of Sight is also Out of ____
22. Affirmative answer
26. They were hung under the roof to serve as boats
28. If Absalom had opened his, he wouldn't have kissed Alison's behind
29. One who rents a room
31. Definite article
32. Alison threatened to throw one at Absalom
33. Nicholas yelled for it when his behind got burned

DOWN
1. Place Nicholas and Alison ran off to when the carpenter fell asleep
2. Musical instrument played by Nicholas
3. Student boarder with the carpenter and Alison
4. Absalom's job
5. Hobby/interest of Nicholas
7. The village people thought the carpenter was this
8. Condition of the Miller as he told the tale
10. Carpenters wife
11. He told this tale about the carpenter, his wife and the student boarder
15. Who takes ____ shall never fare the worse
16. Absalom chewed this to get rid of his bad breath
18. The carpenter built these to provide access to the hanging tubs
20. Alison's relationship to the carpenter
23. Nicholas is one; one who studies
24. The tubs were hung just under there
25. Absalom -----ed the hot iron from the smith
27. From whom Absalom borrowed the iron
30. The tub was to act as a ---- in the water

CROSSWORD ANSWER KEY - *The Miller's Tale*

CROSSWORD - *The Pardoner's Tale*

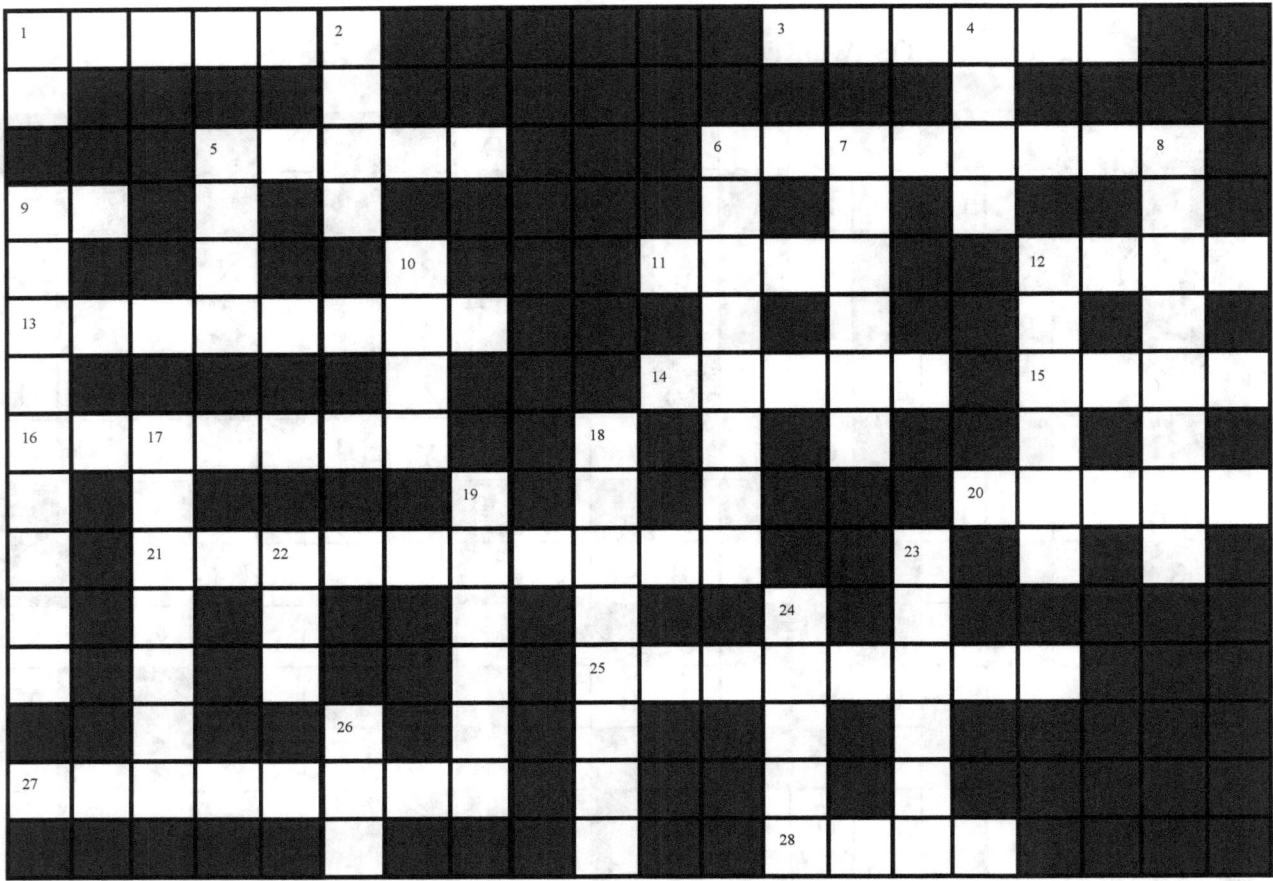

ACROSS
1. The youngest was sent back for food and ---
3. He tried to smooth things over between the Host and the pardoner
5. The three young men went to find and conquer ----
6. Stilbon refused to ally with these
9. Pronoun for that youth
11. The youths ----ed for Death; to track down
12. The old man sent the young men to an oak ----
13. He forgives people's sins (for a small fee!)
14. Each of the youths tried to figure out how to kill the -----s
15. Adjective meaning in a great amount
16. Author
20. Main stem of the tree; the youths leaned against it to rest
21. Where the young man got the poison
25. One must be made to receive a pardon
27. The pardoner does this to advise people to mend their ways
28. Beverage in which the poison was put

DOWN
1. Act
2. The older youths planned to do this to the youngest upon his return
4. It was under the tree
5. What happened to all three youths
6. Overindulgence in food
7. It would multiply grain
8. Vice warned against in the third commandment
9. Word to describe the pardoner
10. The youths showed none of this; fright
12. Three young rioters were sitting in a -----
17. Pardoner's vice
18. The bone could cure everything from sores to this
19. Pardoner sells them as remedies
22. The three young men met an --- man
23. The youngest planned to --- the other two youths
24. Underneath; the gold was --- the tree
26. Definite article

CROSSWORD ANSWER KEY - *The Pardoner's Tale*

D	R	I	N	K	S						K	N	I	G	H	T	
O					T									O			
			D	E	A	T	H			G	A	M	B	L	E	R	S
H	E		I		B					L		I		D			W
Y			E		F			H	U	N	T			T	R	E	E
P	A	R	D	O	N	E	R			T				A			A
O					A			O	T	H	E	R		V	E	R	Y
C	H	A	U	C	E	R		J		O				E		I	
R		V			R			E		N			T	R	U	N	K
I		A	P	O	T	H	E	C	A	R	Y		P		N		G
T		R			L			L			B		O				
E		I			D			I	O	F	F	E	R	I	N	G	
		C		T		C		U		L		S					
P	R	E	A	C	H	E	S			O		O					
				E				Y		W	I	N	E				

CROSSWORD - *The Nun's Priest's Tale*

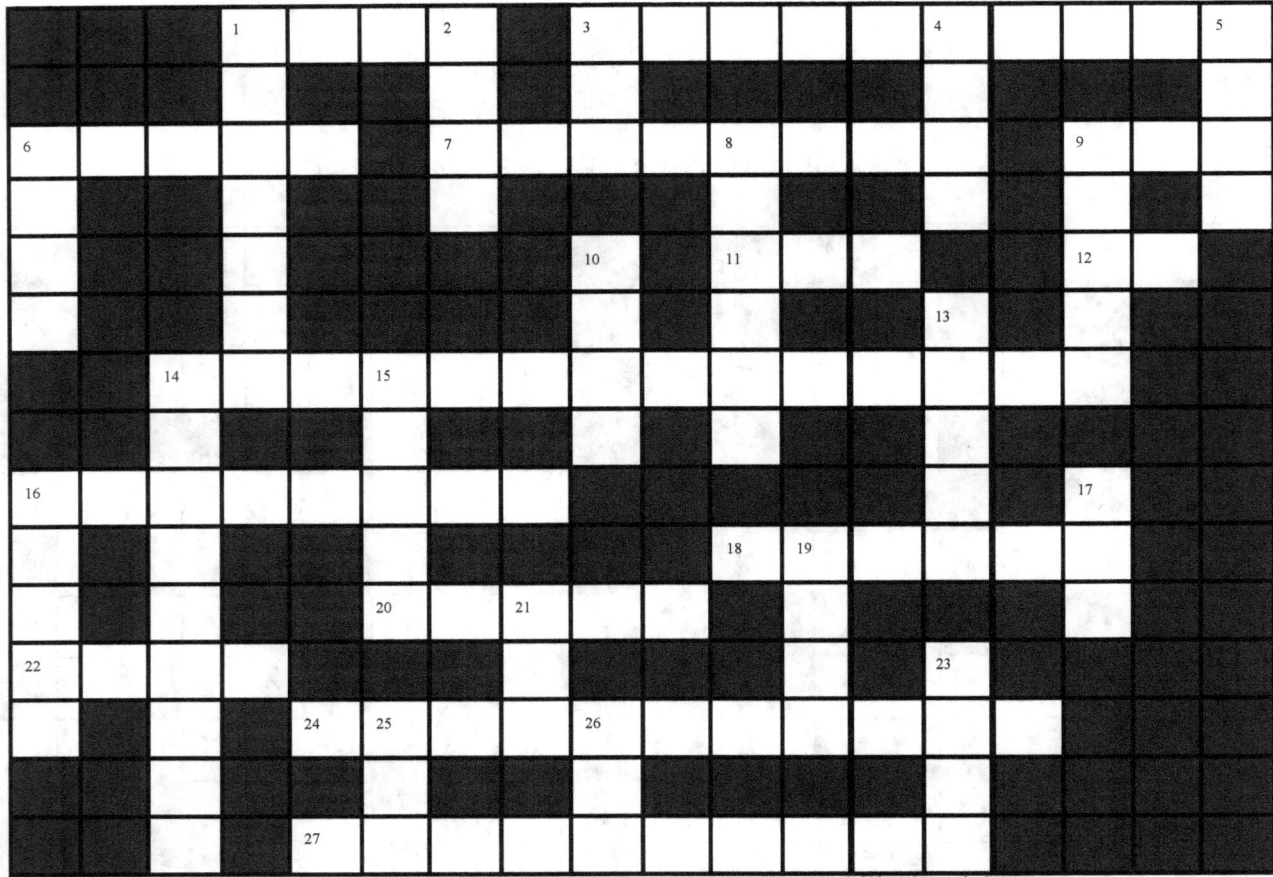

ACROSS
1. Where the man's friend's body was hidden
3. Be on guard against the ----- of this world
6. Chanticleer escaped when the fox opened its mouth to ---
7. Pertilote recommended this remedy
9. Chanticleer --- his battle with the fox
11. Affirmative answer
12. Belonging to me
14. Belief that one's fate is already decided
16. Chanticleer thought dreams could --- the future; predict
18. Nun's ----'s Tale
20. The man's friend was murdered for his ---
22. To deceive into trustfulness
24. The cock
27. Hector's wife who warned him not to go to battle

DOWN
1. Author
2. Nun's Priest's ---
3. It came to kill Chanticleer
4. Chanticleer closed his when he began to sing
5. The fox said he came to hear Chanticleer do this
6. It sank, drowning all on board
8. Chanticleer was --- to get away from the fox; attempting
9. --- is man's delight and all his bliss
10. He said, 'Take no account of dreams'
13. Chanticleer quoted from this Book relating stories about dreams
14. The hen
15. Chanticleer had one that scared him
16. Type of story where animals act as people
17. The fox almost --- Chanticleer
19. Chanticleer's dream was vivid; it seemed almost ----
21. -----'s Priest's Tale
23. Chanticleer and the fox --- being chased by others
25. Pertilote, for example
26. Also

CROSSWORD ANSWER KEY - *The Nun's Priest's Tale*

CROSSWORD - *The Prioress's Tale*

ACROSS
1. The story is --- a boy who sang a song
4. O ---- Redemptoris
7. Place where they took the boy
10. Place where the boy walked to and from each day
11. Belonging to the boy
13. He took the grain of seed from the boy's mouth
14. What the boy's mother did when he did not come home
16. The prologue to the Prioress's Tale is a ---
17. Also
18. The boy's mother was a ---
21. She searched for the boy
22. The boy passed by the Jewish --- on his way to and from school
25. The Christian --- gathered to hear the boy sing
26. The Prioress refers to the Blessed Mother as ----
27. Troubled; agitated; bothered
28. The boy sang a ----

DOWN
2. He sang
3. Language of the song
5. Setting of Prioress's Tale
6. It was His will that the boy should sing to honor His mother
7. Place the boy was attacked
8. The child lay upon one
9. What happened to the boy in the end
12. These people gathered to see the boy singing in the alley
13. Hail ----
15. The ------'s Tale
19. Cry
20. The boy's was cut
23. They hired a murderer to kill the boy
24. The monk took it from the boy's mouth

CROSSWORD ANSWER KEY - *The Prioress's Tale*

													A	B	O	U	T
		L												O			
		A	L	M	A		C			A	B	B	E	Y		D	
		T			S	C	H	O	O	L		I			H	I	S
		I			I		R			L		E			C		E
	M	O	N	K	A		I		S	E	A	R	C	H	E	D	
	A			P			S		Y				R				
P	R	A	Y	E	R		T	O	O			W	I	D	O	W	
	Y			I		T							S			E	
			M	O	T	H	E	R				S	T	R	E	E	T
	J			R		R				S		I				P	
P	E	O	P	L	E					E		A					
	W			E	S				Q	U	E	E	N				
	S		U	P	S	E	T			D		S	O	N	G		

229

CROSSWORD - *The Reeve's Tale*

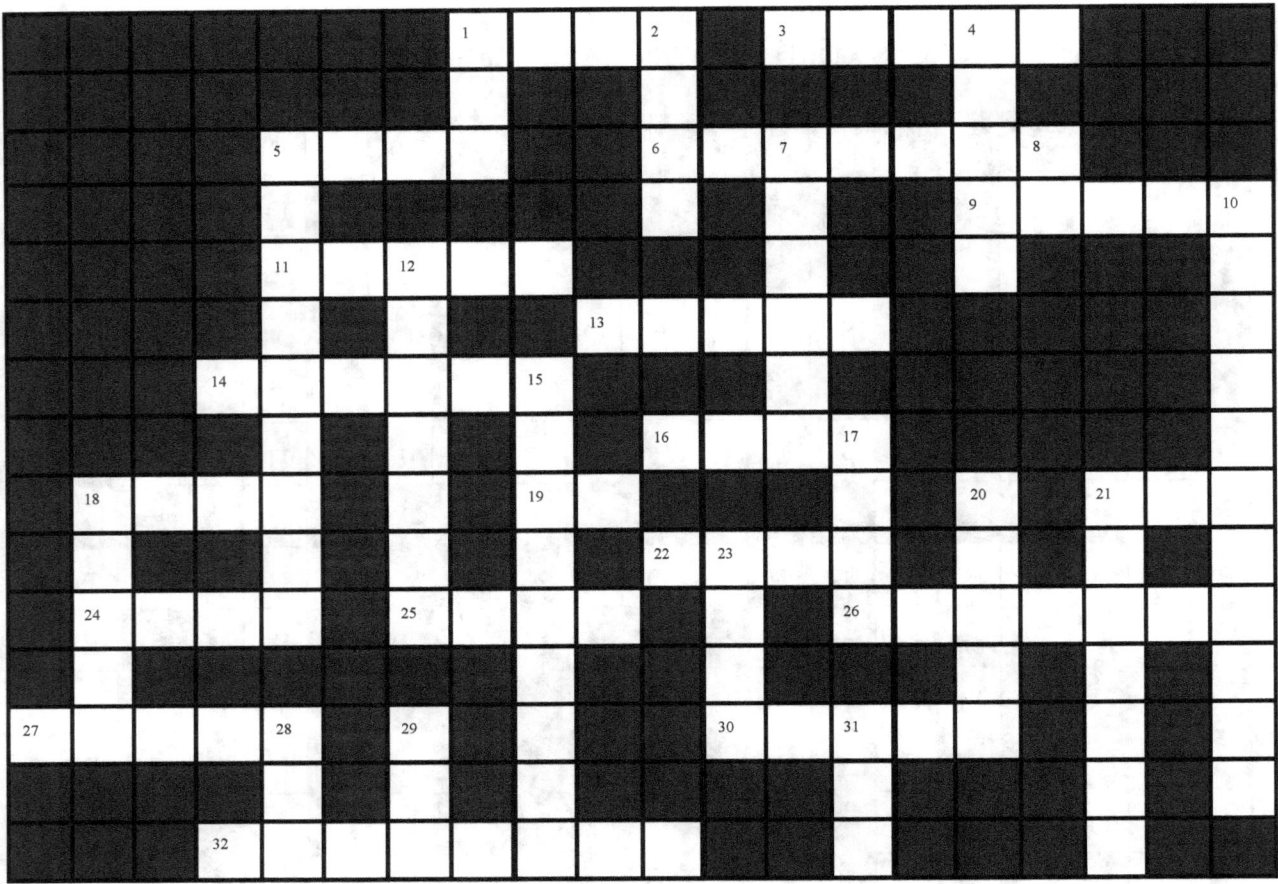

ACROSS
1. He slept with the miller's daughter
3. Dinner meat at the miller's house
5. What the miller's wife made with the stolen flour
6. The miller
9. Add up; --- the bags of grain to make sure they're all there
11. Simpkin's daughter
13. Word describing the miller
14. The baby was in one
16. What Alan & John brought to have ground
18. Where the miller's wife hit him
19. They got -- in the morning; out of bed
21. Prefix meaning three
22. He tricked the miller's wife into sleeping with him
24. Alan and John --- in on a horse
25. Take; snatch
26. What the miller's family was doing to keep Alan & John awake
27. The ---'s tale is about two students who trick a greedy miller
30. ---- Hall
32. John & Alan were — at the college

DOWN
1. Alcoholic drink
2. Alan bashed the miller in the ---
4. The miller's wife mistakenly hit him with one
5. Town where the college was located
7. Simpkin's occupation
8. Negative reply
10. Town near the mill
12. A place to stay overnight
15. Molly received her ---- at the nunnery
17. Women who educated Molly
18. The miller untied it and let it go
20. Product after milling grain
21. John ---- the miller's wife into sleeping with him
23. Belonging to us
28. The miller's wife invited John and Alan to --- supper with them
29. John moved the cradle from next to it
31. Allow

CROSSWORD ANSWER KEY - *The Reeve's Tale*

						A	L	A	N		G	O	O	S	E		
						L			O				T				
			C	A	K	E		S	I	M	P	K	I	N			
			A					E		I			C	O	U	N	T
			M	O	L	L	Y			L			K				R
			B		O		B	U	L	L	Y						U
		C	R	A	D	L	E			E							M
			I		G		D		C	O	R	N					P
H	E	A	D		I		U	P			U		F		T	R	I
O			G		N		C		J	O	H	N		L		R	N
R	O	D	E		G	R	A	B		U		S	N	O	R	I	N	G
S							T			R			U		C		T
R	E	E	V	E		B	I		S	O	L	A	R		K		O
				A		E				E					E		N
			S	T	U	D	E	N	T	S		T			D		

CROSSWORD - *The Shipman's Tale*

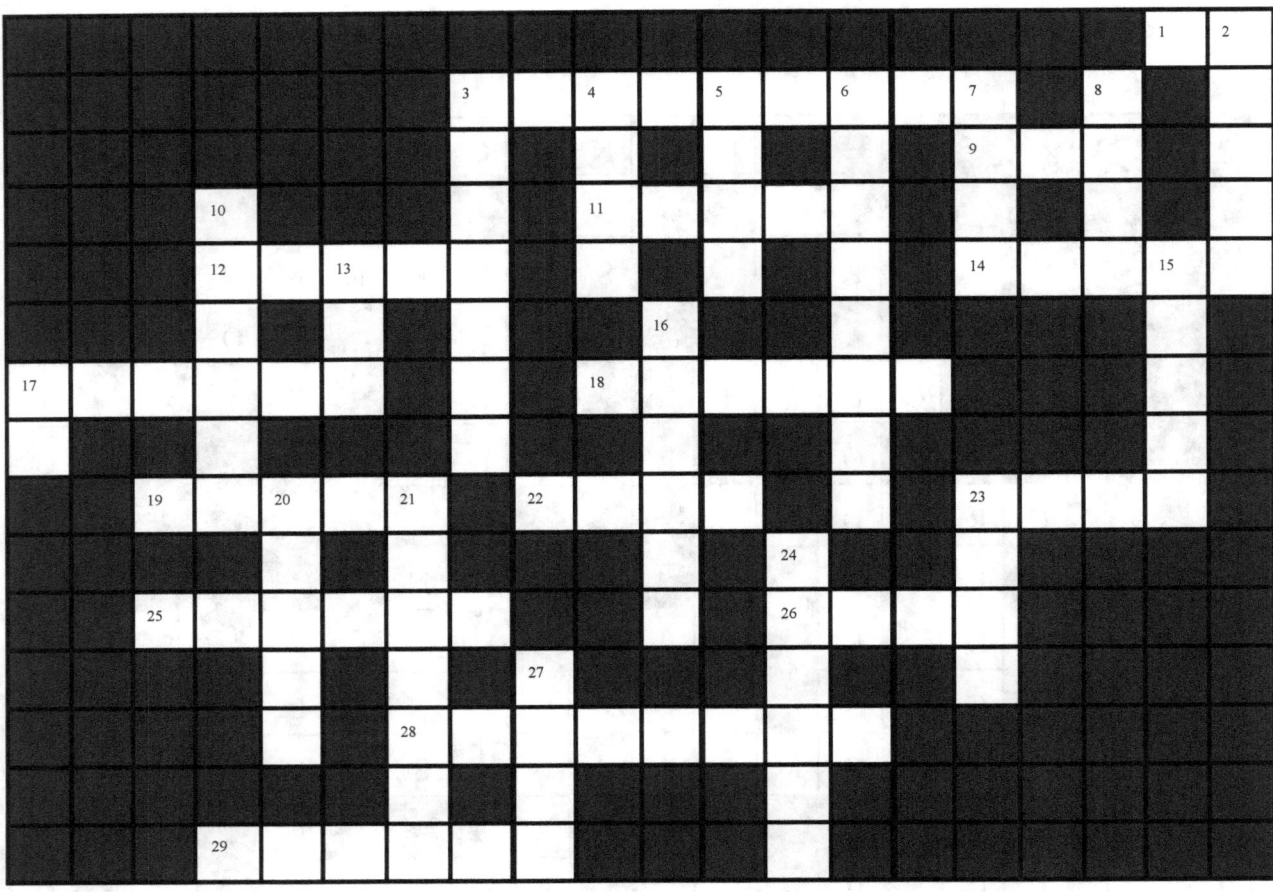

ACROSS
1. Present singular of 'to be'
3. The merchant's wife told her --- to Sir John
9. Present plural of 'to be'
11. Begin
12. He gave permission for Sir John to go to St. Denys
14. Double ----
17. Sir John ---- the merchant's wife; got the best of; outwitted
18. Place of merchant's first business trip
19. Town where merchant lived; St. ---
22. Bruges or St. Denys, for example
23. Seventh month
25. Friendly nickname between merchant and monk
26. Having lots of money
28. The monk and he were best friends
29. The loan amount: 100 ---

DOWN
2. The merchant's wife asked for a loan from Sir John while the merch. was counting his ---
3. What the merchant's wife wanted to buy with her loan money
4. They all went there and prayed before dinner
5. The merchant's wife asked for one from Sir John
6. Fee for lending money
7. The Shipman's ____
8. Amount owing
10. What Sir John said he wanted a loan to buy
13. Where the merchant's wife promised to pay the merchant back
15. Pay back
16. The merchant needed 20,000 of these for a business deal
17. To exist
20. People, places or things; part of speech
21. The --- Tale
23. The monk; Sir ---
24. Country of setting of Shipman's story
27. The merchant's wife requited Sir John by lying in his --- all night

CROSSWORD ANSWER KEY - *The Shipman's Tale*

CROSSWORD - *The Summoner's Tale*

ACROSS
1. Place where souls go between heaven and hell
6. The friar --- for money; begs; inquires
9. The Summoner wants to get --- with the Friar
10. Place where the friars were hidden in hell; under the devil's ----
11. Going without food
16. The friar called the summoner this
17. The boy was shot with one
18. The friar's convent had --- to be filled; it ---- money
20. The friar wanted the people to give ---- to pay for the trentals
21. Three of them were sentenced to be killed by an angry judge
25. The part before the tale begins
27. The marshy district
30. Day after today
31. Thrifty; careful with money
32. What the friar preaches

DOWN
2. An ---- thing is stronger than when it is scattered

DOWN (continued)
3. Thomas's gift to the friar
4. Masses for the souls in purgatory
5. Over there
7. He thought of a solution to the problem of dividing the gift
8. Thomas's wife invited the friar to --- dinner with them
11. The friar told Thomas he had to little of it
12. The noble man's --- was killed
13. Thomas's gift to the friar
14. Anger
15. The friar
19. Where the marshy district lies
22. Vice of overeating
23. The ----'s Tale is about a friar
24. Wished for the possessions of others longingly
26. Place where the friar went in the prologue
28. Appendage attaching your foot to your body
29. Amount of money

CROSSWORD ANSWER KEY - *The Summoner's Tale*

CROSSWORD - *The Wife of Bath's Tale*

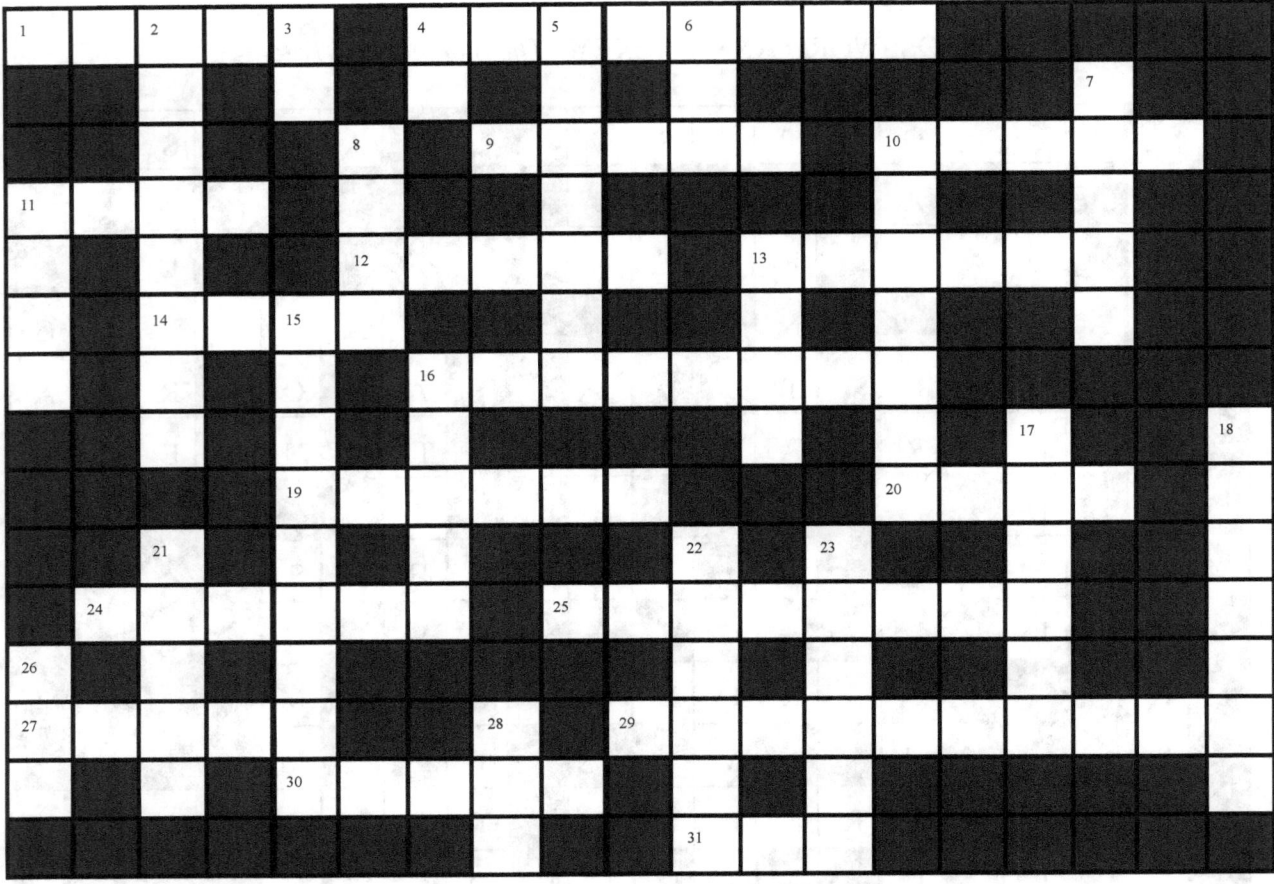

ACROSS
1. The Wife of Bath loved this husband best
4. The knight left the final --- to the old woman
9. The knight had to ---- the old woman
10. He grew ass's ears
11. The Wife of ---
12. The old woman had an ugly --- to speak with
13. The knight was to find the thing that women most ----
14. Number of husbands the Wife of Bath had
16. It is a misery and a woe
19. --- is he that does a ---- deed
20. The knight had one --- and one day to find an answer
24. The fifth husband; the boy from Oxford
25. His wife tricked him into setting himself on fire
27. The knight had to --- the old woman's request; allow
29. It is not 'annexed in nature to possessions'
30. The old woman became ---- and beautiful
31. Unhappy

DOWN
2. The knight and his wife were --- to each other

DOWN (continued)
3. Pronoun for the knight
4. Act
5. Author
6. Title for a knight
7. Midas's wife told her secret to it
8. Wife of Bath married Johnny for this, not money
10. What women most desire is -- over husbands & lovers
11. Johnny hit his wife for tearing pages out of his ----
13. The clout Johnny gave her made the wife of bath ----; suffer loss of hearing
15. Topic of the first part of the prologue
16. Wife of Bath married first husbands for this, not love
17. His wife cut off his hair and he lost his strength
18. The knight had to --- to do the first thing the old woman asked of him
21. The old --- gave the knight the right answer
22. The Queen gave the knight --- to go get the answer; directions; commands
23. The knight --- for the right answer; tracked it down; looked
26. Long time past; long ---
28. The ---; there is no more; the tale is done

CROSSWORD ANSWER KEY - *The Wife of Bath's Tale*

F	I	F	T	H		D	E	C	I	S	I	O	N				
		A		E		O		H		I						W	
		I		L		M	A	R	R	Y		M	I	D	A	S	
B	A	T	H			U						A				T	
O		H		V	O	I	C	E		D	E	S	I	R	E		
O		F	I	V	E			E		E		T			R		
K		U			M	A	R	R	I	A	G	E					
		L			R			O		F		R		S		P	
				G	E	N	T	L	E			Y	E	A	R		
		W		I		E			O		H			M		R	
	J	O	H	N	N	Y		H	E	R	C	U	L	E	S	O	
A		M		I				D		N				O		M	
G	R	A	N	T		E		G	E	N	T	L	E	N	E	S	S
O		N		Y	O	U	N	G		R							E
						D		S	A	D							

237

CROSSWORD 1 - *The Canterbury Tales*

CROSSWORD CLUE SHEET - *The Canterbury Tales*

ACROSS

2. Good navigator, didn't ride well, from Dartmouth
7. Forked beard, good negotiator, always told his opinions
9. Had sores, master chef
11. Carpenter broke his when he fell
12. Pertelote, for example
13. Marquis' new wife
14. Son of the knight
15. Wife of ---
18. Anger
20. Old, thin, brought up the rear, good manager
23. It branded Nicholas
24. Place where they took the singing boy
26. Chanticleer closed his when he began to sing
27. ----'s Priest's Tale
29. The yeoman's true identity
31. From whom Absalom borrowed an iron
32. Squire's servant
34. He tricked the miller's wife into sleeping with him
35. Emily's brother-in-law; he captured two knights
40. Had been in many battles, was a gentleman
41. The merchant's wife asked for one from Sir John
42. He tried to rid the coast of rocks for Dorigen
44. The knight had one -- and one day to find an answer
45. They were hung under the roof to serve as boats
47. The monk took this from the boy's mouth
49. It came to kill Chanticleer
50. Number of husbands the Wife of Bath had
51. He married Emily after his cousin died
52. It was under the tree

DOWN

1. Liked to eat, drink and be merry
2. Garland of flowers on head; insulted the Friar

DOWN (continued)

3. May claimed to desperately want one of this fruit
4. Carpenter's wife
5. Aristocratic, takes bribes for easy penance
6. Arveragus tried to help save Dorigen's
7. Football-player build, cheated customers, plays bagpipes
8. Place where the friars were hidden in hell
9. Loved to learn for the sake of learning
10. Walter brought the --- back to Griselda
13. Thomas's gift to the friar
14. Arveragus's castle was near the ---
15. Host
16. Number of years Arveragus was gone
17. January's wife
19. Griselda was beautiful in looks and ----
21. The queen's sister; two knights loved her
22. Pardoner sells them as remedies
24. He slept with the miller's daughter
25. He sang
28. Student boarder with Alison and the carpenter
30. Author
33. Bald & fat, didn't like work
34. The fifth husband of the Wife of Bath
35. Place where Theseus kept Arcita and Palamon
36. Alison agreed to do this to Absalom to make him go away
37. Fiends take different ones to catch their prey
38. Christ-like, patient, giving, holy, virtuous
39. The miller
42. He won the contest for Emily's hand
43. The older youths planned to do this to the youngest upon his return
46. Where the merchant's wife was going to pay him back
48. What happened to all three youths who found Death

CROSSWORD ANSWER KEY 1 - *The Canterbury Tales*

MATCHING QUIZ/WORKSHEET 1 - *The Canterbury Tales*

____ 1. COOK   A. He tricked the miller's wife into sleeping with him

____ 2. SIMPKIN   B. Condition of the Miller as he told his tale

____ 3. LOVE   C. Marquis' new wife

____ 4. DAMIAN   D. Arveragus's castle was near the ---

____ 5. JOHN   E. The monk took this from the boy's mouth

____ 6. SEED   F. May meets him in a tree

____ 7. STAB   G. Alison agreed to do this to Absalom to make him go away

____ 8. SEA   H. Emily's brother-in-law; he captured two knights

____ 9. CHAUCER   I. The Wife of Bath married Johnny for this, not money

____ 10. CHANTICLEER   J. Thomas's gift to the friar

____ 11. IRON   K. Had sores, master chef

____ 12. GRISELDA   L. The cock

____ 13. PARSON   M. Author

____ 14. KISS   N. Christ-like, patient, giving, holy, virtuous

____ 15. THESEUS   O. Place where Theseus kept Arcita and Palamon

____ 16. ARVERAGUS   P. The older youths planned to do this to the youngest upon his return

____ 17. GAS   Q. It branded Nicholas

____ 18. MASTERY   R. Dorigen's husband

____ 19. DRUNK   S. What women most desire is --- over husbands

____ 20. TOWER   T. The miller

KEY: MATCHING QUIZ/WORKSHEET 1 - *The Canterbury Tales*

__K__ 1. COOK
__T__ 2. SIMPKIN
__I__ 3. LOVE
__F__ 4. DAMIAN
__A__ 5. JOHN
__E__ 6. SEED
__P__ 7. STAB
__D__ 8. SEA
__M__ 9. CHAUCER
__L__ 10. CHANTICLEER
__Q__ 11. IRON
__C__ 12. GRISELDA
__N__ 13. PARSON
__G__ 14. KISS
__H__ 15. THESEUS
__R__ 16. ARVERAGUS
__J__ 17. GAS
__S__ 18. MASTERY
__B__ 19. DRUNK
__O__ 20. TOWER

A. He tricked the miller's wife into sleeping with him
B. Condition of the miller as he told his tale
C. Marquis' new wife
D. Arveragus's castle was near the ---
E. The monk took this from the boy's mouth
F. May meets him in a tree
G. Alison agreed to do this to Absalom to make him go away
H. Emily's brother-in-law; he captured two knights
I. The Wife of Bath married Johnny for this, not money
J. Thomas's gift to the friar
K. Had sores, master chef
L. The cock
M. Author
N. Christ-like, patient, giving, holy, virtuous
O. Place where Theseus kept Arcita and Palamon
P. The older youths planned to do this to the youngest upon his return
Q. It branded Nicholas
R. Dorigen's husband
S. What women most desire is --- over husbands
T. The miller

MATCHING QUIZ/WORKSHEET 2 - *The Canterbury Tales*

____ 1. BRIBE   A. Griselda was beautiful in looks and ----

____ 2. MAY   B. He slept with the miller's daughter

____ 3. DEEDS   C. He married Emily after his cousin died

____ 4. REEVE   D. What women most desire is --- over husbands

____ 5. ALISON   E. The knight's old woman wife became --- and beautiful

____ 6. PRAYER   F. Squire's servant

____ 7. ALAN   G. Carpenter's wife

____ 8. DIED   H. Squire's suggestion as to how to divide the gift

____ 9. PALAMON   I. He tried to rid the coast of rocks for Dorigen

____ 10. GAS   J. A young wife would help January from committing this sin

____ 11. YOUNG   K. Old, thin, brought up the rear, good manager

____ 12. YEOMAN   L. Thomas's gift to the friar

____ 13. TAIL   M. Place where the friars were hidden in hell

____ 14. ADULTERY   N. Money paid to the summoner to keep him from making an arrest

____ 15. WHEEL   O. What happened to all three youths who found Death

____ 16. STAB   P. Liked to eat, drink and be merry

____ 17. AURELIUS   Q. The prologue to the Prioress's Tale is a ---

____ 18. ABBEY   R. The older youths planned to do this to the youngest upon his return

____ 19. MASTERY   S. January's wife

____ 20. FRANKLIN   T. Place where they took the singing boy

KEY: MATCHING QUIZ/WORKSHEET 2 - *The Canterbury Tales*

_N_ 1. BRIBE	A.	Griselda was beautiful in looks and ----
_S_ 2. MAY	B.	He slept with the miller's daughter
_A_ 3. DEEDS	C.	He married Emily after his cousin died
_K_ 4. REEVE	D.	What women most desire is --- over husbands
_G_ 5. ALISON	E.	The knight's old woman wife became --- and beautiful
_Q_ 6. PRAYER	F.	Squire's servant
_B_ 7. ALAN	G.	Carpenter's wife
_O_ 8. DIED	H.	Squire's suggestion as to how to divide the gift
_C_ 9. PALAMON	I.	He tried to rid the coast of rocks for Dorigen
_L_ 10. GAS	J.	A young wife would help January from committing this sin
_E_ 11. YOUNG	K.	Old, thin, brought up the rear, good manager
_F_ 12. YEOMAN	L.	Thomas's gift to the friar
_M_ 13. TAIL	M.	Place where the friars were hidden in hell
_J_ 14. ADULTERY	N.	Money paid to the summoner to keep him from making an arrest
_H_ 15. WHEEL	O.	What happened to all three youths who found Death
_R_ 16. STAB	P.	Liked to eat, drink and be merry
_I_ 17. AURELIUS	Q.	The prologue to the Prioress's Tale is a ---
_T_ 18. ABBEY	R.	The older youths planned to do this to the youngest upon his return
_D_ 19. MASTERY	S.	January's wife
_P_ 20. FRANKLIN	T.	Place where they took the singing boy

WORD SHEET - *The Canterbury Tales*

WORD	CLUE
KNIGHT	Had been in many battles, was a gentleman
SQUIRE	Son of the knight
YEOMAN	Squire's servant
PRIORESS	Dainty, pleasant, sensitive, medieval beauty
MONK	Bald & fat, didn't like work
FRIAR	Aristocratic, takes bribes for easy penance
MERCHANT	Forked beard, good negotiator, always told his opinions
CLERK	Loved to learn for the sake of learning
FRANKLIN	Liked to eat, drink and be merry
COOK	Had sores, master chef
SHIPMAN	Good navigator, didn't ride well, from Dartmouth
BATH	Wife of ---
PARSON	Christ-like, patient, giving, holy, virtuous
PARDONER	Sells false relics, bulging eyes, long yellow hair
MILLER	Football-player build, cheated customers, plays bagpipes
REEVE	Old, thin, brought up the rear, good manager
SUMMONER	Garland of flowers on head; insulted Friar
BAILLY	Host
CHILDREN	Walter brought the --- back to Griselda
GRISELDA	Marquis' new wife
DEEDS	Griselda was beautiful in looks and ----
ARVERAGUS	Dorigen's husband
AURELIUS	He tried to rid the coast of rocks for Dorigen
CHAUCER	Author
HONOR	Arveragus tried to help save Dorigen's
SEA	Arveragus's castle was near the ---
TWO	Number of years Arveragus was gone
DORIGEN	She missed Arveragus
CURSE	The farmer didn't mean his, but the widow did
FIEND	The yeoman's true identity
SHAPES	Fiends take different ones to catch their prey
ARCITA	He won the contest for Emily's hand
EMILY	The queen's sister; two knights loved her
PALAMON	He married Emily after his cousin died
THESEUS	Emily's brother-in-law; he captured two knights
TOWER	Place where Theseus kept Arcita and Palamon
ADULTERY	A young wife would help January from committing this sin
DAMIAN	May meets him in a tree
MAY	January's wife
PEAR	May claimed to desperately want one of this fruit
ABSALOM	Parish clerk who lusts after Alison
ALISON	Carpenter's wife
ARM	Carpenter broke his when he fell
IRON	It branded Nicholas
KISS	Alison agreed to do this to Absalom to make him go away
NICHOLAS	Student boarder with Alison and the carpenter
TUBS	They were hung under the roof to serve as boats
RELICS	Pardoner sells them as remedies

Canterbury Tales Word Sheet Page 2

STAB	The older youths planned to do this to the youngest upon his return
CHANTICLEER	The cock
EYES	Chanticleer closed his when he began to sing
FOX	It came to kill Chanticleer
HEN	Pertelote, for example
NUN	----'s Priest's Tale
ABBEY	Place where they took the singing boy
ALLEY	Place where the singing boy was attacked
BOY	He sang
PRAYER	The prologue to the Prioress's Tale is a ---
THROAT	The boy's was cut
ALAN	He slept with the miller's daughter
JOHN	He tricked the miller's wife into sleeping with him
MOLLY	Simpkin's daughter
SIMPKIN	The miller
BED	Where the merchant's wife was going to pay him back
CLOTHES	What the merchant's wife wanted to buy with her loan
FRANCS	The loan amount: 100 ---
LOAN	The merchant's wife asked for one from Sir John
FAITH	The friar told Thomas he had too little of it
GAS	Thomas's gift to the friar
MONEY	The friar wanted the people to give --- to pay for trentals
DESIRE	The knight was sent to find the thing women most ---
FIVE	Number of husbands the Wife of Bath had
JOHNNY	The fifth husband of the Wife of Bath
LOVE	The Wife of Bath married Johnny for this, not money
MASTERY	What women most desire is --- over husbands
YEAR	The knight had one -- and one day to find an answer
BRIBE	Money paid to the summoner to keep him from making an arrest
BOW	Arcita fell onto his and broke his breast
PROLOGUE	The part that comes before the story
DRUNK	Condition of the Miller as he told his tale
SMITH	From whom Absalom borrowed an iron
DIED	What happened to all three youths who found Death
GOLD	It was under the tree
SEED	The monk took this from the boy's mouth
CAKE	What the miller's wife made from the flour he took from A & J
IRE	Anger
TAIL	Place where the friars were hidden in hell
WHEEL	Squire's suggestion as to how to divide the gift
YOUNG	The knight's old woman wife became --- and beautiful

JUGGLE LETTER REVIEW GAME CLUE SHEET - *The Canterbury Tales*

SCRAMBLED	WORD	CLUE
THINKG	KNIGHT	Had been in many battles, was a gentleman
RIQUES	SQUIRE	Son of the knight
MEONAY	YEOMAN	Squire's servant
SIROPER	PRIORESS	Dainty, pleasant, sensitive, medieval beauty
KMON	MONK	Bald & fat, didn't like work
RIFAR	FRIAR	Aristocratic, takes bribes for easy penance
THEMARNC	MERCHANT	Forked beard, good negotiator, told his opinions
KRLCE	CLERK	Loved to learn for the sake of learning
NARFINKL	FRANKLIN	Liked to eat, drink and be merry
KOCO	COOK	Had sores, master chef
MISHPAN	SHIPMAN	Good navigator, didn't ride well, from Dartmouth
HATB	BATH	Wife of ---
NORSAP	PARSON	Christ-like, patient, giving, holy, virtuous
RADRENOP	PARDONER	Sells false relics, bulging eyes, long yellow hair
LIMREL	MILLER	Football-player build, cheated customers, s
EVERE	REEVE	Old, thin, brought up the rear, good manager
RUMMONES	SUMMONER	Garland of flowers on head; insulted Friar
YABILL	BAILLY	Host
HENRLIDC	CHILDREN	Walter brought the --- back to Griselda
ALSDEGIR	GRISELDA	Marquis' new wife
SEEDD	DEEDS	Griselda was beautiful in looks and ----
GRRVSAAEU	ARVERAGUS	Dorigen's husband
SURLUAIE	AURELIUS	He tried to rid the coast of rocks for Dorigen
HAUCREC	CHAUCER	Author
RHOON	HONOR	Arveragus tried to help save Dorigen's
EAS	SEA	Arveragus's castle was near the ---
WTO	TWO	Number of years Arveragus was gone
GORDINE	DORIGEN	She missed Arveragus
SECUR	CURSE	The farmer didn't mean his, but the widow did
NIDEF	FIEND	The yeoman's true identity
PASSEH	SHAPES	Fiends take different ones to catch their prey
CARTIA	ARCITA	He won the contest for Emily's hand
YELIM	EMILY	The queen's sister; two knights loved her
NMALOPA	PALAMON	He married Emily after his cousin died
SHUTEES	THESEUS	Emily's brother-in-law; he captured two knights
WROTE	TOWER	Place where Theseus kept Arcita and Palamon
LETRADUY	ADULTERY	A young wife would keep January from this sin
NAMDAI	DAMIAN	May meets him in a tree
YAM	MAY	January's wife
REAP	PEAR	May claimed to desperately want one of this fruit
BALMASO	ABSALOM	Parish clerk who lusts after Alison
NILASO	ALISON	Carpenter's wife
MAR	ARM	Carpenter broke his when he fell

NOIR	IRON	It branded Nicholas
SIKS	KISS	Alison agreed to do this to make Absalom go away
SHILCOAN	NICHOLAS	Student boarder with Alison and the carpenter
STUB	TUBS	They were hung under the roof to serve as boats
SRICEL	RELICS	Pardoner sells them as remedies
BAST	STAB	The older youths planned to do this to the youngest
HECNRITACEL	CHANTICLEER	The cock
YEES	EYES	Chanticleer closed his when he began to sing
OXF	FOX	It came to kill Chanticleer
NEH	HEN	Pertelote, for example
UNN	NUN	----'s Priest's Tale
BABEY	ABBEY	Place where they took the singing boy
LALEY	ALLEY	Place where the singing boy was attacked
YOB	BOY	He sang
YAPRER	PRAYER	The prologue to the Prioress's Tale is a ---
ROTHTA	THROAT	The boy's was cut
NAAL	ALAN	He slept with the miller's daughter
HNOJ	JOHN	He tricked the miller's wife into sleeping with him
YOLLM	MOLLY	Simpkin's daughter
KIPMINS	SIMPKIN	The miller
EBD	BED	Where the merchant's wife was going to repay him
SCHOLCET	CLOTHES	What the merchant's wife wanted to buy
SCANRF	FRANCS	The loan amount: 100 ---
NOAL	LOAN	The merchant's wife asked for one from Sir John
AFHTI	FAITH	The friar told Thomas he had too little of it
SGA	GAS	Thomas's gift to the friar
YONEM	MONEY	The friar wanted the people to give --- for trentals
REIEDS	DESIRE	The knight was sent to find the thing women most
IEVF	FIVE	Number of husbands the Wife of Bath had
HYNJON	JOHNNY	The fifth husband of the Wife of Bath
VOLE	LOVE	The Wife of Bath married Johnny for this
STERYMA	MASTERY	What women most desire is --- over husbands
EARY	YEAR	The knight had one -- and one day to find an answer
RIBBE	BRIBE	Money paid to the summoner to keep him from making an arrest
OWB	BOW	Arcita fell onto his and broke his breast
GOLUROPE	PROLOGUE	The part that comes before the story
KURDN	DRUNK	Condition of the Miller as he told his tale
SHTIM	SMITH	From whom Absalom borrowed an iron
EDDI	DIED	What happened to all three youths who found Death
DOLG	GOLD	It was under the tree
EEDS	SEED	The monk took this from the boy's mouth
KAEC	CAKE	What the miller's wife made from the A & J's flour
RIE	IRE	Anger
LTAI	TAIL	Place where the friars were hidden in hell
EEWLH	WHEEL	Squire's suggestion as to how to divide the gift

VOCABULARY RESOURCE MATERIALS

VOCABULARY WORD SEARCH 1 - *The Canterbury Tales*

All words in this list are associated with *The Canterbury Tales* with an emphasis on the vocabulary words chosen for study in the text. The words are placed backwards, forward, diagonally, up and down. The clues below the word search will help you find the words.

```
C O N S T A N C Y T I C I L E F D A I S C H E W
L Z B G U K V R O L R X H R Y N L E A Z C O T T
Q E S S I P D A W N I O I I C W T G N E W E Y C
A Y C R T N P P I Z T R T E D A E H E G E N O D
G C M H U I E L E L O R E X M E P S R R I N Q Q
P L Q S E O N B I L U D I V E I E R C A U E A K
P R U U R R M A L C F S A V E B N S I N L M F T
Y R E T I E E A T A A T U U E L I E D C I L E H
C I O D T E P T R E T T R R N D B R N S E K E D
L A N F E O S R I A C T I E Y T U L S T Z S W D
C A I C F S N C E N P A I O N M E T I U Q E R S
T Z N S I E T Y E H U R R U N C H D F T H S R R
F G V G I T R I T H E E E O Q S H Q D C H E K N
M E N C U D I I N I T N K P U C Q A S H D E W S
D E R I S I O N N A L A S F L S A E N R M Q L Q
B D L U T Z S R G G T A E I N E E M E T P Z X Y
F G K V C A S H H P B I G U B N T S M G Q W N S
V V D T H S R N I P S M O U Q L S I L P W P Z N
X B G R N S B P T N A S Q N R E E P O S N C B L
P R O D I G I O U S G W T X D F B Q G N S R Q P
```

A cause of suffering or harm
A drug or food having the effect of arousing sexual desire
A man who overindulges in sexual activities
A mystery; a puzzle
A raised platform
Agree; consent
Anger
Appeals; pleas
Artificial; counterfeited; faked
Behaves riotously; revels
Belief that one's fate is already decided
Chattering; jabbering
Consisting of many different kinds
Deprived of courage as a result of fear, anxiety or disgust
Deserving condemnation; despicable
Diplomatic; politic; tactful
Enchanted; fascinated
Even; indeed
Extreme paleness
Faithfulness; fidelity
Full to or beyond satisfaction
Given to flirting
Group of attendants or followers
Happiness; bliss
Kindhearted, considerate
Lacking energy or strength
Lending money & charging outrageously high interest

Lightheartedly; festively; merrily
Loot; goods seized unlawfully
Lovers
Make an earnest request
Mockery; ridicule
Not readily noticed or seen; unknown
Of extraordinary size and/or power
Plan
Repay
Reserved in manner; shy; modest
Sharp
Stirring to action
Stubborn
The vice of continually overeating
Thriftiness; careful use of material goods
To behave festively; frolic
To criticize for a fault or offense
To free from a charge or accusation
To get revenge for
To leave material goods by will
To obtain from another by intimidation or blackmail
To put before another for acceptance
To stay away from
Usefulness
Whims
Widely known; famous
Wise; wise person; scholarly
Wrong; awry

KEY: VOCABULARY WORD SEARCH 1 - *The Canterbury Tales*

All words in this list are associated with *The Canterbury Tales* with an emphasis on the vocabulary words chosen for study in the text. The words are placed backwards, forward, diagonally, up and down. The included words are listed below the word search.

```
C O N S T A N C Y T I C I L E F D A I S C H E
L   B G U   V R O L R   H R   N   E A   C O T
  E S S I P D A   N I O I I C   T G N E W E Y C
A   C R T N P P I   T R T E D A E H E G E   O
G C   H U I E L E L O R E X M E P S R R I N
P L Q S E O N B I L U D I V E I E R C A U E A
P R U U R R M A L C F S A V E B N S I N L M F
  R E T I E E A T A A T U U E L I E D C I L E
C I O D T E P T R E T T R R N D B R N S E   E D
L A N F E O S R I A C T I E Y T U L S T     S W D
  A I C F S N C E N P A I O N M E T I U Q E R
    N S I E T Y E H U R R U N C   D   T H   R
  G   G I T R I T H E E E O Q S H     C H E
  E N   U D I I N I T N   P U C   A S   D E
D E R I S I O N N A L A S   L S A E N R     L
    U T   S R G G T A E I   E E   E T       Y
      C A   H H     I G U B   T S
        S R   I P     O U Q L S I
          B P   N A     N R E E   O
P R O D I G I O U S G     D F B       N
```

WOE
APHRODISIAC
LECHER
CONUNDRUM
DIAS
ACQUIESCE
IRE
SUPPLICATIONS
FEIGNED
CAROUSES
PREDESTINATION
PRATING
SUNDRY
DAUNTED
REPREHENSIBLE
DISCREET
ENTHRALLED
VERILY
PALLOR
CONSTANCY
REPLETION
COY
RETINUE
FELICITY
BENIGN
LANGUISHING
USURY

BLITHELY
PELF
PARAMOURS
BESEECH
DERISION
OBSCURE
PRODIGIOUS
CONTRIVE
REQUITE
DEMURE
TRENCHANT
INCITING
OBSTINATE
GLUTTONY
FRUGALITY
REVEL
CHIDE
ACQUITTAL
REDRESSED
BEQUEATH
EXTORT
PROFFERING
ESCHEW
AVAIL
CAPRICES
EMINENT
SAGE
AMISS

VOCABULARY WORD SEARCH 2 - *The Canterbury Tales*

All words in this list are associated with *The Canterbury Tales* with an emphasis on the vocabulary words chosen for study in the text. The words are placed backwards, forward, diagonally, up and down. The included words are listed below.

```
P R O D I G I O U S E N T H R A L L E D P E L F
T R P B A R B N F P D L Y E M E I U E S C C A Z
P R E R S U E E C Y A V B I X A Q S S C C P Q R
I A E R A C N P N I J L S A V H S U G U H H W N
E N R N O T U T L I T S L A N E O N I R R E E W
C X E A C G I R E E G I T O R I I R O T G Y R W
C O T B M H A N E D T N N D R R M D T L E S J X
Q A N O R O A T G S C I E G E K I O K A E D Q W
N N P T R I U N I R N R O F K S L V B S T Y C V
W Z O R R T A R T V L O F N I A F M U A T I H S
J B Z B I I B T S Y E O I A T R F O B E B X O M
M M L T S C V D E B R H C T U X R E E B E Z S N
K U P V V T E E W P V C I G A A Q R L C R N M Y
G S R F E R I S T I P U A R C U C R N I Z R D K
H D Z D I R X N C W Q L E H E S N E E C C E N S
Y Z R S N G I T A C I V I A I R G I W T N I A V
C S I V G U U L A T E D T D G I U F S G I G T D
C O N S T A N C Y L E H T I L B E M I N E N T Y
N W Y Q L Y N O T T U L G I R Y S E E F I H U B
L B E S E E C H C S I A D W O E F Y R D N U S E
```

ABOMINABLE	COY	GLUTTONY	REDRESSED
ACQUITTAL	DAIS	INCITING	REPLETION
AMISS	DAUNTED	INEBRIATE	REQUITE
APHRODISIAC	DEMURE	INSINUATIONS	RETINUE
AVAIL	DERISION	IRE	REVEL
BENIGN	DILIGENCE	LECHER	SAGE
BEQUEATH	DISCREET	OBSCURE	SUNDRY
BESEECH	EMINENT	OBSTINATE	TRENCHANT
BLITHELY	ENTHRALLED	PALLOR	USURY
CAPRICES	ESCHEW	PARAMOURS	VERILY
CAROUSES	EXHORTATION	PELF	VICTUALS
CHIDE	EXTORT	PRATING	WOE
CONSTANCY	FEIGNED	PREROGATIVE	
CONTRIVE	FELICITY	PRODIGIOUS	
CONUNDRUM	FRUGALITY	PROFFERING	

KEY: VOCABULARY WORD SEARCH 2 - *The Canterbury Tales*

All words in this list are associated with *The Canterbury Tales* with an emphasis on the vocabulary words chosen for study in the text. The words are placed backwards, forward, diagonally, up and down. The included words are listed below.

```
            P R O D I G I O U S E N T H R A L L E D P E L F
            T R P B A R B N   P   L   E M E I U E S       A
            P R E R S U E E C   A   B I X A Q S S C C     P
            I A E R A C N P N I   L S A V H S U G U H H
            E N R N O T U T L I T S L A N E O N I R R E E
            C X E A C G I R E E G I   O R I I R O T   Y R W
            C O T B M H A N E D T N N D R R M D T   E S
              A N O R O A T G S   I E G E   I O   A E
              P T R I U N I   N R O F   S L   B S T
              O R R T A R T V   O F N I A F   U A T I
              B I I   T S   E O I A T R F O B E     O
            M     S C V D E   R   C T U   R E E   E     N
              U   V   T E E   P V   I G A A Q R L C
                  R   E R I S   I   U A R C U C R N I     D
                    D I R   N C   Q L E H E S N E E   C E S
                        S N   I T A C I V I A I R G I   T N I A
            C   I     U U L A T E D T D   I U   S G I G T
            C O N S T A N C Y L E H T I L B E M I N E N T Y
            N   Y   L Y N O T T U L G I R     E E   I   U
              B E S E E C H C S I A D W O E F Y R D N U S E
```

ABOMINABLE	COY	GLUTTONY	REDRESSED
ACQUITTAL	DAIS	INCITING	REPLETION
AMISS	DAUNTED	INEBRIATE	REQUITE
APHRODISIAC	DEMURE	INSINUATIONS	RETINUE
AVAIL	DERISION	IRE	REVEL
BENIGN	DILIGENCE	LECHER	SAGE
BEQUEATH	DISCREET	OBSCURE	SUNDRY
BESEECH	EMINENT	OBSTINATE	TRENCHANT
BLITHELY	ENTHRALLED	PALLOR	USURY
CAPRICES	ESCHEW	PARAMOURS	VERILY
CAROUSES	EXHORTATION	PELF	VICTUALS
CHIDE	EXTORT	PRATING	WOE
CONSTANCY	FEIGNED	PREROGATIVE	
CONTRIVE	FELICITY	PRODIGIOUS	
CONUNDRUM	FRUGALITY	PROFFERING	

VOCABULARY CROSSWORD - *The Canterbury Tales*

VOCABULARY CROSSWORD CLUE SHEET - *The Canterbury Tales*

ACROSS
1. Happiness; bliss
4. Alison agreed to do this to Absalom to make him go away
6. He sang
7. Number of years Arveragus was gone
8. Carpenter broke his when he fell
10. Lightheartedly; festively; merrily
12. He won the contest for Emily's hand
14. Lending money & charging outrageously high interest
16. To stay away from
21. Arveragus's castle was near the ---
22. Place where the friars were hidden in hell
25. Kindhearted, considerate
27. Wrong; awry
28. A man who overindulges in sexual activities
31. Usefulness
33. The queen's sister; two knights loved her
34. Food for humans
37. Anger
38. Group of attendants or followers
39. A raised platform
41. What the miller's wife made from the flour he took from A & J
42. It branded Nicholas
44. Loot; goods seized unlawfully
45. Extreme paleness
46. ----'s Priest's Tale
47. Not readily noticed or seen; unknown
48. To get revenge for

DOWN
1. It came to kill Chanticleer
2. To criticize for a fault or offense
3. January's wife
4. Had been in many battles, was a gentleman
5. The older youths planned to do this to the youngest upon his return
6. Wife of ---
9. Bald & fat, didn't like work
10. Make an earnest request
11. Speech that incites
13. Thriftiness; careful use of material goods
15. Consisting of many different kinds
17. Wise; wise person; scholarly
18. A cause of suffering or harm
19. Widely known; famous
20. Stubborn
23. Place where they took the singing boy
24. Lacking energy or strength
26. Steady attention and effort
29. Given to flirting
30. To obtain from another by intimidation or blackmail
32. Hateful; horrid; awful
35. Stirring to action
36. Mockery; ridicule
38. To behave festively; frolic
39. Reserved in manner; shy; modest
40. Arcita fell onto his and broke his breast
43. Thomas's gift to the friar

VOCABULARY CROSSWORD ANSWER KEY - *The Canterbury Tales*

VOCABULARY WORKSHEET 1 - *The Canterbury Tales*

____ 1. Stirring to action
    A. Inciting   B. Frugality   C. Obscure   D. Sage

____ 2. To free from a charge or accusation
    A. Usury   B. Trenchant   C. Acquittal   D. Amiss

____ 3. To criticize for a fault or offense
    A. Prating   B. Obstinate   C. Predestination   D. Chide

____ 4. Innuendoes; indirect hints; implications
    A. Sundry   B. Diligence   C. Felicity   D. Insinuations

____ 5. Wise; wise person; scholarly
    A. Gluttony   B. Sage   C. Prerogative   D. Abominable

____ 6. A man who overindulges in sexual activities
    A. Redressed   B. Avail   C. Lecher   D. Carouses

____ 7. Wrong; awry
    A. Woe   B. Amiss   C. Lecher   D. Beseech

____ 8. Thriftiness; careful use of material goods
    A. Insinuations   B. Frugality   C. Repletion   D. Revel

____ 9. To behave festively; frolic
    A. Enthralled   B. Revel   C. Beseech   D. Aphrodisiac

____ 10. Drunk
    A. Proffering   B. Languishing   C. Redressed   D. Inebriate

____ 11. Consisting of many different kinds
    A. Daunted   B. Gluttony   C. Sundry   D. Reprehensible

____ 12. Behaves riotously; revels
    A. Blithely   B. Extort   C. Usury   D. Carouses

____ 13. The vice of continually overeating
    A. Constancy   B. Demure   C. Gluttony   D. Enthralled

____ 14. Even; indeed
    A. Amiss   B. Eminent   C. Verily   D. Obstinate

____ 15. Extreme paleness
    A. Carouses   B. Pallor   C. Reprehensible   D. Extort

____ 16. A raised platform
    A. Redressed   B. Dais   C. Conundrum   D. Diligence

____ 17. Reserved in manner; shy; modest
    A. Caprices   B. Requite   C. Demure   D. Pelf

____ 18. Mockery; ridicule
    A. Pelf   B. Derision   C. Chide   D. Trenchant

____ 19. Deprived of courage as a result of fear, anxiety or disgust
    A. Requite   B. Diligence   C. Daunted   D. Blithely

____ 20. Lacking energy or strength
    A. Languishing   B. Supplications   C. Insinuations   D. Inebriate

KEY: VOCABULARY WORKSHEET 1 - *The Canterbury Tales*

__A__ 1. Stirring to action
    A. Inciting   B. Frugality   C. Obscure   D. Sage

__C__ 2. To free from a charge or accusation
    A. Usury   B. Trenchant   C. Acquittal   D. Amiss

__D__ 3. To criticize for a fault or offense
    A. Prating   B. Obstinate   C. Predestination   D. Chide

__D__ 4. Innuendoes; indirect hints; implications
    A. Sundry   B. Diligence   C. Felicity   D. Insinuations

__B__ 5. Wise; wise person; scholarly
    A. Gluttony   B. Sage   C. Prerogative   D. Abominable

__C__ 6. A man who overindulges in sexual activities
    A. Redressed   B. Avail   C. Lecher   D. Carouses

__B__ 7. Wrong; awry
    A. Woe   B. Amiss   C. Lecher   D. Beseech

__B__ 8. Thriftiness; careful use of material goods
    A. Insinuations   B. Frugality   C. Repletion   D. Revel

__B__ 9. To behave festively; frolic
    A. Enthralled   B. Revel   C. Beseech   D. Aphrodisiac

__D__ 10. Drunk
    A. Proffering   B. Languishing   C. Redressed   D. Inebriate

__C__ 11. Consisting of many different kinds
    A. Daunted   B. Gluttony   C. Sundry   D. Reprehensible

__D__ 12. Behaves riotously; revels
    A. Blithely   B. Extort   C. Usury   D. Carouses

__C__ 13. The vice of continually overeating
    A. Constancy   B. Demure   C. Gluttony   D. Enthralled

__C__ 14. Even; indeed
    A. Amiss   B. Eminent   C. Verily   D. Obstinate

__B__ 15. Extreme paleness
    A. Carouses   B. Pallor   C. Reprehensible   D. Extort

__B__ 16. A raised platform
    A. Redressed   B. Dais   C. Conundrum   D. Diligence

__C__ 17. Reserved in manner; shy; modest
    A. Caprices   B. Requite   C. Demure   D. Pelf

__B__ 18. Mockery; ridicule
    A. Pelf   B. Derision   C. Chide   D. Trenchant

__C__ 19. Deprived of courage as a result of fear, anxiety or disgust
    A. Requite   B. Diligence   C. Daunted   D. Blithely

__A__ 20. Lacking energy or strength
    A. Languishing   B. Supplications   C. Insinuations   D. Inebriate

VOCABULARY WORKSHEET 2 - *The Canterbury Tales*

____ 1. VERILY   A. Lightheartedly; festively; merrily

____ 2. CONUNDRUM   B. Behaves riotously; revels

____ 3. REQUITE   C. Wise; wise person; scholarly

____ 4. LECHER   D. Even; indeed

____ 5. EMINENT   E. To free from a charge or accusation

____ 6. CAROUSES   F. Repay

____ 7. REDRESSED   G. A man who overindulges in sexual activities

____ 8. PROFFERING   H. A mystery; a puzzle

____ 9. ACQUITTAL   I. Steady attention and effort

____ 10. SAGE   J. To put before another for acceptance

____ 11. DILIGENCE   K. To get revenge for

____ 12. BLITHELY   L. To leave material goods by will

____ 13. AMISS   M. Happiness; bliss

____ 14. ABOMINABLE N. A raised platform

____ 15. BEQUEATH   O. Widely known; famous

____ 16. DAIS   P. Consisting of many different kinds

____ 17. FELICITY   Q. Hateful; horrid; awful

____ 18. ESCHEW   R. Wrong; awry

____ 19. SUNDRY   S. To stay away from

____ 20. REVEL   T. To behave festively; frolic

KEY: VOCABULARY WORKSHEET 2 - *The Canterbury Tales*

__D__ 1. VERILY   A. Lightheartedly; festively; merrily

__H__ 2. CONUNDRUM   B. Behaves riotously; revels

__F__ 3. REQUITE   C. Wise; wise person; scholarly

__G__ 4. LECHER   D. Even; indeed

__O__ 5. EMINENT   E. To free from a charge or accusation

__B__ 6. CAROUSES   F. Repay

__K__ 7. REDRESSED   G. A man who overindulges in sexual activities

__J__ 8. PROFFERING   H. A mystery; a puzzle

__E__ 9. ACQUITTAL   I. Steady attention and effort

__C__ 10. SAGE   J. To put before another for acceptance

__I__ 11. DILIGENCE   K. To get revenge for

__A__ 12. BLITHELY   L. To leave material goods by will

__R__ 13. AMISS   M. Happiness; bliss

__Q__ 14. ABOMINABLE   N. A raised platform

__L__ 15. BEQUEATH   O. Widely known; famous

__N__ 16. DAIS   P. Consisting of many different kinds

__M__ 17. FELICITY   Q. Hateful; horrid; awful

__S__ 18. ESCHEW   R. Wrong; awry

__P__ 19. SUNDRY   S. To stay away from

__T__ 20. REVEL   T. To behave festively; frolic

VOCABULARY WORD SHEET - *The Canterbury Tales*

WORDS	CLUES
BENIGN	Kindhearted, considerate
OBSTINATE	Stubborn
SUNDRY	Consisting of many different kinds
COY	Given to flirting
EMINENT	Widely known; famous
FELICITY	Happiness; bliss
LANGUISHING	Lacking energy or strength
RETINUE	Group of attendants or followers
EXHORTATION	Speech that incites
LECHER	A man who overindulges in sexual activities
PROFFERING	To put before another for acceptance
PARAMOURS	Lovers
BESEECH	Make an earnest request
TRENCHANT	Sharp
FRUGALITY	Thriftiness; careful use of material goods
AMISS	Wrong; awry
INCITING	Stirring to action
WOE	A cause of suffering or harm
CONTRIVE	Plan
BLITHELY	Lightheartedly; festively; merrily
CHIDE	To criticize for a fault or offense
USURY	Lending money & charging outrageously high interest
DILIGENCE	Steady attention and effort
REDRESSED	To get revenge for
AVAIL	Usefulness
REPLETION	Full to or beyond satisfaction
DISCREET	Diplomatic; politic; tactful
ABOMINABLE	Hateful; horrid; awful
DERISION	Mockery; ridicule
PREDESTINATION	Belief that one's fate is already decided
CAROUSES	Behaves riotously; revels
GLUTTONY	The vice of continually overeating
PALLOR	Extreme paleness
PRATING	Chattering; jabbering
DAUNTED	Deprived of courage as a result of fear, anxiety or disgust
APHRODISIAC	A drug or food having the effect of arousing sexual desire
EXTORT	To obtain from another by intimidation or blackmail
BEQUEATH	To leave material goods by will
OBSCURE	Not readily noticed or seen; unknown
FEIGNED	Artificial; counterfeited; faked
INEBRIATE	Drunk
ACQUITTAL	To free from a charge or accusation

Canterbury Tales Vocabulary Word Sheet Page 2

WORDS	CLUES
IRE	Anger
SUPPLICATIONS	Appeals; pleas
PRODIGIOUS	Of extraordinary size and/or power
CONUNDRUM	A mystery; a puzzle
PREROGATIVE	The right to command or decide
CONSTANCY	Faithfulness; fidelity
ACQUIESCE	Agree; consent
CAPRICES	Whims
DEMURE	Reserved in manner; shy; modest
ESCHEW	To stay away from
PELF	Loot; goods seized unlawfully
DAIS	A raised platform
REPREHENSIBLE	Deserving condemnation; despicable
INSINUATIONS	Innuendoes; indirect hints; implications
REVEL	To behave festively; frolic
VERILY	Even; indeed
ENTHRALLED	Enchanted; fascinated
VICTUALS	Food for humans
SAGE	Wise; wise person; scholarly
REQUITE	Repay

VOCABULARY JUGGLE LETTER REVIEW GAME CLUES - *The Canterbury Tales*

SCRAMBLED	WORD	CLUE
NEGIBN	BENIGN	Kindhearted, considerate
SOBTAEIN	OBSTINATE	Stubborn
RUNDSY	SUNDRY	Consisting of many different kinds
OCY	COY	Given to flirting
TIMEENN	EMINENT	Widely known; famous
LIYFETIC	FELICITY	Happiness; bliss
GALUHNISGIN	LANGUISHING	Lacking energy or strength
ETIRUEN	RETINUE	Group of attendants or followers
NOTIHROTAEX	EXHORTATION	Speech that incites
HERCEL	LECHER	A man who overindulges in sexual activities
FORGINERP	PROFFERING	To put before another for acceptance
MARUSAPO	PARAMOURS	Lovers
SHEEBEC	BESEECH	Make an earnest request
THANRENTC	TRENCHANT	Sharp
LUGYRFITA	FRUGALITY	Thriftiness; careful use of material goods
SIMSA	AMISS	Wrong; awry
TININCG	INCITING	Stirring to action
OEW	WOE	A cause of suffering or harm
NICEVOTR	CONTRIVE	Plan
TLIBLEHY	BLITHELY	Lightheartedly; festively; merrily
HEDCI	CHIDE	To criticize for a fault or offense
SYURU	USURY	Lending money & charging outrageously high interest
GINILECDE	DILIGENCE	Steady attention and effort
DESDRESER	REDRESSED	To get revenge for
LAVIA	AVAIL	Usefulness
PLONTEEIR	REPLETION	Full to or beyond satisfaction
TREDISEC	DISCREET	Diplomatic; politic; tactful
MABELIBONA	ABOMINABLE	Hateful; horrid; awful
SIRENIDO	DERISION	Mockery; ridicule
NITDESERPAOTNI	PREDESTINATION	Belief that one's fate is already decided
SOURACSE	CAROUSES	Behaves riotously; revels
TULNOGYT	GLUTTONY	The vice of continually overeating
LAPROL	PALLOR	Extreme paleness
TRANPIG	PRATING	Chattering; jabbering
DENTADU	DAUNTED	Deprived of courage as a result of fear, anxiety or disgust
DORAHIPACIS	APHRODISIAC	A drug or food having the effect of arousing sexual desire
TEXROT	EXTORT	To obtain from another by intimidation or blackmail
QUETEBHA	BEQUEATH	To leave material goods by will

Canterbury Tales Vocabulary Word Sheet Page 2

WORDS	CLUES	
BESORUC	OBSCURE	Not readily noticed; unknown
FIGDENE	FEIGNED	Artificial; counterfeited; faked
RIBINETAE	INEBRIATE	Drunk
TIQULACA	ACQUITTAL	To free from a charge or accusation
RIE	IRE	Anger
CAPTINOSSPULI	SUPPLICATIONS	Appeals; pleas
DORISIPUO	PRODIGIOUS	Of extraordinary size and/or power
MURDNOCNU	CONUNDRUM	A mystery; a puzzle
GRATERVIREO	PREROGATIVE	The right to command or decide
SOCNAYTC	CONSTANCY	Faithfulness; fidelity
SEQUCIAEC	ACQUIESCE	Agree; consent
SEPRACIC	CAPRICES	Whims
RUMEED	DEMURE	Reserved in manner; shy; modest
SHECEW	ESCHEW	To stay away from
FELP	PELF	Loot; goods seized unlawfully
SAID	DAIS	A raised platform
BENPERSHEERI	REPREHENSIBLE	Deserving condemnation; despicable
TINUSONISAIN	INSINUATIONS	Innuendoes; indirect hints; implications
LEVER	REVEL	To behave festively; frolic
RELYVI	VERILY	Even; indeed
LLHDRANTEE	ENTHRALLED	Enchanted; fascinated
SLITCUV	VICTUALS	Food for humans
GASE	SAGE	Wise; wise person; scholarly
QTRUEIE	REQUITE	Repay

www.ingramcontent.com/pod-product-compliance
Lightning Source LLC
Chambersburg PA
CBHW051402070526
44584CB00023B/3260